AMERICAN
DEMOCRACY

AMERICAN DEMOCRACY

21 Historic Answers *to* 5 Urgent Questions

NICHOLAS LEMANN, *editor*

A SPECIAL PUBLICATION OF
THE LIBRARY OF AMERICA

Contents

QUESTION 4

The Power of Money: How to Control It?   169

QUESTION 5

Protest: Can We Disobey the Law?   221

Introduction

By Nicholas Lemann

It is hard to remember a time when people were discussing the future of the United States as a well-functioning democracy, as if that were an open question, as urgently as they are now. The news is full of evidence to make one wonder. The President can, and regularly does, push past the official boundaries of the power of the office—by spending money without congressional approval, selectively enforcing the immigration laws, undermining the independence of federal agencies, and unilaterally ordering assassinations overseas, even of American citizens. It has always been possible for someone who lost the popular vote by a significant margin to win a presidential election, but that has now happened twice in two decades. The Electoral College, and the way representation in the Senate is structured, were designed to give some states political power out of proportion to their population, but the discrepancy between the largest and smallest states is now greater than it has ever been. There are never-ending battles, which we really shouldn't still be having, over who has the right to vote and what obstacles stand in the way of casting a ballot. The outsize political influence of the rich and powerful seems impervious to limitation. The two political parties, which are supposed to function as broad coalitions that have come together to get the government's work done, behave instead like opposing armies bent on annihilating each other. And if democracy implies something beyond elections and the operations of government—something like a universal guarantee of a decently provisioned life, individual opportunity, and personal freedom—then America isn't functioning so well in that way either.

Many of us were raised on a series of bromides about American democracy: Ours is the world's oldest functioning democracy. The United States provides a model of governance to which the rest of the world aspires. We have a moral obligation to try to bring every other country's system closer in design to our own. If we are now questioning these comfortable assumptions, that is useful, because they were always automatic and never fully warranted. Our new disquiet about our democracy may be a sign that this is an especially alarming moment, or it may simply be that, for the past few decades, we have been in a kind of national slumber about shortcomings of American democracy that were always there. In that case, looking under the surface of our politics and into the structure in which it takes place is vitally important. The results of political systems are a product of their design, which doesn't usually get the attention it deserves because it isn't immediately obvious.

This book is meant to serve as a tool in the effort to understand American democracy—the fundamental challenges that our system faces and the questions it has never been fully able to resolve. The book's perspective is historical. It is not very useful, as we'll see, to think of the United States as a once perfect democracy that only recently went astray. Instead, nearly all the essential aspects of our democracy have been in dispute from the very beginning. That is not meant as a devastating revelation, but, instead, as a prod to ongoing thought and engagement. With the great exception of the Civil War, Americans have been able to agree enough about what our democracy should be for us to continue to function as a single nation. Otherwise we have disagreed vehemently, often violently, about most of democracy's major aspects. That will surely continue. To understand some of the major disagreements is a way of preparing yourself to play your own part in the necessary and never-ending struggle over them.

There are twenty-one historical texts in this book, which were originally produced across a long span of time beginning in the eighteenth century and ending in the twenty-first. Any such selection must be partial. You won't find here some texts that are usually considered to be canonical, like the Declaration of Independence, the Gettysburg Address, and Martin Luther King's "I Have a Dream" speech. The principle governing the selections is that each one is meant to illuminate an issue that was in dispute when it was produced and is still salient today. Together they are meant to convey the idea that American democracy is dynamic, not static—that is has changed continuously and will continue to change, sometimes for the better, sometimes not.

The selections are organized around five major and never fully settled questions about American democracy. They are:

Citizenship: Who Are "We the People"? *Democracy* literally means, in Greek, rule by the people. The ancient inventors of the term were highly skeptical about it as an ideal, and at the outset of the United States as a nation, democracy was the furthest thing from a global norm. The Framers' suspicion of rule by the people was based on the idea that they would be ill-informed, motivated by passion rather than reason, and prone to impose their prejudices too forcefully on people who did not share them. We still hear versions of these concerns. By the standards of their time, the Framers were pushing forward the idea of elected government, but they did so with some caution. Initially, only a small minority of Americans, white and male, had the right to vote, and only one part of the national government, the House of Representatives, was chosen by direct election.

The selections in this section show a gradually ascendant argument for a redefinition of democracy, so that it would entail much wider participation and a more expansive concept of the rights of American citizens. George Washington's letter to the Hebrew Congregation of Newport announced that in the United States, Jews, and by implication others, would be able to practice their religion freely and openly without being in any way excluded from citizenship. The selections by Frederick Douglass and Elizabeth Cady Stanton—towering figures in the nineteenth-century movements to win rights for black people and women—show the ways the American tradition, exclusionary as it was, could be used rhetorically to argue for more inclusion. The final two selections, by the long-serving Massachusetts senator Henry Cabot Lodge and the early twentieth-century radical intellectual Randolph Bourne, display complete disagreement about a matter that is still deeply in dispute today: In what numbers, and on what political and cultural terms, people from other countries should be permitted to come to the United States? Immigration, voting rights, multiculturalism—all these are pressing present-day concerns that are deeply rooted in the historical debates about American democracy.

Equality: How Can It Be Achieved? Democracy, narrowly defined, is political. But in the United States and elsewhere, people assume that if we have moved haltingly toward a system in which all Americans would have full citizenship and the ability to participate in choosing their government, then something beyond political rights should result: a decent life for everyone. The Constitution has almost nothing to say about this, beyond giving Congress the power to provide for the "general welfare," but it is the daily material of our political lives, discussed constantly by candidates for the highest office, by legislators at all levels, and by ordinary voters. Equality is an especially contested concept, and because its meaning is not formally, legally enshrined in one document, it has been put into effect in many different forms and to highly varying degrees. In the twenty-first century, ever higher economic inequality is one of the main animating concerns of our politics.

Most people today would probably say that after voting and respect for the rule of law, public education is the next essential aspect of democracy. If we want to give everyone an equal start in life, education is the best means. Horace Mann, one of the pioneers in establishing public school for all as a government responsibility, which it was not in the early republic, shows us how the argument had to be made to a skeptical public in Massachusetts in the mid-nineteenth century—as a promise that education would produce both equality and prosperity. A not very well-known set of remarks that Abraham Lincoln gave to a regiment of Union soldiers who visited the White House during the Civil War introduces us to the powerful American notion—sometimes an aspiration, sometimes an illusion, sometimes a reality—that anyone should be able to rise from the humblest origins to the highest office. Jane Addams, the great Progressive-era reformer, writes with painful honesty about the corrosive effects of class in America, noting specifically the skepticism that the poor people she worked with in settlement houses had about the middle-class, individualistic values that social workers tried to impart to them there. W.E.B. Du Bois, the first major twentieth-century intellectual to present the empowerment of African Americans in the South during Reconstruction in positive terms, reminds us that without true political equality, all other kinds of equality are vulnerable to being ruthlessly dismantled.

A More Perfect Union: What Is the Government For? After the Declaration of Independence, before the Constitution, there were the Articles of Confederation, which created a national government that was too minimal to be able to function effectively. The Constitution was meant to give the national government greater, but still limited, power; governance still resided mainly with the states, and the early constitutional system looks to us today as if it is more concerned with constraining than enhancing the federal government's power. Over the years, as the country became geographically larger, more populous, and more economically and militarily powerful, the federal government grew—not so much gradually as in periodic bursts, and never without vigorous dispute.

The first selections in this section come from the time when government was, by today's standards, meant to be very small indeed. James Madison's Federalist No. 51, written in support of the as yet unratified Constitution, is the classic statement of separation of powers within the structure of the government, to prevent any one part of it from becoming threateningly large in its scope and influence. Chief Justice John Marshall's opinion in the landmark Supreme Court case of *McCulloch v. Maryland* reaffirmed the supremacy of the federal government's constitutional power over the state governments. Alexis de Tocqueville, the French aristocrat who was the early republic's most perceptive visitor, warns of American democracy's capacity to generate a new kind of popular despotism, with government taking on responsibilities that, in Tocqueville's view, should rest with individuals. The later selections illuminate moments of significant government expansion—moments that coincided with a national sense of crisis, as enlargements of government's powers usually have. A speech Franklin Roosevelt made during his first presidential campaign establishes a rhetorical framework for a greatly enhanced government role in the economic life of the country, and a seminal national security document from the early days of the Cold War shows the rationale for creating a vast permanent peacetime military establishment. Today one of American democracy's most unusual features, given where we started, is the immense and lightly checked power of the President to conduct domestic and foreign affairs, including the power to initiate wars and to violate the rights of citizens.

The Power of Money: How to Control It? The full force of the Industrial Revolution came to America relatively late, after the Civil War. It produced concentrated wealth on a scale the country had never seen. As great fortunes were transformed into disproportionate political power, what to do about money in politics became one of the major questions about American democracy—as it still is today. A long series of reforms have mainly failed to stem the outsize influence that rich people and organizations have in our political system. That doesn't mean one should lose hope. It does mean that being familiar with the historical debates about money and politics is a prerequisite to understanding where we are and trying to create a better system in the future.

There have always been strong tensions between America's financial interests and the country's plain folk. Andrew Jackson's veto message for the re-chartering of the Second Bank of the United States has a forceful, emotional populist charge that shows how politically potent those tensions already were by the 1830s. Jackson imagined himself to be waging war against moneyed interests, not trying to clean up politics. The civil service system, elaborately praised by Carl Schurz in this section, was meant to make government more a profession and less a spoils system based on the exchange of money, jobs, contracts, and favors. Even as the civil service took over most employment in the federal government, the power of money persisted. Theodore Roosevelt's "The New Nationalism," a speech from 1910, proposed to give the government significant new capabilities that would let it establish control over big business, rather than being controlled by it. Even then there was, and still is, the problem of money finding its entry point through contributions to political campaigns, which over time have become ever more expensive. The most recent selection in this book is an excerpt from Justice John Paul Stevens's dissent in a 2010 Supreme Court case that found crucial limits on political spending by corporations to be in violation of the First Amendment—a decision that unleashed a fresh flood of political money. The system is awash in it now.

Protest: Can We Disobey the Law? Democracy is not only about electoral politics and government. When a political system is failing to respond to the urgent concerns of its people, protest is an essential avenue for action. Today we are experiencing an unprecedented, massive wave of protests, and that is a sign not just of widespread anger, but also of the health of one aspect of American democracy. Protest is a venerable American tradition, extending back to our colonial past, and it has taken many different forms: nonviolent and violent, legal and extralegal, individual and mass. One should begin to worry not when mass protests appear, but when the state tries to suppress them.

Henry David Thoreau's "Civil Disobedience" is often treated as the sacred text of American protest, but it is actually atypical in a number of ways. Thoreau, reflecting on a night he spent in jail for refusing to pay taxes, objects to government policies, but he insists that he is not trying to change them, or even to work in concert with others who agree with him—he is merely following the dictates of his conscience. Martin Luther King's "Letter from Birmingham Jail" also was the product of a violation of the law (demonstrating without a permit). There the similarity to Thoreau's essay ends. King presents himself as a member of a painstakingly organized movement with an explicit political goal, ending the Jim Crow system of legal segregation, and he associates himself with the major heroes of the American political tradition. Hannah Arendt, the German émigré political philosopher, is explicitly critical of Thoreau. Writing at a time when hundreds of thousands of people were protesting the Vietnam War, she imagined protest to be an expression of the American civic impulse—something specific to a situation, which would disappear after the protesters had achieved their goals. That may assume a more orderly national character than we have. Protest waxes and wanes in response to political conditions, but it has never disappeared, and it never will.

* * *

Democracy is a system. Because the word carries such a positive charge, people naturally assume that when, by their lights, the good guys are winning, it must mean that American democracy is in a healthy state. That is a temptation to be avoided: it mistakes an outcome for a process. It's most useful to try to think about the condition of our democracy by pretending that we don't know who's on top at the moment. What, regardless of current events, should a high-functioning American system look like?

First and most of all, everyone should have an ironclad right to vote. Elections should be freely contested and conducted openly and fairly, and ballots should be counted accurately, without malfunctions or tampering. Outside of electoral politics, every citizen should have an inviolable set of basic rights, including the right to speak, write, and assemble freely, the right to due process of law, and the right to privacy. To say that these are the fundamental conditions of a good democracy doesn't mean that they don't have to be protected. They do not firmly exist everywhere in the United States today. But the underlying principles are straightforward.

It takes a greater effort to pay attention to the less obvious aspects of democracy, the ones that can be more difficult to embrace wholeheartedly and whose failings do not give rise to news coverage. One of these is representation. "The people" is an appealing construct. Originally, it would have been logistically impossible to empower the public to adjudicate every issue that arises. Now that is easier, so we should remind ourselves that we elect representatives in what is meant to be a spirit of trust that they can make specific decisions on their own, subject to our overall review when they run for reelection. Do we really want elected officials to be precisely attuned and responsive to overall public opinion on every issue, even in cases where the public opinion of the moment does not align with the right and necessary course for government? Politicians are representatives, not proxies. They need room to think about their constituencies', and the country's, long-term needs, and to protect the rights of minorities whose rights and interests the majority has a well-demonstrated capacity to ignore, especially at times when passions run high, such as national crises or periods of seductive demagogic leadership.

A healthy democracy requires a diversity of government institutions that hold each other in check, and also a set of strong civic institutions outside of government. Within government, we should be grateful that we have a bewildering welter of state, local, and federal entities, operating by different principles, and we should think of many-membered legislatures, not singular mayors, governors, and presidents, as the heart of democratic governance. In society, interest groups, political parties, an independent and varied press, and organizations that conduct policy research and advocacy are all essential actors in American democracy. It can be tempting to dream of a false ideal of democracy, one that either pursues the public interest without interference, or that always operates in accordance with the will of the people. This is a temptation to be avoided.

Politics is messy, politicians are often ignoble, interest groups are greedy, the press is sensational, parties are controlled by insiders. In the American system, all of that is a feature, not a bug. In the aggregate, an impure and varied democracy should produce spirited ongoing engagement combined with a shared commitment by all the players to abide by the outcome, at least until it's time to try to achieve a different outcome next time around. It's when everyone seems to agree, when one part of government (usually the presidency) seems all-powerful, and when the institutions outside government seem weak—as is the case now, for example, with America's local news organizations—that we are right to worry about the health of our democracy.

There has never been a time when American democracy was in perfect shape. There have been times when that was the perception, at least of people at the top of the society, but in historical perspective those moments look like examples of willful blindness—to slavery and segregation, to the denial of rights to women, to unacceptable conditions for the poor and vulnerable, and to many other woes. It is essential always to allow for multiple and conflicting perspectives on the health of our democracy. Many of the selections in this book were written by outsiders who were motivated by their exclusion from the system.

This is *our* country. To be an American citizen is to bear a personal responsibility for improving American democracy. Everyone can do something. In deciding what to do, history helps. This book should serve as a spur to political reflection and action. The themes highlighted here—citizenship, equality, governance, money in politics, and protest—are long-running, essential flash points in American democracy, sources of vital debate, conflict, and creativity. They will still be flash points well into the future. The stakes are too high, and our opinions too varied, for any of them easily to be put to rest. Although the authors of the selections here are major historical figures, readers have a real commonality with them. All of them participated actively in American democracy. All of us can too.

QUESTION 1

Citizenship:
Who Are "We the People"?

★ ★ ★

It is tempting, at a moment when the most basic questions about what it means to be an American are in play—who gets to come to the country, who gets to vote, who has civil rights—to wonder in exasperation why we are still arguing about them. Weren't they settled long ago? Well, no, they weren't. The Constitution did not define citizenship until the ratification of the Fourteenth Amendment in 1868. Even then, if we understand citizenship as entailing at an absolute minimum the right to vote, women were not citizens until decades later, and most African Americans in the South were citizens only briefly before the end of Jim Crow. There really isn't one place where the precise meaning of being an American has been clearly enshrined for all time. Citizenship is so valuable and so consequential that it is also inescapably controversial. Because it is the most fundamental of political issues, it entails never-ending struggle.

The first selection in this section, George Washington's celebrated letter to one of America's earliest Jewish congregations, in Newport, Rhode Island, in 1790, is in a way the most radical: here was the first President affirming that all Americans have a fundamental right to freedom of religious practice, as an aspect of citizenship—including even "the Children of the Stock of Abraham," who at that time were denied full citizenship rights almost everywhere else. A year later, the ratification of the First Amendment to the Constitution banned the nationwide establishment of a state religion, a feature of most of the pre-Revolutionary American colonies (and some post-Revolutionary American states) and of almost every other country in the world at the time. There is a significant difference between coming to America to have the freedom to practice your own religion, as the Massachusetts Puritans did, and granting every other religious group the same freedom, as the Puritans most certainly did not. Now Washington was saying that this new principle was not just American practice, but an example for the whole world to follow.

Washington's statement doesn't mean that from the very beginning of the United States, other examples, by our lights, of what Washington called "an enlarged and liberal policy" abounded. Voting rights in the early republic were entirely (and still are substantially) controlled by the states, not the national government, and were mostly restricted to white male property owners. The last state to eliminate property requirements, North Carolina, did not do so until 1856. And of course women, Native Americans, enslaved African Americans, and many free African Americans could not vote. Only in 1869, with the passage of the Fifteenth Amendment, did the federal government establish itself as a guarantor of voting rights—but not for women, and, after the end of Reconstruction in 1877, not for black men in the former Confederate states either. Women didn't have a federally guaranteed right to vote until the ratification of the Nineteenth Amendment, in 1920, and it took until the enactment of the Voting Rights Act, in 1965, for the federal government to begin addressing the Jim Crow era's decades of severe limitations on black voting rights.

While citizenship policy during the first century of the United States was restrictive, immigration policy was permissive: although legislation excluded black people (until 1870) and Asians from being naturalized, the country had no formal system for limiting entry from abroad. The two are related, because the fewer rights citizenship confers, the easier it is to admit immigrants without controversy. Through the first half of the nineteenth century, the balance shifted, toward a gradually enhanced conception of citizenship and a rising suspicion of immigration, especially by Catholics. As voting rights were extended to white men who didn't own property, and as immigration from Europe increased, immigrants acquired a measure of political power. They helped make voting a broad phenomenon and fueled the rise of mass political parties, an essential element in American democracy that the Constitution doesn't mention. By the 1830s, the much more democratic form that American politics was taking pushed government to do more that would benefit ordinary people—for example, providing education and free land—and this made citizenship more valuable. It wasn't an accident that anti-immigrant political movements, like the Know Nothings, arose not long afterward.

The expansion of citizenship rights was useful to those engaged in the long and difficult campaign to undo the denial of rights to the majority of Americans who were not white men. Frederick Douglass's supremely eloquent address, "What to the Slave is the 4th of July," presents slavery as the complete negation of the American project. He reminds his audience that George Washington emancipated his slaves; that the Constitution is a "GLORIOUS LIBERTY DOCUMENT," which never mentions slavery by name; and that slavery is incompatible with the soaring language of the Declaration of Independence. Abolition and the extension of civil rights were anything but inevitable, but we can see how the rising tide of full citizenship for white men provided Douglass with an opportunity to frame his searing indictment of the country's treatment of black people.

From its beginning, the women's rights movement was related to abolitionism—sometimes as an ally, sometimes as a rival for the attention of reformers—and it too rooted its arguments in the necessity of having legal rights as an American citizen in order to live in dignity, safety, and fulfillment as an individual. Elizabeth Cady Stanton's "Solitude of Self," an address delivered in Stanton's old age after decades of ceaseless battling for women's rights, paints a picture of women as unjustly forced into dependence on men, and denied "the whole round of human duties and pleasures," because of not being full American citizens. Women, we should remember, often lacked not just voting rights but other basic aspects of citizenship as well, including access to education, the right to own property, the right to sue, and the right to be protected against domestic violence and sexual exploitation. As more men came to have these rights, the case became stronger that women should have them too.

Nativist sentiment, always present in the United States, began to find expression in new laws in the late nineteenth century. In 1882, Congress passed the Chinese Exclusion Act, the first piece of national legislation aimed at restricting immigration by an entire ethnic group. A much more wide-ranging piece of legislation was the Immigration Act of 1924, which severely restricted immigration, especially from Southern and Eastern Europe, for four decades. Immigrants have never all joined in common cause—Irish immigrants were among those who pushed for the Chinese Exclusion Act—but through the late nineteenth and early twentieth centuries, when immigration was high, its most significant opponents were prosperous, established Americans descended from British colonists, like Massachusetts senator Henry Cabot Lodge, whose 1896 speech calling for immigration restrictions appears in this section. These restrictionists were made intensely uncomfortable by the spectacle of a rapidly industrializing America, with big-city slums, parvenu fortunes, political machines, and a decreasingly Protestant and Northern European population. Our current idea of white people as a single distinct category meant nothing to Lodge—he saw instead a broad spectrum of white races, arrayed in rank order with those whose origins were English or German at the top and those who were arriving in great numbers from Southern and Eastern Europe at the bottom.

Many of the notes that Lodge sounded are still being sounded today, loud and clear. These include the idea that there are, as Lodge put it, desirable and undesirable immigrants and the former should be treated more favorably than the latter; the idea that immigrants will drive down the wages of unskilled laborers; and the idea that immigrants will always live in poverty and disorder and so will represent a permanent drain on public resources. In the twenty-first century, the Democratic Party has reaped the political benefits from the broad opening of immigration policy that a Democratic Congress and President passed back in 1965, and the Republican Party has increasingly become hostile to immigration. In this area more than any other, President Donald Trump has chosen to violate longstanding conventions of political rhetoric and public policy and to treat immigrants, especially those who are Muslim or from Mexico and Central America, as dangerous criminals who deserve the harshest possible treatment, including even separating children from their parents. He has claimed to have the authority to abolish by executive order the Fourteenth Amendment's guarantee of birthright citizenship. And this strategy has worked, at least electorally. It's hard to imagine that without his demagogic and relentless attacks on immigrants, Trump would have been elected President in 2016. He aggressively tapped into sentiments that are unlikely ever to disappear entirely.

There is an alternative tradition, though. Randolph Bourne's century-old essay "Trans-National America" speaks to us with uncanny resonance today, so much so that it can serve as an inspiration. Bourne was one of the leading intellectual opponents of America's entry into the First World War. His passions at the moment he was writing led him to imagine a United States that would be different from the rest of the world, especially Europe, in its refusal to have any one mainstream culture. He also imagined that this quality would exempt America from the national rivalries that were tearing Europe apart. That idea is dated. What's prescient, considering that Bourne was writing at a moment when the debate about immigration was between nativists and advocates of a monocultural melting pot that immigrants would be expected to join, was Bourne's vision of the country as "a federation of cultures." Rather than expecting that everyone who came would join the original Anglo-Saxon national culture, Bourne believed that "we may have to accept some form of that dual citizenship which meets with so much articulate horror among us." Immigrants might retain a home-country identity in addition to their American one. They might move back and forth between their old and new national homes. Better that than our trying to turn the country into "a tasteless, colorless fluid of uniformity." Bourne did not include in his complaints about American nativism the strict restrictions on immigration from Asia, and he offered no examples, in his celebration of transnationalism, of non-European cultures. Still, he was far ahead of most American intellectuals of the day, including liberals, in his attitudes.

All of this prefigures what we'd now call multiculturalism, which is a far more realistic way to include immigrants in American life than to expect their origins to disappear. We should not permit the current moment to give rise to despair. The same sentiments that Trump has publicly unleashed have always existed, here and abroad. So have sentiments like Randolph Bourne's. These sentiments are always going to compete; they both run deep in the national character, and in human nature. The unexpected and contentious rise of mass citizenship, including legal rights, social benefits, and political power, enhanced the value of being an American, and so intensified the contention over who gets to be one. Defining Americanness capaciously is a cause worth fighting for—and one that will always require fighting for.

George Washington to the Hebrew Congregation of Newport, Rhode Island

Gentlemen.

While I receive, with much satisfaction, your Address replete with expressions of affection and esteem; I rejoice in the opportunity of assuring you, that I shall always retain a grateful remembrance of the cordial welcome I experienced in my visit to Newport, from all classes of Citizens.

The reflection on the days of difficulty and danger which are past is rendered the more sweet, from a consciousness that they are succeeded by days of uncommon prosperity and security. If we have wisdom to make the best use of the advantages with which we are now favored, we cannot fail, under the just administration of a good Government, to become a great and a happy people.

The Citizens of the United States of America have a right to applaud themselves for having given to mankind examples of an enlarged and liberal policy: a policy worthy of imitation. All possess alike liberty of conscience and immunities of citizenship. It is now no more that toleration is spoken of, as if it was by the indulgence of one class of people, that another enjoyed the exercise of their inherent natural rights. For happily the Government of the United States, which gives to bigotry no sanction, to persecution no assistance requires only that they who live under its protection should demean themselves as good citizens, in giving it on all occasions their effectual support.

It would be inconsistent with the frankness of my character not to avow that I am pleased with your favorable opinion of my Administration, and fervent wishes for my felicity. May the Children of the Stock of Abraham, who dwell in this land,

continue to merit and enjoy the good will of the other Inhabitants; while every one shall sit in safety under his own vine and
figtree, and there shall be none to make him afraid. May the
father of all mercies scatter light and not darkness in our paths,
and make us all in our several vocations useful here, and in his
own due time and way everlastingly happy.

Go: Washington

August 18, 1790

Frederick Douglass: from What to the Slave is the 4th of July?

My business, if I have any here to-day, is with the present. The accepted time with God and his cause is the ever-living now.

> "Trust no future, however pleasant,
>   Let the dead past bury its dead;
> Act, act in the living present,
>   Heart within, and God overhead."

We have to do with the past only as we can make it useful to the present and to the future. To all inspiring motives, to noble deeds which can be gained from the past, we are welcome. But now is the time, the important time. Your fathers have lived, died, and have done their work, and have done much of it well. You live and must die, and you must do your work. You have no right to enjoy a child's share in the labor of your fathers, unless your children are to be blest by your labors. You have no right to wear out and waste the hard-earned fame of your fathers to cover your indolence. Sydney Smith tells us that men seldom eulogize the wisdom and virtues of their fathers, but to excuse some folly or wickedness of their own. This truth is not a doubtful one. There are illustrations of it near and remote, ancient and modern. It was fashionable, hundreds of year ago, for the children of Jacob to boast, we have "Abraham to our father," when they had long lost Abraham's faith and spirit. That people contented themselves under the shadow of Abraham's great name, while they repudiated the deeds which made his name great. Need I remind you that a similar thing is being done all over this country to-day? Need I tell you that the Jews are not the only people who built the tombs of the prophets, and garnished the sepulchres of the righteous? Washington could not die till he had broken the chains of his slaves. Yet his monument is built up by the price of human blood, and the traders in the bodies and souls of men, shout—"We have Washington to "*our father*."—Alas! that it should be so; yet so it is.

> "The evil that men do, lives after them,
> The good is oft' interred with their bones."

Fellow-citizens, pardon me, allow me to ask, why am I called upon to speak here to-day? What have I, or those I represent, to do with your national independence? Are the great principles of political freedom and of natural justice, embodied in that Declaration of Independence, extended to us? and am I, therefore, called upon to bring our humble offering to the national altar, and to confess the benefits and express devout gratitude for the blessings resulting from your independence to us?

Would to God, both for your sakes and ours, that an affirmative answer could be truthfully returned to these questions! Then would my task be light, and my burden easy and delightful. For *who* is there so cold, that a nation's sympathy could not warm him? Who so obdurate and dead to the claims of gratitude, that would not thankfully acknowledge such priceless benefits? Who so stolid and selfish, that would not give his voice to swell the hallelujahs of a nation's jubilee, when the chains of servitude had been torn from his limbs? I am not that man. In a case like that, the dumb might eloquently speak, and the "lame man leap as an hart."

But, such is not the state of the case. I say it with a sad sense of the disparity between us. I am not included within the pale of this glorious anniversary! Your high independence only reveals the immeasurable distance between us. The blessings in which you, this day, rejoice, are not enjoyed in common.—The rich inheritance of justice, liberty, prosperity and independence, bequeathed by your fathers, is shared by you, not by me. The sunlight that brought life and healing to you, has brought stripes and death to me. This Fourth July is *yours*, not *mine*. *You* may rejoice, *I* must mourn. To drag a man in fetters into the grand illuminated temple of liberty, and call upon him to join you in joyous anthems, were inhuman mockery and sacrilegious irony. Do you mean, citizens, to mock me, by asking me to speak to-day? If so, there is a parallel to your conduct. And let me warn you that it is dangerous to copy the example of a nation whose crimes, towering up to heaven, were thrown down by the breath of the Almighty, burying that nation in irrecoverable ruin! I can to-day take up the plaintive lament of a peeled and woe-smitten people!

"By the rivers of Babylon, there we sat down. Yea! we wept when we remembered Zion. We hanged our harps upon the willows in the midst thereof. For there, they that carried us away captive, required of us a song; and they who wasted us required of us mirth, saying, Sing us one of the songs of Zion. How can we sing the Lord's song in a strange land? If I forget thee, O Jerusalem, let my right hand forget her cunning. If I do not remember thee, let my tongue cleave to the roof of my mouth."

Fellow-citizens; above your national, tumultuous joy, I hear the mournful wail of millions! whose chains, heavy and grievous yesterday, are, to-day, rendered more intolerable by the jubilee shouts that reach them. If I do forget, if I do not faithfully remember those bleeding children of sorrow this day, "may my right hand forget her cunning, and may my tongue cleave to the roof of my mouth!" To forget them, to pass lightly over their wrongs, and to chime in with the popular theme, would be treason most scandalous and shocking, and would make me a reproach before God and the world. My subject, then, fellow-citizens, is AMERICAN SLAVERY. I shall see, this day, and its popular characteristics, from the slave's point of view. Standing, there, identified with the American bondman, making his wrongs mine, I do not hesitate to declare, with all my soul, that the character and conduct of this nation never looked blacker to me than on this 4th of July! Whether we turn to the declarations of the past, or to the professions of the present, the conduct of the nation seems equally hideous and revolting. America is false to the past, false to the present, and solemnly binds herself to be false to the future. Standing with God and the crushed and bleeding slave on this occasion, I will, in the name of humanity which is outraged, in the name of liberty which is fettered, in the name of the constitution and the Bible, which are disregarded and trampled upon, dare to call in question and to denounce, with all the emphasis I can command, everything that serves to perpetuate slavery—the great sin and shame of America! "I will not equivocate; I will not excuse;" I will use the severest language I can command; and yet not one word shall escape me that any man, whose judgment is not blinded by prejudice, or who is not at heart a slaveholder, shall not confess to be right and just.

But I fancy I hear some one of my audience say, it is just in this circumstance that you and your brother abolitionists fail to make a favorable impression on the public mind. Would you argue more, and denounce less, would you persuade more, and rebuke less, your cause would be much more likely to suc-ceed. But, I submit, where all is plain there is nothing to be argued. What point in the anti-slavery creed would you have me argue? On what branch of the subject do the people of this country need light? Must I undertake to prove that the slave is a man? That point is conceded already. Nobody doubts it. The slaveholders themselves acknowledge it in the enactment of laws for their government. They acknowledge it when they punish disobedience on the part of the slave. There are seventy-two crimes in the State of Virginia, which, if committed by a black man, (no matter how ignorant he be,) subject him to the punishment of death; while only two of the same crimes will subject a white man to the like punishment.—What is this but the acknowledgement that the slave is a moral, intellectual and responsible being. The manhood of the slave is conceded. It is admitted in the fact that Southern statute books are covered with enactments forbidding, under severe fines and penalties, the teaching of the slave to read or to write.—When you can point to any such laws, in reference to the beasts of the field, then I may consent to argue the manhood of the slave. When the dogs in your streets, when the fowls of the air, when the cattle on your hills, when the fish of the sea, and the reptiles that crawl, shall be unable to distinguish the slave from a brute, *then* will I argue with you that the slave is a man!

For the present, it is enough to affirm the equal manhood of the negro race. Is it not astonishing that, while we are plough-ing, planting and reaping, using all kinds of mechanical tools, erecting houses, constructing bridges, building ships, working in metals of brass, iron, copper, silver and gold; that, while we are reading, writing and cyphering, acting as clerks, merchants and secretaries, having among us lawyers, doctors, ministers, poets, authors, editors, orators and teachers; that, while we are engaged in all manner of enterprises common to other men, digging gold in California, capturing the whale in the Pacific, feeding sheep and cattle on the hill-side, living, moving, acting, thinking, planning, living in families as husbands, wives and children, and, above all, confessing and worshipping the Christian's God, and looking hopefully for life and immortality beyond the grave, we are called upon to prove that we are men!

Would you have me argue that man is entitled to liberty? that he is the rightful owner of his own body? You have already declared it. Must I argue the wrongfulness of slavery? Is that a question for Republicans? Is it to be settled by the rules of logic and argumentation, as a matter beset with great difficulty, involving a doubtful application of the principle of justice, hard to be understood? How should I look to-day, in the presence of Americans, dividing, and subdividing a discourse, to show that men have a natural right to freedom? speaking of it relatively, and positively, negatively, and affirmatively. To do so, would be to make myself ridiculous, and to offer an insult to your under-standing.—There is not a man beneath the canopy of heaven, that does not know that slavery is wrong *for him*.

What, am I to argue that it is wrong to make men brutes, to rob them of their liberty, to work them without wages, to keep them ignorant of their relations to their fellow men, to beat them with sticks, to flay their flesh with the lash, to load their limbs with irons, to hunt them with dogs, to sell them at auction, to sunder their families, to knock out their teeth, to burn their flesh, to starve them into obedience and submission to their masters? Must I argue that a system thus marked with blood, and stained with pollution, is *wrong*? No! I will not. I have better employment for my time and strength, than such arguments would imply.

What, then, remains to be argued? Is it that slavery is not divine; that God did not establish it; that our doctors of divinity are mistaken? There is blasphemy in the thought. That which is inhuman, cannot be divine! *Who* can reason on such a proposition? They that can, may; I cannot. The time for such argument is past.

At a time like this, scorching irony, not convincing argument, is needed. O! had I the ability, and could I reach the nation's ear, I would, to-day, pour out a fiery stream of biting ridicule, blasting reproach, withering sarcasm, and stern rebuke. For it is not light that is needed, but fire; it is not the gentle shower, but thunder. We need the storm, the whirlwind, and the earthquake. The feeling of the nation must be quickened; the conscience of the nation must be roused; the propriety of the nation must be startled; the hypocrisy of the nation must be exposed; and its crimes against God and man must be proclaimed and denounced.

What, to the American slave, is your 4th of July? I answer; a day that reveals to him, more than all other days in the year, the gross injustice and cruelty to which he is the constant victim. To him, your celebration is a sham; your boasted liberty, an unholy license; your national greatness, swelling vanity; your sounds of rejoicing are empty and heartless; your denunciations of tyrants, brass fronted impudence; your shouts of liberty and equality, hollow mockery; your prayers and hymns, your sermons and thanksgivings, with all your religious parade, and solemnity, are, to him, mere bombast, fraud, deception, impiety, and hypocrisy—a thin veil to cover up crimes which would disgrace a nation of savages. There is not a nation on the earth guilty of practices, more shocking and bloody, than are the people of these United States, at this very hour.

Go where you may, search where you will, roam through all the monarchies and despotisms of the old world, travel through South America, search out every abuse, and when you have found the last, lay your facts by the side of the every day practices of this nation, and you will say with me, that, for revolting barbarity and shameless hypocrisy, America reigns without a rival.

July 5, 1852

Elizabeth Cady Stanton: Solitude of Self

Mr. Chairman and gentlemen of the committee: We have been speaking before Committees of the Judiciary for the last twenty years, and we have gone over all the arguments in favor of a sixteenth amendment which are familiar to all you gentlemen; therefore, it will not be necessary that I should repeat them again.

The point I wish plainly to bring before you on this occasion is the individuality of each human soul; our Protestant idea, the right of individual conscience and judgment—our republican idea, individual citizenship. In discussing the rights of woman, we are to consider, first, what belongs to her as an individual, in a world of her own, the arbiter of her own destiny, an imaginary Robinson Crusoe with her woman Friday on a solitary island. Her rights under such circumstances are to use all her faculties for her own safety and happiness.

Secondly, if we consider her as a citizen, as a member of a great nation, she must have the same rights as all other members, according to the fundamental principles of our Government.

Thirdly, viewed as a woman, an equal factor in civilization, her rights and duties are still the same—individual happiness and development.

Fourthly, it is only the incidental relations of life, such as mother, wife, sister, daughter, that may involve some special duties and training. In the usual discussion in regard to woman's sphere, such men as Herbert Spencer, Frederic Harrison, and Grant Allen uniformly subordinate her rights and duties as an individual, as a citizen, as a woman, to the necessities of these incidental relations, some of which a large class of women may never assume. In discussing the sphere of man we do not decide his rights as an individual, as a citizen, as a man by his duties as a father, a husband, a brother, or a son, relations some of which he may never fill. Moreover he would be better fitted for these very relations and whatever special work he might choose to do to earn his bread by the complete development of all his faculties as an individual.

Just so with woman. The education that will fit her to discharge the duties in the largest sphere of human usefulness will best fit her for whatever special work she may be compelled to do.

The isolation of every human soul and the necessity of self-dependence must give each individual the right to choose his own surroundings.

The strongest reason for giving women all the opportunities for higher education, for the full development of her faculties, forces of mind and body; for giving her the most enlarged freedom of thought and action; a complete emancipation from all forms of bondage, of custom, dependence, superstition; from all the crippling influences of fear, is the solitude and personal responsibility of her own individual life. The strongest reason why we ask for woman a voice in the government under which she lives; in the religion she is asked to believe; equality in social life, where she is the chief factor; a place in the trades and professions, where she may earn her bread, is because of her birthright to self-sovereignty; because, as an individual, she must rely on herself. No matter how much women prefer to lean, to be protected and supported, nor how much men desire to have them do so, they must make the voyage of life alone, and for safety in an emergency they must know something of the laws of navigation. To guide our own craft, we must be captain, pilot, engineer; with chart and compass to stand at the wheel; to watch the wind and waves and know when to take in the sail, and to read the signs in the firmament over all. It matters not whether the solitary voyager is man or woman. Nature having endowed them equally, leaves them to their own skill and judgment in the hour of danger, and, if not equal to the occasion, alike they perish.

To appreciate the importance of fitting every human soul for independent action, think for a moment of the immeasurable solitude of self. We come into the world alone, unlike all who have gone before us; we leave it alone under circumstances peculiar to ourselves. No mortal ever has been, no mortal ever will be like the soul just launched on the sea of life. There can never again be just such a combination of prenatal influences; never again just such environments as make up the infancy, youth, and manhood of this one. Nature never repeats herself, and the possibilities of one human soul will never be found in another. No one has ever found two blades of ribbon grass alike, and no one will ever find two human beings alike. Seeing, then, what must be the infinite diversity in human character, we can in a measure appreciate the loss to a nation when any large class of the people is uneducated and unrepresented in the government. We ask for the complete development of every individual, first, for his own benefit and happiness. In fitting out an army we give each soldier his own knapsack, arms, powder, his blanket, cup, knife, fork and spoon. We provide alike for all their individual necessities, then each man bears his own burden.

Again we ask complete individual development for the general good; for the consensus of the competent on the whole round of human interests; on all questions of national life, and here each man must bear his share of the general burden. It is sad to see how soon friendless children are left to bear their own burdens before they can analyze their feelings; before they can even tell their joys and sorrows, they are thrown on their own resources. The great lesson that nature seems to teach us at all ages is self-dependence, self-protection, self-support. What a touching instance of a child's solitude; of that hunger of the heart for love and recognition, in the case of the little girl who helped to dress a Christmas tree for the children of the family in which she served. On finding there was no present for herself she slipped away in the darkness and spent the night in an open field sitting on a stone, and when found in the morning was weeping as if her heart would break. No mortal will ever know the thoughts that passed through the mind of that friendless child in the long hours of that cold night, with only the silent stars to keep her company. The mention of her case in the daily papers moved many generous hearts to send her presents, but in the hours of her keenest suffering she was thrown wholly on herself for consolation.

In youth our most bitter disappointments, our brightest hopes and ambitions are known only to ourselves; even our friendship and love we never fully share with another; there is something of every passion in every situation we conceal. Even so in our triumphs and our defeats. The successful candidate for the Presidency and his opponent each have a solitude peculiarly his own, and good form forbids either to speak of his pleasure or regret. The solitude of the king on his throne and the prisoner in his cell differs in character and degree, but it is solitude nevertheless.

We ask no sympathy from others in the anxiety and agony of a broken friendship or shattered love. When death sunders our nearest ties, alone we sit in the shadow of our affliction. Alike mid the greatest triumphs and darkest tragedies of life we walk alone. On the divine heights of human attainments, eulogized and worshiped as a hero or saint, we stand alone. In ignorance, poverty, and vice, as a pauper or criminal, alone we starve or steal; alone we suffer the sneers and rebuffs of our fellows; alone we are hunted and hounded through dark courts and alleys, in by-ways and highways; alone we stand in the judgment seat; alone in the prison cell we lament our crimes and misfortunes; alone we expiate them on the gallows. In hours like these we realize the awful solitude of individual life, its pains, its penalties, its responsibilities; hours in which the youngest and most helpless are thrown on their own resources for guidance and consolation. Seeing then that life must ever be a march and a battle, that each soldier must be equipped for his own protection, it is the height of cruelty to rob the individual of a single natural right.

To throw obstacles in the way of a complete education is like putting out the eyes; to deny the rights of property, like cutting off the hands. To deny political equality is to rob the ostracised of all self-respect; of credit in the market place; of recompense in the world of work; of a voice in those who make and administer the law; a choice in the jury before whom they are tried, and in the judge who decides their punishment. Shakespeare's play of Titus and Andronicus contains a terrible satire on woman's position in the nineteenth century—"Rude men" (the play tells us) "seized the king's daughter, cut out her tongue, cut off her hands, and then bade her go call for water and wash her hands." What a picture of woman's position. Robbed of her natural rights, handicapped by law and custom at every turn, yet compelled to fight her own battles, and in the emergencies of life to fall back on herself for protection.

The girl of sixteen, thrown on the world to support herself, to make her own place in society, to resist the temptations that surround her and maintain a spotless integrity, must do all this by native force or superior education. She does not acquire this power by being trained to trust others and distrust herself. If she wearies of the struggle, finding it hard work to swim upstream, and allows herself to drift with the current, she will find plenty of company, but not one to share her misery in the hour of her deepest humiliation. If she tries to retrieve her position, to conceal the past, her life is hedged about with fears lest willing hands should tear the veil from what she fain would hide. Young and friendless, *she* knows the bitter solitude of self.

How the little courtesies of life on the surface of society, deemed so important from man towards woman, fade into utter insignificance in view of the deeper tragedies in which she must play her part alone, where no human aid is possible.

The young wife and mother, at the head of some establishment with a kind husband to shield her from the adverse winds of life, with wealth, fortune and position, has a certain harbor of safety, secure against the ordinary ills of life. But to manage a household, have a desirable influence in society, keep her friends and the affections of her husband, train her children and servants well, she must have rare common sense, wisdom, diplomacy, and a knowledge of human nature. To do all this she needs the cardinal virtues and the strong points of character that the most successful statesman possesses.

An uneducated woman, trained to dependence, with no resources in herself must make a failure of any position in life. But society says women do not need a knowledge of the world; the liberal training that experience in public life must give, all the advantages of collegiate education; but when for the lack of all this, the woman's happiness is wrecked, alone she bears her humiliation; and the solitude of the weak and the ignorant is indeed pitiable. In the wild chase for the prizes of life they are ground to powder.

In age, when the pleasures of youth are passed, children grown up, married and gone, the hurry and bustle of life in a measure over, when the hands are weary of active service, when the old armchair and the fireside are the chosen resorts, then men and women alike must fall back on their own resources. If they cannot find companionship in books, if they have no interest in the vital questions of the hour, no interest in watching the consummation of reforms, with which they might have been identified, they soon pass into their dotage. The more fully the faculties of the mind are developed and kept in use, the longer the period of vigor and active interest in all around us continues. If from a lifelong participation in public affairs a woman feels responsible for the laws regulating our system of education, the discipline of our jails and prisons, the sanitary condition of our private homes, public buildings, and thoroughfares, an interest in commerce, finance, our foreign relations, in any or all these questions, her solitude will at least be respectable, and she will not be driven to gossip or scandal for entertainment.

The chief reason for opening to every soul the doors to the whole round of human duties and pleasures is the individual development thus attained, the resources thus provided under all circumstances to mitigate the solitude that at times must come to everyone. I once asked Prince Krapotkin, a Russian nihilist, how he endured his long years in prison, deprived of books, pen, ink, and paper. "Ah," he said, "I thought out many questions in which I had a deep interest. In the pursuit of an idea I took no note of time. When tired of solving knotty problems I recited all the beautiful passages in prose or verse I had ever learned. I became acquainted with myself and my own resources. I had a world of my own, a vast empire, that no Russian jailor or Czar could invade." Such is the value of liberal thought and broad culture when shut off from all human companionship, bringing comfort and sunshine within even the four walls of a prison cell.

As women ofttimes share a similar fate, should they not have all the consolation that the most liberal education can give? Their suffering in the prisons of St. Petersburg; in the long, weary marches to Siberia, and in the mines, working side by side with men, surely call for all the self-support that the most exalted sentiments of heroism can give. When suddenly roused at midnight, with the startling cry of "fire! fire!" to find the house over their heads in flames, do women wait for men to point the way to safety? And are the men, equally bewildered and half suffocated with smoke, in a position to do more than try to save themselves?

At such times the most timid women have shown a courage and heroism in saving their husbands and children that has surprised everybody. Inasmuch, then, as woman shares equally the joys and sorrows of time and eternity, is it not the height of presumption in man to propose to represent her at the ballot box and the throne of grace, to do her voting in the state, her praying in the church, and to assume the position of high priest at the family altar?

Nothing strengthens the judgment and quickens the conscience like individual responsibility. Nothing adds such dignity to character as the recognition of one's self-sovereignty; the right to an equal place, everywhere conceded; a place earned by personal merit, not an artificial attainment, by inheritance, wealth, family, and position. Seeing, then, that the responsibilities of life rest equally on man and woman, that their destiny is the same, they need the same preparation for time and eternity. The talk of sheltering woman from the fierce storms of life is the sheerest mockery, for they beat on her from every point of the compass, just as they do on man, and with more fatal results, for he has been trained to protect himself, to resist, to conquer. Such are the facts in human experience, the responsibilities of individual sovereignty. Rich and poor, intelligent and ignorant, wise and foolish, virtuous and vicious, man and woman, it is ever the same, each soul must depend wholly on itself.

Whatever the theories may be of woman's dependence on man, in the supreme moments of her life he can not bear her burdens. Alone she goes to the gates of death to give life to every man that is born into the world. No one can share her fears, no one can mitigate her pangs; and if her sorrow is greater than she can bear, alone she passes beyond the gates into the vast unknown.

From the mountain tops of Judea, long ago, a heavenly voice bade His disciples "Bear ye one another's burdens," but humanity has not yet risen to that point of self-sacrifice, and if ever so willing, how few the burdens are that one soul can bear for another. In the highways of Palestine; in prayer and fasting on the solitary mountain top; in the Garden of Gethsemane; before the judgment seat of Pilate; betrayed by one of His trusted disciples at His last supper; in His agonies on the cross, even Jesus of Nazareth, in these last sad days on earth, felt the awful solitude of self. Deserted by man, in agony he cries, "My God! My God! why hast Thou forsaken me?" And so it ever must be in the conflicting scenes of life, in the long, weary march, each one walks alone. We may have many friends, love, kindness, sympathy, and charity to smoothe our pathway in everyday life, but in the tragedies and triumphs of human experience each mortal stands alone.

But when all artificial trammels are removed, and women are recognized as individuals, responsible for their own environments, thoroughly educated for all positions in life they may be called to fill; with all the resources in themselves that liberal thought and broad culture can give; guided by their own conscience and judgment; trained to self-protection by a healthy development of the muscular system and skill in the use of weapons of defense, and stimulated to self-support by a knowledge of the business world and the pleasure that pecuniary independence must ever give; when women are trained in this way they will, in a measure, be fitted for those hours of solitude that come alike to all, whether prepared or otherwise. As in our extremity we must depend on ourselves, the dictates of wisdom point to complete individual development.

In talking of education how shallow the argument, that each class must be educated for the special work it proposes to do, and all those faculties not needed in this special walk must lie dormant and utterly wither for want of use, when, perhaps, these will be the very faculties needed in life's greatest emergencies. Some say, Where is the use of drilling girls in the languages, the sciences, in law, medicine, theology? As wives, mothers, housekeepers, cooks, they need a different curriculum from boys who are to fill all positions. The chief cooks in our great hotels and ocean steamers are men. In our large cities men run the bakeries; they make our bread, cake and pies. They manage the laundries; they are now considered our best milliners and dressmakers. Because some men fill these departments of usefulness, shall we regulate the curriculum in Harvard and Yale to their present necessities? If not, why this talk in our best colleges of a curriculum for girls who are crowding into the trades and professions; teachers in all our public schools, rapidly filling many lucrative and honorable positions in life? They are showing, too, their calmness and courage in the most trying hours of human experience.

You have probably all read in the daily papers of the terrible storm in the Bay of Biscay when a tidal wave made such havoc on the shore, wrecking vessels, unroofing houses, and carrying destruction everywhere. Among other buildings the woman's prison was demolished. Those who escaped saw men struggling to reach the shore. They promptly by clasping hands made a chain of themselves and pushed out into the sea, again and again, at the risk of their lives, until they had brought six men to shore, carried them to a shelter, and did all in their power for their comfort and protection.

What special school training could have prepared these women for this sublime moment in their lives? In times like this humanity rises above all college curriculums and recognizes Nature as the greatest of all teachers in the hour of danger and death. Women are already the equals of men in the whole realm of thought, in art, science, literature, and government. With telescopic vision they explore the starry firmament and bring back the history of the planetary world. With chart and compass they pilot ships across the mighty deep, and with skillful finger send electric messages around the globe. In galleries of art the beauties of nature and the virtues of humanity are immortalized by them on canvas and by their inspired touch dull blocks of marble are transformed into angels of light.

In music they speak again the language of Mendelssohn, Beethoven, Chopin, Schumann, and are worthy interpreters of their great thoughts. The poetry and novels of the century are theirs, and they have touched the keynote of reform in religion, politics, and social life. They fill the editor's and professor's chair, and plead at the bar of justice, walk the wards of the hospital, and speak from the pulpit and the platform; such is the type of womanhood that an enlightened public sentiment welcomes to-day, and such the triumph of the facts of life over the false theories of the past.

Is it, then, consistent to hold the developed woman of this day within the same narrow political limits as the dame with the spinning wheel and knitting needle occupied in the past? No! no! Machinery has taken the labors of woman as well as man on its tireless shoulders; the loom and the spinning wheel are but dreams of the past; the pen, the brush, the easel, the chisel, have taken their places, while the hopes and ambitions of women are essentially changed.

We see reason sufficient in the outer conditions of human beings for individual liberty and development, but when we consider the self dependence of every human soul we see the need of courage, judgment, and the exercise of every faculty of mind and body, strengthened and developed by use, in woman as well as man.

Whatever may be said of man's protecting power in ordinary conditions, mid all the terrible disasters by land and sea, in the supreme moments of danger, alone woman must ever meet the horrors of the situation; the Angel of Death even makes no royal pathway for her. Man's love and sympathy enter only into the sunshine of our lives. In that solemn solitude of self, that links us with the immeasurable and the eternal, each soul lives alone forever. A recent writer says:

I remember once, in crossing the Atlantic, to have gone upon the deck of the ship at midnight, when a dense black cloud enveloped the sky, and the great deep was roaring madly under the lashes of demoniac winds. My feeling was not of danger or fear (which is a base surrender of the immortal soul), but of utter desolation and loneliness; a little speck of life shut in by a tremendous darkness. Again I remember to have climbed the slopes of the Swiss Alps, up beyond the point where vegetation ceases, and the stunted conifers no longer struggle against the unfeeling blasts. Around me lay a huge confusion of rocks, out of which the gigantic ice peaks shot into the measureless blue of the heavens, and again my only feeling was the awful solitude.

And yet, there is a solitude, which each and every one of us has always carried with him more inaccessible than the ice-cold mountains, more profound than the midnight sea; the solitude of self. Our inner being, which we call ourself, no eye nor touch of man or angel has ever pierced. It is more hidden than the caves of the gnome; the sacred adytum of the oracle; the hidden chamber of eleusinian mystery, for to it only omniscience is permitted to enter.

Such is individual life. Who, I ask you, can take, dare take, on himself the rights, the duties, the responsibilities of another human soul?

January 18, 1892

★ ★ ★

Henry Cabot Lodge: Speech in the Senate on Immigration

MR. PRESIDENT: This bill is intended to amend the existing law so as to restrict still further immigration to the United States. Paupers, diseased persons, convicts, and contract laborers are now excluded. By this bill it is proposed to make a new class of excluded immigrants, and add to those which have just been named the totally ignorant. The bill is of the simplest kind. The first section excludes from the country all immigrants who cannot read and write either their own or some other language. The second section merely provides a simple test for determining whether the immigrant can read or write, and is added to the bill so as to define the duties of the immigrant inspectors, and to assure to all immigrants alike perfect justice and a fair test of their knowledge.

Two questions arise in connection with this bill. The first is as to the merits of this particular form of restriction; the second as to the general policy of restricting immigration at all. I desire to discuss briefly these two questions in the order in which I have stated them. The smaller question as to the merits of this particular bill comes first. The existing laws of the United States now exclude, as I have said, certain classes of immigrants who, it is universally agreed, would be most undesirable additions to our population. These exclusions have been enforced, and the results have been beneficial; but the excluded classes are extremely limited and do not by any means cover all or even any considerable part of the immigrants whose presence here is undesirable or injurious, nor do they have any adequate effect in properly reducing the great body of immigration to this country. There can be no doubt that there is a very earnest desire on the part of the American people to restrict further, and much more extensively than has yet been done, foreign immigration to the United States. The question before the committee was how this could best be done; that is, by what method the largest number of undesirable immigrants and the smallest possible number of desirable immigrants could be shut out. Three methods of obtaining this further restriction have been widely discussed of late years, and in various forms have been brought to the attention of Congress. The first was the imposition of a capitation tax on all immigrants. There can be no doubt as to the effectiveness of this method if the tax is made sufficiently heavy. But although exclusion by a tax would be thorough, it would be undiscriminating, and your committee did not feel that the time had yet come for its application. The second scheme was to restrict immigration by requiring consular certification of immigrants. This plan has been much advocated, and if it were possible to carry it out thoroughly and to add very largely to the number of our consuls in order to do so, it would no doubt be effective and beneficial. But the committee was satisfied that consular certification was, under existing circumstances, impractical; that the necessary machinery could not be provided; that it would lead to many serious questions with foreign governments; that it could not be properly and justly enforced; and that it would take a long time to put it in operation. It is not necessary to go further into the details which brought the committee to this conclusion. It is sufficient to say here that the opinion of the committee is shared, they believe, by all expert judges who have given the most careful attention to the question.

The third method was to exclude all immigrants who could neither read nor write, and this is the plan which was adopted by the committee and which is embodied in this bill. In their report the committee have shown by statistics, which have been collected and tabulated with great care, the emigrants who would be affected by this illiteracy test. It is not neces- sary for me here to do more than summarize the results of the committee's investigation, which have been set forth fully in their report. It is found, in the first place, that the illiteracy test will bear most heavily upon the Italians, Russians, Poles, Hungarians, Greeks, and Asiatics, and very lightly, or not at all, upon English-speaking emigrants, or Germans, Scandinavians, and French. In other words, the races most affected by the illiteracy test are those whose emigration to this country has begun within the last twenty years and swelled rapidly to enormous proportions, races with which the English-speaking people have never hitherto assimilated, and who are most alien to the great body of the people of the United States. On the other hand, immigrants from the United Kingdom and of those races which are most closely related to the English-speaking people, and who with the English-speaking people themselves founded the American colonies and built up the United States, are affected but little by the proposed test. These races would not be prevented by this law from coming to this country in practically undiminished numbers. These kindred races also are those who alone go to the Western and Southern States, where immigrants are desired, and take up our unoccupied lands. The races which would suffer most seriously by exclusion under the proposed bill furnish the immigrants who do not go to the West or South, where immigration is needed, but who remain on the Atlantic seaboard, where immigration is not needed and where their presence is most injurious and undesirable.

The statistics prepared by the committee show further that the immigrants excluded by the illiteracy test are those who remain for the most part in congested masses in our great cities. They furnish, as other tables show, a large proportion of the population of the slums. The committee's report proves that illiteracy runs parallel with the slum population, with criminals, paupers, and juvenile delinquents of foreign birth or parentage, whose percentage is out of all proportion to their share of the total population when compared with the percentage of the same classes among the native born. It also appears from investigations which have been made that the immigrants who would be shut out by the illiteracy test are those who bring least money to the country and come most quickly upon private or public charity for support. The replies of the governors of twenty-six states to the Immigration Restriction League show that in only two cases are immigrants of the classes affected by the illiteracy test desired, and those are of a single race. All the other immigrants mentioned by the governors as desirable belong to the races which are but slightly affected by the provisions of this bill. It is also proved that the classes now excluded by law—the criminals, the diseased, the paupers, and the contract laborers—are furnished chiefly by the same races as those most affected by the test of illiteracy. The same is true as to those immigrants who come to this country for a brief season and return to their native land, taking with them the money they have earned in the United States. There is no more hurtful and undesirable class of immigrants from every point of view than these "birds of passage," and the tables show that the races furnishing the largest number of "birds of passage" have also the greatest proportion of illiterates.

These facts prove to demonstration that the exclusion of immigrants unable to read or write, as proposed by this bill, will operate against the most undesirable and harmful part of our present immigration, and shut out elements which no thoughtful or patriotic man can wish to see multiplied among the people of the United States. The report of the committee also proves that this bill meets the great requirement of all legislation of this character, in excluding the greatest proportion possible of thoroughly undesirable and dangerous immigrants and the smallest proportion of immigrants who are unobjectionable.

I have said enough to show what the effects of this bill would be, and that if enacted into law it would be fair in its operation and highly beneficial in its results. It now remains for me to discuss the second and larger question, as to the advisability of restricting immigration at all. This is a subject of the greatest magnitude and the most far-reaching importance. It has two sides, the economic and the social. As to the former, but few words are necessary. There is no one thing which does so much to bring about a reduction of wages and to injure the American wage earner as the unlimited introduction of cheap foreign labor through unrestricted immigration. Statistics show that the change in the race character of our immigration has been accompanied by a corresponding decline in its quality. The number of skilled mechanics and of the persons trained to some occupation or pursuit has fallen off, while the number of those without occupation or training, that is, who are totally unskilled, has risen in our recent immigration to enormous proportions. This low, unskilled labor is the most deadly enemy of the American wage earner, and does more than anything else toward lowering his wages and forcing down his standard of living. An attempt was made, with the general assent of both political parties, to meet this crying evil some years ago by the passage of what are known as the contract-labor laws. That legislation was excellent in intention, but has proved of but little value in practice. It has checked to a certain extent the introduction of cheap, low-class labor in large masses into the United States. It has made it a little more difficult for such labor to come here; but the labor of this class continues to come, even if not in the same way, and the total amount of it has not been materially reduced. Even if the contract-labor laws were enforced intelligently and thoroughly, there is no reason to suppose that they would have any adequate effect in checking the evil which they were designed to stop. It is perfectly clear, after the experience of several years, that the only relief which can come to the American wage earner from the competition of low-class immigrant labor must be by general laws restricting the total amount of immigration, and framed in such a way as to affect most strongly those elements of the immigration which furnish the low, unskilled, and ignorant foreign labor.

It is not necessary to enter further into a discussion of the economic side of the general policy of restricting immigration. In this direction the argument is unanswerable. If we have any regard for the welfare, the wages, or the standard of life of American workingmen, we should take immediate steps to restrict foreign immigration. There is no danger, at present at all events, to our workingmen from the coming of skilled mechanics or trained and educated men with a settled occupation or pursuit, for immigrants of this class will never seek to lower the American standard of life and wages. On the contrary, they desire the same standard for themselves. But there is an appalling danger to the American wage earner from the flood of low, unskilled, ignorant, foreign labor which has poured into the country for some years past, and which not only takes lower wages, but accepts a standard of life and living so low that the American workingman cannot compete with it.

I now come to the aspect of this question which is graver and more serious than any other. The injury of unrestricted immigration to American wages and American standards of living is sufficiently plain and is bad enough, but the danger which this immigration threatens to the quality of our citizenship is far worse. That which it concerns us to know, and that which is more vital to us as a people than all possible questions of tariff or currency, is whether the quality of our citizenship is endangered by the present course and character of immigration to the United States. To determine this question we must look into the history of our race.

Two hundred years ago Daniel Defoe, in some very famous verses called the "True-born Englishman," defended William III, the greatest ruler, with the exception of Cromwell, whom England has had since the days of the Plantagenets, against the accusation so constantly made at the time that he was a foreigner. The line taken by Defoe is the highly characteristic one of a fierce attack upon his opponents. He declared, in lines which were as forcible as they were rough, that the English-speaking people drew their descent from many sources; that there was no such thing as a pure-blooded Englishman; and that King William was as much an Englishman as any of them. The last proposition, in regard to the King, whose mother was a Stuart, was undoubtedly true. It was also superficially true that

Englishmen drew their blood from many strains; but the rest of the argument was ludicrously false if the matter is considered in the light of modern history and modern science.

For practical purposes in considering the question of race and in dealing with the civilized peoples of western Europe and of America, there is no such thing as a race of original purity according to the divisions of ethnical science. In considering the practical problems of the present time we can deal only with artificial races,—that is, races like the English-speaking people, the French, or the Germans,—who have been developed as races by the operation during a long period of time of climatic influences, wars, migrations, conquests, and industrial development. To the philologist and the ethnologist it is of great importance to determine the ethnical divisions of mankind in the earliest historic times. To the scientific modern historian, to the student of social phenomena, and to the statesman alike, the early ethnic divisions are of little consequence; but the sharply marked race divisions which have been gradually developed by the conditions and events of the last thousand years are absolutely vital. It is by these conditions and events that the races or nations which to-day govern the world have been produced, and it is their characteristics which it is important for us to understand.

How, then, has the English-speaking race, which to-day controls so large a part of the earth's surface, been formed? Great Britain and Ireland at the time of the Roman conquest were populated by Celtic tribes. After the downfall of the Roman Empire these tribes remained in possession of the islands, with probably but very slight infusion of Latin blood. Then came what is commonly known as the Saxon invasion. Certain North German tribes, own brothers to those other tribes which swept southward and westward over the whole Roman Empire, crossed the English Channel and landed in the corner of England known as the Isle of Thanet. They were hard fighters, pagans, and adventurers. They swept over the whole of England and the Lowlands of Scotland. A few British words like basket, relating to domestic employments, indicate that only women of the conquered race, and not many of those, were spared. The extermination was fierce and thorough. The native Celts were driven back into the Highlands of Scotland and to the edge of the sea in Cornwall and Wales, while all the rest of the land became Saxon.

The conquerors established themselves in their new country, were converted to Christianity, and began to advance in civilization. Then came a fresh wave from the Germanic tribes. This time it was the Danes. They were of the same blood as the Saxons, and the two kindred races fought hard for the possession of England, until the last comers prevailed and their chiefs reached the throne. Then in 1066 there was another invasion, this time from the shores of France. But the new invaders and conquerors were not Frenchmen. As Carlyle says, they were only Saxons who spoke French. A hundred years before, these Normans, or Northmen, northernmost of all the Germanic tribes, had descended from their land of snow and ice upon Europe. They were the most remarkable of all the people who poured out of the Germanic forests. They came upon Europe in their long, low ships, a set of fighting pirates and buccaneers; and yet these same pirates brought with them out of the darkness and cold of the north a remarkable literature and a strange and poetic mythology. Wherever they went they conquered, and wherever they stopped they set up for themselves dukedoms, principalities, and kingdoms. To them we owe the marvels of Gothic architecture, for it was they who were the great builders and architects of mediæval Europe. They were great military engineers as well, and revived the art of fortified defense, which had been lost to the world. They were great statesmen and great generals, and they had only been in Normandy about a hundred years when they crossed the English Channel, conquered the country, and gave to England for many generations to come her kings and nobles. But the Normans in their turn were absorbed or blended with the great mass of the Danes and the still earlier Saxons. In reality, they were all one people. They had different names and spoke differing dialects, but their blood and their characteristics were the same. And so this Germanic people of one blood, coming through various channels, dwelt in England, assimilating more or less and absorbing to a greater or less degree their neighbors of the northern and western Celtic fringe, with an occasional fresh infusion from their own brethren who dwelt in the low sea-girt lands at the mouths of the Scheldt and Rhine. In the course of the centuries these people were welded together and had made a new speech and a new race, with strong and well-defined qualities, both mental and moral.

When the Reformation came this work was pretty nearly done; and after that great movement had struck off the shackles from the human mind, the English-speaking people were ready to come forward and begin to play their part in a world where the despotism of the church had been broken, and where political despotism was about to enter on its great struggle against the forces of freedom. Let me describe what these English people were at the close of the sixteenth century, when the work of race making had been all done and the achievements of the race so made were about to begin. I will take for this purpose, not words of my own, but the brilliant sentences of one of the greatest of modern English writers:—

> In those past silent centuries, among those silent classes, much had been going on. Not only had red deer in the New and other forests been got preserved, and shot; and treacheries of Simon de Montfort, wars of Red and White Roses, battles of Crecy, battles of Bosworth, and many other battles been got transacted, and adjusted; but England wholly, not without sore toil and aching bones to the millions of sires and the millions of sons these eighteen generations, had been got drained, and tilled, covered with yellow harvests, beautiful and rich possessions; the mud-wooden Ceasters and Chesters had become steepled, tile-roofed, compact towns. Sheffield had taken to the manufacture of Sheffield

whittles; Worstead could from wool spin yarn, and knit or weave the same into stockings or breeches for men. England had property valuable to the auctioneer; but the accumulate manufacturing, commercial, economic skill which lay impalpably warehoused in English hands and heads, what auctioneer could estimate?

Hardly an Englishman to be met with but could do something—some cunninger thing than break his fellow-creature's head with battle-axes. The seven incorporated trades, with their million guild brethren, with their hammers, their shuttles, and tools; what an army—fit to conquer that land of England, as we say, and to hold it conquered. Nay, strangest of all, the English people had acquired the faculty and habit of thinking, even of believing; individual conscience had unfolded itself among them; conscience, and intelligence its handmaid. Ideas of innumerable kinds were circulating among these men; witness one Shakespeare, a wool-comber, poacher, or whatever else, at Stratford, in Warwickshire, who happened to write books—the finest human figure, as I apprehend, that nature has hitherto seen fit to make of our widely diffused Teutonic clay. Saxon, Norman, Celt, or Sarmat, I find no human soul so beautiful these fifteen hundred known years—our supreme modern European man. Him England had contrived to realize. Were there not ideas—ideas poetic and also puritanic, that had to seek utterance in the notablest way? England had got her Shakespeare, but was now about to get her Milton and Oliver Cromwell. This, too, we will call a new expansion, hard as it might be to articulate and adjust; this, that a man could actually have a conscience for his own behoof, and not for his priest's only; that his priest, be who he might, would henceforth have to take that fact along with him. One of the hardest things to adjust. It is not adjusted down to this hour. It lasts onward to the time they call "glorious revolution" before so much as a reasonable truce can be made and the war proceed by logic mainly. And still it is war, and no peace, unless we call waste vacancy peace. But it needed to be adjusted, as the others had done, as still others will do.

This period, when the work of centuries which had resulted in the making of the English people was complete, and when they were entering upon their career of world conquest, is of peculiar interest to us. Then it was that from the England of Shakespeare and Bacon and Raleigh, and later from the England of Pym and Hampden and Cromwell and Milton, Englishmen fared forth across the great ocean to the North American Continent. The first Englishmen to come and to remain here settled on the James River, and there laid the foundation of the great State of Virginia. The next landed much farther to the north. I will again borrow the words of Carlyle to describe the coming of this second English migration:—

> But now on the industrial side, while this great constitutional controversy and revolt of the middle class had not ended, had yet but begun, what a shoot was that that England, carelessly, in quest of other objects, struck out across the ocean, into the waste land, which it named New England. Hail to thee, poor little ship Mayflower, of Delft-Haven! poor common-looking ship, hired by common charter party for coined dollars; calked with mere oakum and tar; provisioned with vulgarest biscuit and bacon; yet what ship Argo, or miraculous epic ship built by the sea gods, was other than a foolish bumbarge in comparison? Golden fleeces or the like these sailed for, with or without effect; thou, little Mayflower, hadst in thee a veritable Promethean spark; the life spark of the largest nation on our earth, so we may already name the transatlantic Saxon nation. They went seeking leave to hear sermon in their own method, these Mayflower Puritans; a most honest indispensable search; and yet, like Saul the son of Kish, seeking a small thing, they found this unexpected great thing. Honor to the brave and true! they verily, we say, carry fire from heaven, and have a power that themselves dream not of. Let all men honor Puritanism, since God has so honored it.

At the period of these two English settlements, and just about at the same time, the Dutch settled at the mouth of the Hudson and the Swedes upon the Delaware. Both, be it remembered, were of the same original race stock as the English settlers of Virginia and New England, who were destined to be so predominant in the North American colonies. At the close of the seventeenth century and during the eighteenth there came to America three other migrations of people sufficiently numerous to be considered in estimating the races from which the colonists were derived. These were the Scotch-Irish, the Germans, and the French Huguenots. The Scotch-Irish, as they are commonly called with us, were immigrants from the north of Ireland. They were chiefly descendants of Cromwell's soldiers, who had been settled in Ulster, and of the Lowland Scotch, who had come to the same region. They were the men who made the famous defense of Londonderry against James II, and differed in no essential respect either of race or language from the English who had preceded them in America. Some of them settled in New Hampshire, but most of them in the western part of Pennsylvania, Maryland, and Virginia. They were found in all the colonies in a greater or less degree, and were a vigorous body of men, who have contributed very largely to the upbuilding of the United States and played a great part in our history. The German immigrants were the Protestants of the Palatinate, and they settled in large numbers in western Pennsylvania, Maryland, and Virginia. The Huguenots, although not very numerous, were a singularly fine body of people. They had shown the highest moral qualities in their long struggle for religious freedom. They had faced war, massacre, and persecution for nearly two centuries, and had never wavered in their constancy to the creed in which they believed. Harried and driven out of France by Louis XIV, they had sought refuge in Holland, in England, and in the New World. They were to be found in this country in all our colonies, and everywhere they became a most valuable addition to our population.

Such, then, briefly were the people composing the colonies when we faced England in the war for independence. It will be observed that, with the exception of the Huguenot French, who formed but a small percentage of the total population, the people of the thirteen colonies were all of the same original race stocks. The Dutch, the Swedes, and the Germans simply blended again with the English-speaking people, who like them were descended from the Germanic tribes whom Cæsar fought and Tacitus described.

During the present century, down to 1875, there have been three large migrations to this country in addition to the always steady stream from Great Britain; one came from Ireland about the middle of the century, and somewhat later one from Germany and one from Scandinavia, in which is included Sweden, Denmark, and Norway. The Irish, although of a different race stock originally, have been closely associated with the English-speaking people for nearly a thousand years. They speak the same language, and during that long period the two races have lived side by side, and to some extent intermarried. The Germans and Scandinavians are again people of the same race stock as the English who founded and built up the colonies. During this century, down to 1875, then, as in the two which preceded it, there had been scarcely any immigration to this country except from kindred or allied races, and no other which was sufficiently numerous to have produced any effect on the national characteristics, or to be taken into account here. Since 1875, however, there has been a great change. While the people who for two hundred and fifty years have been migrating to America have continued to furnish large numbers of immigrants to the United States, other races of totally different race origin, with whom the English-speaking people have never hitherto been assimilated or brought in contact, have suddenly begun to immigrate to the United States in large numbers. Russians, Hungarians, Poles, Bohemians, Italians, Greeks, and even Asiatics, whose immigration to America was almost unknown twenty years ago, have during the last twenty years poured in in steadily increasing numbers, until now they nearly equal the immigration of those races kindred in blood or speech, or both, by whom the United States has hitherto been built up and the American people formed.

This momentous fact is the one which confronts us to-day, and if continued, it carries with it future consequences far deeper than any other event of our times. It involves, in a word, nothing less than the possibility of a great and perilous change in the very fabric of our race.

The English-speaking race, as I have shown, has been made slowly during the centuries. Nothing has happened thus far to change it radically here. In the United States, after allowing for the variations produced by new climatic influences and changed conditions of life and of political institutions, it is still in the great essentials fundamentally the same race. The additions in this country until the present time have been from kindred people, or from those with whom we have been long allied and who speak the same language. By those who look at this question superficially, we hear it often said that the English-speaking people, especially in America, are a mixture of races. Analysis shows that the actual mixture of blood in the English-speaking race is very small, and that while the English-speaking people are derived through different channels, no doubt, there is among them none the less an overwhelming preponderance of the same race stock, that of the great Germanic tribes who reached from Norway to the Alps. They have been welded together by more than a thousand years of wars, conquests, migrations, and struggles, both at home and abroad, and in so doing they have attained a fixity and definiteness of national character unknown to any other people. Let me quote on this point a disinterested witness of another race and another language, M. Gustave Le Bon, a distinguished French writer of the highest scientific training and attainments, who says in his very remarkable book on the Evolution of Races:—

Most of the historic races of Europe are still in process of formation, and it is important to realize this fact in order to understand their history. The English alone represent a race almost entirely fixed. In them, the ancient Briton, the Saxon, and the Norman have been effaced to form a new and very homogeneous type.

It being admitted, therefore, that a historic race of fixed type has been developed, it remains to consider what this means, what a race is, and what a change would portend. That which identifies a race and sets it apart from others is not to be found merely or ultimately in its physical appearance, its institutions, its laws, its literature, or even its language. These are in the last analysis only the expression or the evidence of race. The achievements of the intellect pass easily from land to land and from people to people. The telephone, invented but yesterday, is used to-day in China, in Australia, or in South Africa as freely as in the United States. The book which the press to-day gives to the world in English is scattered to-morrow throughout the earth in every tongue, and the thoughts of the writer become the property of mankind. You can take a Hindoo and give him the highest education the world can afford. He has a keen intelligence. He will absorb the learning of Oxford, he will acquire the manners and habits of England, he will sit in the British Parliament, but you cannot make him an Englishman. Yet, he, like his conqueror, is of the great Indo-European family. But it has taken six thousand years and more to create the differences which exist between them. You cannot efface those differences thus made, by education in a single life, because they do not rest upon the intellect. What, then, is the matter of race which separates the Englishman from the Hindoo and the American from the Indian? It is something deeper and more fundamental than anything which concerns the intellect. We all know it instinctively, although it is so impalpable that we can scarcely define it, and yet is so deeply marked that even the physiological differences between the Negro, the Mongol, and the Caucasian are not more persistent or more obvious. When we speak of a race, then, we do not mean its expressions in art or in language, or its achievements in knowledge. We mean the moral and intellectual characters, which in their association make the soul of a race, and which represent the product of all its past, the inheritance of all its ancestors, and the motives of all its conduct. The men of each race possess an indestructible stock of ideas, traditions, sentiments, modes of thought, an unconscious inheritance from their ancestors, upon which argument has no effect. What makes a race are their mental and, above all, their moral characteristics, the slow growth and accumulation of centuries of toil and conflict. These are the qualities which determine their social efficiency as a people, which make one race rise and another fall, which we draw out of a dim past through many generations of ancestors, about which we cannot argue, but in which we blindly believe, and which guide us in our short-lived generation as they have guided the race itself across the centuries.

I have cited a witness of the highest authority and entire disinterestedness to support what I have said as to the fixed and determinate character of the English-speaking race. Now that I come to show what that race is by recounting its qualities and characteristics, I will not trust myself to speak, for I might be accused of prejudice, but I will quote again M. Le Bon, who is not of our race nor of our speech.

He says:—

Inability to foresee the remote consequences of actions and the tendency to be guided only by the instinct of the moment, condemn an individual as well as a race to remain always in a very inferior condition. It is only in proportion as they have been able to master their instincts—that is to say, as they have acquired strength of will and consequently empire over themselves—that nations have been able to understand the importance of discipline, the necessity of sacrificing themselves to an ideal and lifting themselves up to civilization. If it were necessary to determine by a single test the social level of races in history, I would take willingly as a standard the aptitude displayed by each in controlling their impulses. The Romans in antiquity, the Anglo-Americans in modern times, represent the people who have possessed this quality in the highest degree. It has powerfully contributed to assure their greatness.

Again he says, speaking now more in detail:—

Let us summarize, then, in a few words the characteristics of the Anglo-Saxon race, which has peopled the United States. There is not perhaps in the world one which is more homogeneous and whose mental constitution is more easy to define in its great outline. The dominant qualities of this mental constitution are, from the standpoint of character, a will power which scarcely any people except perhaps the Romans have possessed, an unconquerable energy, a very great initiative, an absolute empire over self, a sentiment of independence pushed even to excessive unsociability, a puissant activity, very keen religious sentiments, a very fixed morality, a very clear idea of duty.

Again he says:—

But, above all, it is in a new country like America that we must follow the astonishing progress due to the mental constitution of the English race. Transported to a wilderness inhabited only by savages and having only itself to count upon, we know what that race has done. Scarcely a century has been necessary to those people to place themselves in the first rank of the great powers of the world, and to-day there is hardly one who could struggle against them.

Such achievements as M. Le Bon credits us with are due to the qualities of the American people, whom he, as a man of science looking below the surface, rightly describes as homogeneous. Those qualities are moral far more than intellectual, and it is on the moral qualities of the English-speaking race that our history, our victories, and all our future rest. There is only one way in which you can lower those qualities or weaken those characteristics, and that is by breeding them out. If a lower race mixes with a higher in sufficient numbers, history teaches us that the lower race will prevail. The lower race will absorb the higher, not the higher the lower, when the two strains approach equality in numbers. In other words, there is a limit to the capacity of any race for assimilating and elevating an inferior race; and when you begin to pour in in unlimited numbers people of alien or lower races of less social efficiency and less moral force, you are running the most frightful risk that a people can run. The lowering of a great race means not only its own decline, but that of civilization. M. Le Bon sees no danger to us in immigration, and his reason for this view is one of the most interesting things he says. He declares that the people of the United States will never be injured by immigration, because the moment they see the peril the great race instinct will assert itself and shut the immigration out. The reports of the Treasury for the last fifteen years show that the peril is at hand. I trust that the prediction of science is true, and that the unerring instinct of the race will shut the danger out, as it closed the door upon the coming of the Chinese.

That the peril is not imaginary or the offspring of race prejudice, I will prove by another disinterested witness, also a Frenchman. M. Paul Bourget, the distinguished novelist, visited this country a few years ago, and wrote a book containing his impressions of what he saw. He was not content, as many travelers are, to say that our cabs were high-priced, the streets of New York noisy, the cars hot, and then feel that he had disposed of the United States and the people thereof for time and for eternity. M. Bourget saw here a great country and a great people; in other words, a great fact in modern times. Our ways were not his ways, nor our thoughts his thoughts, and he probably liked his own country and his own ways much better; but he none the less studied us carefully and sympathetically. What most interested him was to see whether the socialistic movements, which now occupy the alarmed attention of Europe, were equally threatening here. His conclusion, which I will state in a few words, is of profound interest. He expected to find signs of a coming war of classes, and he went home believing that if any danger threatened the United States it was not from a war of classes, but a war of races.

Mr. President, more precious even than forms of government are the mental and moral qualities which make what we call our race. While those stand unimpaired all is safe. When those decline all is imperiled. They are exposed to but a single danger, and that is by changing the quality of our race and citizenship through the wholesale infusion of races whose traditions and inheritances, whose thoughts and whose beliefs are wholly alien to ours, and with whom we have never assimilated or even been associated in the past. The danger has begun. It is small as yet, comparatively speaking, but it is large enough to warn us to act while there is yet time and while it can be done easily and efficiently. There lies the peril at the portals of our land; there is pressing the tide of unrestricted immigration. The time has certainly come, if not to stop, at least to check, to sift, and to restrict those immigrants. In careless strength, with generous hand, we have kept our gates wide open to all the world. If we do not close them, we should at least place sentinels beside them to challenge those who would pass through. The gates which admit men to the United States and to citizenship in the great republic should no longer be left unguarded.

> O Liberty, white Goddess! is it well
> To leave the gates unguarded? On thy breast
> Fold Sorrow's children, soothe the hurts of fate,
> Lift the down-trodden, but with hand of steel
> Stay those who to thy sacred portals come
> To waste the gifts of freedom. Have a care
> Lest from thy brow the clustered stars be torn

And trampled in the dust. For so of old
The thronging Goth and Vandal trampled Rome,
And where the temples of the Cæsars stood
The lean wolf unmolested made her lair.[1]

March 16, 1896

---

[1] Aldrich, *Unguarded Gates.*

★ ★ ★

Randolph S. Bourne: Trans-National America

No reverberatory effect of the great war has caused American public opinion more solicitude than the failure of the "melting-pot." The discovery of diverse nationalistic feelings among our great alien population has come to most people as an intense shock. It has brought out the unpleasant inconsistencies of our traditional beliefs. We have had to watch hardhearted old Brahmins virtuously indignant at the spectacle of the immigrant refusing to be melted, while they jeer at patriots like Mary Antin who write about "our forefathers." We have had to listen to publicists who express themselves as stunned by the evidence of vigorous nationalistic and cultural movements in this country among Germans, Scandinavians, Bohemians, and Poles, while in the same breath they insist that the alien shall be forcibly assimilated to that Anglo-Saxon tradition which they unquestioningly label "American."

As the unpleasant truth has come upon us that assimilation in this country was proceeding on lines very different from those we had marked out for it, we found ourselves inclined to blame those who were thwarting our prophecies. The truth became culpable. We blamed the war, we blamed the Germans. And then we discovered with a moral shock that these movements had been making great headway before the war even began. We found that the tendency, reprehensible and paradoxical as it might be, has been for the national clusters of immigrants, as they became more and more firmly established and more and more prosperous, to cultivate more and more assiduously the literature and cultural traditions of their homelands. Assimilation, in other words, instead of washing out the memories of

Europe, made them more and more intensely real. Just as these clusters became more and more objectively American, did they become more and more German or Scandinavian or Bohemian or Polish.

To face the fact that our aliens are already strong enough to take a share in the direction of their own destiny, and that the strong cultural movements represented by the foreign press, schools, and colonies are a challenge to our facile attempts, is not, however, to admit the failure of Americanization. It is not to fear the failure of democracy. It is rather to urge us to an investigation of what Americanism may rightly mean. It is to ask ourselves whether our ideal has been broad or narrow— whether perhaps the time has not come to assert a higher ideal than the "melting-pot." Surely we cannot be certain of our spiritual democracy when, claiming to melt the nations within us to a comprehension of our free and democratic institutions, we fly into panic at the first sign of their own will and tendency. We act as if we wanted Americanization to take place only on our own terms, and not by the consent of the governed. All our elaborate machinery of settlement and school and union, of social and political naturalization, however, will move with friction just in so far as it neglects to take into account this strong and virile insistence that America shall be what the immigrant will have a hand in making it, and not what a ruling class, descendant of those British stocks which were the first permanent immigrants, decide that America shall be made. This is the condition which confronts us, and which demands a clear and general readjustment of our attitude and our ideal.

I

Mary Antin is right when she looks upon our foreign-born as the people who missed the Mayflower and came over on the first boat they could find. But she forgets that when they did come it was not upon other Mayflowers, but upon a "Maiblume," a "Fleur de Mai," a "Fior di Maggio," a "Majblomst." These people were not mere arrivals from the same family, to be welcomed as understood and long-loved, but strangers to the neighborhood, with whom a long process of settling down had to take place. For they brought with them their national and racial characters, and each new national quota had to wear slowly away the contempt with which its mere alienness got itself greeted. Each had to make its way slowly from the lowest strata of unskilled labor up to a level where it satisfied the accredited norms of social success.

We are all foreign-born or the descendants of foreign-born, and if distinctions are to be made between us they should rightly be on some other ground than indigenousness. The early colonists came over with motives no less colonial than the later. They did not come to be assimilated in an American melting-pot. They did not come to adopt the culture of the American Indian. They had not the smallest intention of "giving themselves without reservation" to the new country. They came to get freedom to live as they wanted to. They came to escape from the stifling air and chaos of the old world; they came to make their fortune in a new land. They invented no new social framework. Rather they brought over bodily the old ways to which they had been accustomed. Tightly concentrated on a hostile frontier, they were conservative beyond belief. Their pioneer daring was reserved for the objective conquest of material resources. In their folkways, in their social and political institutions, they were, like every colonial people, slavishly imitative of the mother-country. So that, in spite of the "Revolution," our whole legal and political system remained more English than the English, petrified and unchanging, while in England law developed to meet the needs of the changing times.

It is just this English-American conservatism that has been our chief obstacle to social advance. We have needed the new peoples—the order of the German and Scandinavian, the turbulence of the Slav and Hun—to save us from our own stagnation. I do not mean that the illiterate Slav is now the equal of the New Englander of pure descent. He is raw material to be educated, not into a New Englander, but into a socialized American along such lines as those thirty nationalities are being educated in the amazing schools of Gary. I do not believe that this process is to be one of decades of evolution. The spectacle of Japan's sudden jump from mediævalism to post-modernism should have destroyed that superstition. We are not dealing with individuals who are to "evolve." We are dealing with their children, who, with that education we are about to have, will start level with all of us. Let us cease to think of ideals like democracy as magical qualities inherent in certain peoples. Let us speak, not of inferior races, but of inferior civilizations. We are all to educate and to be educated. These peoples in America are in a common enterprise. It is not what we are now that concerns us, but what this plastic next generation may become in the light of a new cosmopolitan ideal.

We are not dealing with static factors, but with fluid and dynamic generations. To contrast the older and the newer immigrants and see the one class as democratically motivated by love of liberty, and the other by mere money-getting, is not to illuminate the future. To think of earlier nationalities as culturally assimilated to America, while we picture the later as a sodden and resistive mass, makes only for bitterness and misunderstanding. There may be a difference between these earlier and these later stocks, but it lies neither in motive for coming nor in strength of cultural allegiance to the home-land. The truth is that no more tenacious cultural allegiance to the mother country has been shown by any alien nation than by the ruling class of Anglo-Saxon descendants in these American States. English snobberies, English religion, English literary styles, English literary reverences and canons, English ethics, English superiorities, have been the cultural food that we have drunk in from our mothers' breasts. The distinctively American spirit—pioneer, as distinguished from the reminis-cently English—that appears in Whitman and Emerson and James, has had to exist on sufferance alongside of this other cult, unconsciously belittled by our cultural makers of opinion.

No country has perhaps had so great indigenous genius which had so little influence on the country's traditions and expressions. The unpopular and dreaded German-American of the present day is a beginning amateur in comparison with those foolish Anglophiles of Boston and New York and Philadelphia whose reversion to cultural type sees uncritically in England's cause the cause of Civilization, and, under the guise of ethical independence of thought, carries along European traditions which are no more "American" than the German categories themselves.

It speaks well for German-American innocence of heart or else for its lack of imagination that it has not turned the hyphen stigma into a "Tu quoque!" If there were to be any hyphens scattered about, clearly they should be affixed to those English descendants who had had centuries of time to be made American where the German had had only half a century. Most significantly has the war brought out of them this alien virus, showing them still loving English things, owing allegiance to the English Kultur, moved by English shibboleths and prejudice. It is only because it has been the ruling class in this country that bestowed the epithets that we have not heard copiously and scornfully of "hyphenated English-Americans." But even our quarrels with England have had the bad temper, the extravagance, of family quarrels. The Englishman of to-day nags us and dislikes us in that personal, peculiarly intimate way in which he dislikes the Australian, or as we may dislike our younger brothers. He still thinks of us incorrigibly as "colonials." America—official, controlling, literary, political America—is still, as a writer recently expressed it, "culturally speaking, a self-governing dominion of the British Empire."

The non-English American can scarcely be blamed if he sometimes thinks of the Anglo-Saxon predominance in America as little more than a predominance of priority. The Anglo-Saxon was merely the first immigrant, the first to found a colony. He has never really ceased to be the descendant of immigrants, nor has he ever succeeded in transforming that

colony into a real nation, with a tenacious, richly woven fabric
of native culture. Colonials from the other nations have come
and settled down beside him. They found no definite native
culture which should startle them out of their colonialism, and
consequently they looked back to their mother-country, as the
earlier Anglo-Saxon immigrant was looking back to his. What
has been offered the newcomer has been the chance to learn
English, to become a citizen, to salute the flag. And those elements of our ruling classes who are responsible for the public
schools, the settlements, all the organizations for amelioration
in the cities, have every reason to be proud of the care and
labor which they have devoted to absorbing the immigrant. His
opportunities the immigrant has taken to gladly, with almost
a pathetic eagerness to make his way in the new land without
friction or disturbance. The common language has made not
only for the necessary communication, but for all the amenities
of life.

If freedom means the right to do pretty much as one pleases,
so long as one does not interfere with others, the immigrant
has found freedom, and the ruling element has been singularly
liberal in its treatment of the invading hordes. But if freedom
means a democratic coöperation in determining the ideals and
purposes and industrial and social institutions of a country, then
the immigrant has not been free, and the Anglo-Saxon element
is guilty of just what every dominant race is guilty of in every
European country: the imposition of its own culture upon the
minority peoples. The fact that this imposition has been so mild
and, indeed, semi-conscious does not alter its quality. And the
war has brought out just the degree to which that purpose of
"Americanizing," that is, "Anglo-Saxonizing," the immigrant
has failed.

For the Anglo-Saxon now in his bitterness to turn upon
the other peoples, talk about their "arrogance," scold them for
not being melted in a pot which never existed, is to betray the
unconscious purpose which lay at the bottom of his heart. It
betrays too the possession of a racial jealousy similar to that of

which he is now accusing the so-called "hyphenates." Let the Anglo-Saxon be proud enough of the heroic toil and heroic sacrifices which moulded the nation. But let him ask himself, if he had had to depend on the English descendants, where he would have been living to-day. To those of us who see in the exploitation of unskilled labor the strident red *leit-motif* of our civilization, the settling of the country presents a great social drama as the waves of immigration broke over it.

Let the Anglo-Saxon ask himself where he would have been if these races had not come? Let those who feel the inferiority of the non-Anglo-Saxon immigrant contemplate that region of the States which has remained the most distinctively "American," the South. Let him ask himself whether he would really like to see the foreign hordes Americanized into such an Americanization. Let him ask himself how superior this native civilization is to the great "alien" states of Wisconsin and Minnesota, where Scandinavians, Poles, and Germans have self-consciously labored to preserve their traditional culture, while being outwardly and satisfactorily American. Let him ask himself how much more wisdom, intelligence, industry and social leadership has come out of these alien states than out of all the truly American ones. The South, in fact, while this vast Northern development has gone on, still remains an English colony, stagnant and complacent, having progressed culturally scarcely beyond the early Victorian era. It is culturally sterile because it has had no advantage of cross-fertilization like the Northern states. What has happened in states such as Wisconsin and Minnesota is that strong foreign cultures have struck root in a new and fertile soil. America has meant liberation, and German and Scandinavian political ideas and social energies have expanded to a new potency. The process has not been at all the fancied "assimilation" of the Scandinavian or Teuton. Rather has it been a process of their assimilation of us—I speak as an Anglo-Saxon. The foreign cultures have not been melted down or run together, made into some homogeneous Americanism, but have remained distinct but coöperating to the greater glory and benefit, not only of themselves but of all the native "Americanism" around them.

What we emphatically do not want is that these distinctive qualities should be washed out into a tasteless, colorless fluid of uniformity. Already we have far too much of this insipidity,— masses of people who are cultural half-breeds, neither assimilated Anglo-Saxons nor nationals of another culture. Each national colony in this country seems to retain in its foreign press, its vernacular literature, its schools, its intellectual and patriotic leaders, a central cultural nucleus. From this nucleus the colony extends out by imperceptible gradations to a fringe where national characteristics are all but lost. Our cities are filled with these half-breeds who retain their foreign names but have lost the foreign savor. This does not mean that they have actually been changed into New Englanders or Middle Westerners. It does not mean that they have been really Americanized. It means that, letting slip from them whatever native culture they had, they have substituted for it only the most rudimentary American—the American culture of the cheap newspaper, the "movies," the popular song, the ubiquitous automobile. The unthinking who survey this class call them assimilated, Americanized. The great American public school has done its work. With these people our institutions are safe. We may thrill with dread at the aggressive hyphenate, but this tame flabbiness is accepted as Americanization. The same moulders of opinion whose ideal is to melt the different races into Anglo-Saxon gold hail this poor product as the satisfying result of their alchemy.

Yet a truer cultural sense would have told us that it is not the self-conscious cultural nuclei that sap at our American life, but these fringes. It is not the Jew who sticks proudly to the faith of his fathers and boasts of that venerable culture of his who is dangerous to America, but the Jew who has lost the Jewish fire and become a mere elementary, grasping animal. It is not the Bohemian who supports the Bohemian schools in Chicago whose influence is sinister, but the Bohemian who has made money and has got into ward politics. Just so surely as we tend to disintegrate these nuclei of nationalistic culture do we tend to create hordes of men and women without a spiritual country, cultural outlaws, without taste, without standards but those of the mob. We sentence them to live on the most rudimentary planes of American life. The influences at the centre of the nuclei are centripetal. They make for the intelligence and the social values which mean an enhancement of life. And just because the foreign-born retains this expressiveness is he likely to be a better citizen of the American community. The influences at the fringe, however, are centrifugal, anarchical. They make for detached fragments of peoples. Those who came to find liberty achieve only license. They become the flotsam and jetsam of American life, the downward undertow of our civilization with its leering cheapness and falseness of taste and spiritual outlook, the absence of mind and sincere feeling which we see in our slovenly towns, our vapid moving pictures, our popular novels, and in the vacuous faces of the crowds on the city street. This is the cultural wreckage of our time, and it is from the fringes of the Anglo-Saxon as well as the other stocks that it falls. America has as yet no impelling integrating force. It makes too easily for this detritus of cultures. In our loose, free country, no constraining national purpose, no tenacious folk-tradition and folk-style hold the people to a line.

The war has shown us that not in any magical formula will this purpose be found. No intense nationalism of the European plan can be ours. But do we not begin to see a new and more adventurous ideal? Do we not see how the national colonies in America, deriving power from the deep cultural heart of Europe and yet living here in mutual toleration, freed from the age-long tangles of races, creeds, and dynasties, may work out a federated ideal? America is transplanted Europe, but a Europe that has not been disintegrated and scattered in the transplanting as in some Dispersion. Its colonies live here inextricably mingled, yet not homogeneous. They merge but they do not fuse.

America is a unique sociological fabric, and it bespeaks poverty of imagination not to be thrilled at the incalculable potentialities of so novel a union of men. To seek no other goal than the weary old nationalism,—belligerent, exclusive, inbreeding, the poison of which we are witnessing now in Europe,—is to make patriotism a hollow sham, and to declare that, in spite of our boastings, America must ever be a follower and not a leader of nations.

II

If we come to find this point of view plausible, we shall have to give up the search for our native "American" culture. With the exception of the South and that New England which, like the Red Indian, seems to be passing into solemn oblivion, there is no distinctively American culture. It is apparently our lot rather to be a federation of cultures. This we have been for half a century, and the war has made it ever more evident that this is what we are destined to remain. This will not mean, however, that there are not expressions of indigenous genius that could not have sprung from any other soil. Music, poetry, philosophy, have been singularly fertile and new. Strangely enough, American genius has flared forth just in those directions which are least understanded of the people. If the American note is bigness, action, the objective as contrasted with the reflective life, where is the epic expression of this spirit? Our drama and our fiction, the peculiar fields for the expression of action and objectivity, are somehow exactly the fields of the spirit which remain poor and mediocre. American materialism is in some way inhibited from getting into impressive artistic form its own energy with which it bursts. Nor is it any better in architecture, the least romantic and subjective of all the arts. We are inarticulate of the very values which we profess to idealize. But in the finer forms—music, verse, the essay, philosophy—the American genius puts forth work equal to any of its contemporaries. Just in so far as our American genius has expressed the pioneer spirit, the adventurous, forward-looking drive of a colonial empire, is it representative of that whole America of the many races and peoples, and not of any partial or traditional enthusiasm. And only as that pioneer note is sounded can we really speak of the American culture. As long as we thought of Americanism in terms of the "melting-pot," our American cultural tradition lay in the past. It was something to which the new Americans were to be moulded. In the light of our changing ideal of Americanism, we must perpetrate the paradox that our American cultural tradition lies in the future. It will be what we all together make out of this incomparable opportunity of attacking the future with a new key.

Whatever American nationalism turns out to be, it is certain to become something utterly different from the nationalisms of twentieth-century Europe. This wave of reactionary enthusiasm to play the orthodox nationalistic game which is passing over the country is scarcely vital enough to last. We cannot swagger and thrill to the same national self-feeling. We must give new edges to our pride. We must be content to avoid the unnumbered woes that national patriotism has brought in Europe, and that fiercely heightened pride and self-consciousness. Alluring as this is, we must allow our imaginations to transcend this scarcely veiled belligerency. We can be serenely too proud to fight if our pride embraces the creative forces of civilization which armed contest nullifies. We can be too proud to fight if our code of honor transcends that of the schoolboy on the playground surrounded by his jeering mates. Our honor must be positive and creative, and not the mere jealous and negative protectiveness against metaphysical violations of our technical rights. When the doctrine is put forth that in one American flows the mystic blood of all our country's sacred honor, freedom, and prosperity, so that an injury to him is to be the signal for turning our whole nation into that clan-feud of horror and reprisal which would be war, then we find ourselves back among the musty schoolmen of the Middle Ages, and not in any pragmatic and realistic America of the twentieth century.

We should hold our gaze to what America has done, not what mediæval codes of dueling she has failed to observe. We have transplanted European modernity to our soil, without the spirit that inflames it and turns all its energy into mutual destruction. Out of these foreign peoples there has somehow been squeezed the poison. An America, "hyphenated" to bitterness, is somehow non-explosive. For, even if we all hark back in sympathy to a European nation, even if the war has set every one vibrating to some emotional string twanged on the other side of the Atlantic, the effect has been one of almost dramatic harmlessness.

What we have really been witnessing, however unappreciatively, in this country has been a thrilling and bloodless battle of Kulturs. In that arena of friction which has been the most dramatic—between the hyphenated German-American and the hyphenated English-American—there have emerged rivalries of philosophies which show up deep traditional attitudes, points of view which accurately reflect the gigantic issues of the war. America has mirrored the spiritual issues. The vicarious struggle has been played out peacefully here in the mind. We have seen the stout resistiveness of the old moral interpretation of history on which Victorian England thrived and made itself great in its own esteem. The clean and immensely satisfying vision of the war as a contest between right and wrong; the enthusiastic support of the Allies as the incarnation of virtue-on-a-rampage; the fierce envisaging of their selfish national purposes as the ideals of justice, freedom and democracy—all this has been thrown with intensest force against the German realistic interpretations in terms of the struggle for power and the virility of the integrated State. America has been the intellectual battleground of the nations.

III

The failure of the melting-pot, far from closing the great American democratic experiment, means that it has only just begun. Whatever American nationalism turns out to be, we see already that it will have a color richer and more exciting than our ideal has hitherto encompassed. In a world which has dreamed of internationalism, we find that we have all unawares been building up the first international nation. The voices which have cried for a tight and jealous nationalism of the European pattern are failing. From that ideal, however valiantly and disinterestedly it has been set for us, time and tendency have moved us further and further away. What we have achieved has been rather a cosmopolitan federation of national colonies, of foreign cultures, from whom the sting of devastating competition has been removed. America is already the world-federation in miniature, the continent where for the first time in history has been achieved that miracle of hope, the peaceful living side by side, with character substantially preserved, of the most heterogeneous peoples under the sun. Nowhere else has such contiguity been anything but the breeder of misery. Here, notwithstanding our tragic failures of adjustment, the outlines are already too clear not to give us a new vision and a new orientation of the American mind in the world.

It is for the American of the younger generation to accept this cosmopolitanism, and carry it along with self-conscious and fruitful purpose. In his colleges, he is already getting, with the study of modern history and politics, the modern literatures, economic geography, the privilege of a cosmopolitan outlook such as the people of no other nation of to-day in Europe can possibly secure. If he is still a colonial, he is no longer the colonial of one partial culture, but of many. He is a colonial of the world. Colonialism has grown into cosmopolitanism, and his motherland is no one nation, but all who have anything life-enhancing to offer to the spirit. That vague sympathy which the France of ten years ago was feeling for the world—a sympathy which was drowned in the terrible reality of war—may be the modern American's, and that in a positive and aggressive sense. If the American is parochial, it is in sheer wantonness or cowardice. His provincialism is the measure of his fear of bogies or the defect of his imagination.

Indeed, it is not uncommon for the eager Anglo-Saxon who goes to a vivid American university to-day to find his true friends not among his own race but among the acclimatized German or Austrian, the acclimatized Jew, the acclimatized Scandinavian or Italian. In them he finds the cosmopolitan note. In these youths, foreign-born or the children of foreign-born parents, he is likely to find many of his old inbred morbid problems washed away. These friends are oblivious to the repressions of that tight little society in which he so provincially grew up. He has a pleasurable sense of liberation from the stale and familiar attitudes of those whose ingrowing culture has scarcely created anything vital for his America of to-day. He breathes a larger air. In his new enthusiasms for continental literature, for unplumbed Russian depths, for French clarity of thought, for Teuton philosophies of power, he feels himself citizen of a larger world. He may be absurdly superficial, his outward-reaching wonder may ignore all the stiller and homelier virtues of his Anglo-Saxon home, but he has at least found the clue to that international mind which will be essential to all men and women of good-will if they are ever to save this Western world of ours from suicide. His new friends have gone through a similar evolution. America has burned most of the baser metal also from them. Meeting now with this common American background, all of them may yet retain that distinctiveness of their native cultures and their national spiritual slants. They are more valuable and interesting to each other for being different, yet that difference could not be creative were it not for this new cosmopolitan outlook which America has given them and which they all equally possess.

A college where such a spirit is possible even to the smallest degree, has within itself already the seeds of this international intellectual world of the future. It suggests that the contribution of America will be an intellectual internationalism which goes far beyond the mere exchange of scientific ideas and discoveries and the cold recording of facts. It will be an intellectual

sympathy which is not satisfied until it has got at the heart of
the different cultural expressions, and felt as they feel. It may
have immense preferences, but it will make understanding and
not indignation its end. Such a sympathy will unite and not
divide.

Against the thinly disguised panic which calls itself "patriotism" and the thinly disguised militarism which calls itself "pre-
paredness" the cosmopolitan ideal is set. This does not mean
that those who hold it are for a policy of drift. They, too, long
passionately for an integrated and disciplined America. But
they do not want one which is integrated only for domestic
economic exploitation of the workers or for predatory economic
imperialism among the weaker peoples. They do not want one
that is integrated by coercion or militarism, or for the truculent
assertion of a mediæval code of honor and of doubtful rights.
They believe that the most effective integration will be one
which coördinates the diverse elements and turns them consciously toward working out together the place of America in
the world-situation. They demand for integration a genuine
integrity, a wholeness and soundness of enthusiasm and purpose which can only come when no national colony within our
America feels that it is being discriminated against or that its
cultural case is being prejudged. This strength of coöperation,
this feeling that all who are here may have a hand in the destiny
of America, will make for a finer spirit of integration than any
narrow "Americanism" or forced chauvinism.

In this effort we may have to accept some form of that dual
citizenship which meets with so much articulate horror among
us. Dual citizenship we may have to recognize as the rudimentary form of that international citizenship to which, if our words
mean anything, we aspire. We have assumed unquestioningly
that mere participation in the political life of the United States
must cut the new citizen off from all sympathy with his old
allegiance. Anything but a bodily transfer of devotion from one
sovereignty to another has been viewed as a sort of moral treason against the Republic. We have insisted that the immigrant

whom we welcomed escaping from the very exclusive nationalism of his European home shall forthwith adopt a nationalism
just as exclusive, just as narrow, and even less legitimate because
it is founded on no warm traditions of his own. Yet a nation like
France is said to permit a formal and legal dual citizenship even
at the present time. Though a citizen of hers may pretend to cast
off his allegiance in favor of some other sovereignty, he is still
subject to her laws when he returns. Once a citizen, always a
citizen, no matter how many new citizenships he may embrace.
And such a dual citizenship seems to us sound and right. For it
recognizes that, although the Frenchman may accept the formal
institutional framework of his new country and indeed become
intensely loyal to it, yet his Frenchness he will never lose. What
makes up the fabric of his soul will always be of this Frenchness,
so that unless he becomes utterly degenerate he will always to
some degree dwell still in his native environment.

Indeed, does not the cultivated American who goes to
Europe practice a dual citizenship, which, if not formal, is no
less real? The American who lives abroad may be the least expa-
triate of men. If he falls in love with French ways and French
thinking and French democracy and seeks to saturate himself
with the new spirit, he is guilty of at least a dual spiritual citizenship. He may be still American, yet he feels himself through
sympathy also a Frenchman. And he finds that this expansion
involves no shameful conflict within him, no surrender of his
native attitude. He has rather for the first time caught a glimpse
of the cosmopolitan spirit. And after wandering about through
many races and civilizations he may return to America to find
them all here living vividly and crudely, seeking the same
adjustment that he made. He sees the new peoples here with
a new vision. They are no longer masses of aliens, waiting to
be "assimilated," waiting to be melted down into the indistin-
guishable dough of Anglo-Saxonism. They are rather threads of
living and potent cultures, blindly striving to weave themselves
into a novel international nation, the first the world has seen.
In an Austria-Hungary or a Prussia the stronger of these cultures

would be moving almost instinctively to subjugate the weaker. But in America those wills-to-power are turned in a different direction into learning how to live together.

Along with dual citizenship we shall have to accept, I think, that free and mobile passage of the immigrant between America and his native land again which now arouses so much prejudice among us. We shall have to accept the immigrant's return for the same reason that we consider justified our own flitting about the earth. To stigmatize the alien who works in America for a few years and returns to his own land, only perhaps to seek American fortune again, is to think in narrow nationalistic terms. It is to ignore the cosmopolitan significance of this migration. It is to ignore the fact that the returning immigrant is often a missionary to an inferior civilization.

This migratory habit has been especially common with the unskilled laborers who have been pouring into the United States in the last dozen years from every country in southeastern Europe. Many of them return to spend their earnings in their own country or to serve their country in war. But they return with an entirely new critical outlook, and a sense of the superiority of American organization to the primitive living around them. This continued passage to and fro has already raised the material standard of living in many regions of these backward countries. For these regions are thus endowed with exactly what they need, the capital for the exploitation of their natural resources, and the spirit of enterprise. America is thus educating these laggard peoples from the very bottom of society up, awaking vast masses to a new-born hope for the future. In the migratory Greek, therefore, we have not the parasitic alien, the doubtful American asset, but a symbol of that cosmopolitan interchange which is coming, in spite of all war and national exclusiveness.

Only America, by reason of the unique liberty of opportunity and traditional isolation for which she seems to stand, can lead in this cosmopolitan enterprise. Only the American—and in this category I include the migratory alien who has lived with us and caught the pioneer spirit and a sense of new social vistas—has the chance to become that citizen of the world. America is coming to be, not a nationality but a trans-nationality, a weaving back and forth, with the other lands, of many threads of all sizes and colors. Any movement which attempts to thwart this weaving, or to dye the fabric any one color, or disentangle the threads of the strands, is false to this cosmopolitan vision. I do not mean that we shall necessarily glut ourselves with the raw product of humanity. It would be folly to absorb the nations faster than we could weave them. We have no duty either to admit or reject. It is purely a question of expediency. What concerns us is the fact that the strands are here. We must have a policy and an ideal for an actual situation. Our question is, What shall we do with our America? How are we likely to get the more creative America—by confining our imaginations to the ideal of the melting-pot, or broadening them to some such cosmopolitan conception as I have been vaguely sketching?

The war has shown America to be unable, though isolated geographically and politically from a European world-situation, to remain aloof and irresponsible. She is a wandering star in a sky dominated by two colossal constellations of states. Can she not work out some position of her own, some life of being in, yet not quite of, this seething and embroiled European world? This is her only hope and promise. A trans-nationality of all the nations, it is spiritually impossible for her to pass into the orbit of any one. It will be folly to hurry herself into a premature and sentimental nationalism, or to emulate Europe and play fast and loose with the forces that drag into war. No Americanization will fulfill this vision which does not recognize the uniqueness of this trans-nationalism of ours. The Anglo-Saxon attempt to fuse will only create enmity and distrust. The crusade against "hyphenates" will only inflame the partial patriotism of transnationals, and cause them to assert their European traditions in strident and unwholesome ways. But the attempt to weave a wholly novel international nation out of our chaotic America will liberate and harmonize the creative power of all these peoples and give them the new spiritual citizenship, as so many individuals have already been given, of a world.

Is it a wild hope that the undertow of opposition to metaphysics in international relations, opposition to militarism, is less a cowardly provincialism than a groping for this higher cosmopolitan ideal? One can understand the irritated restlessness with which our proud pro-British colonists contemplate a heroic conflict across the seas in which they have no part. It was inevitable that our necessary inaction should evolve in their minds into the bogey of national shame and dishonor. But let us be careful about accepting their sensitiveness as final arbiter. Let us look at our reluctance rather as the first crude beginnings of assertion on the part of certain strands in our nationality that they have a right to a voice in the construction of the American ideal. Let us face realistically the America we have around us. Let us work with the forces that are at work. Let us make something of this trans-national spirit instead of outlawing it. Already we are living this cosmopolitan America. What we need is everywhere a vivid consciousness of the new ideal. Deliberate headway must be made against the survivals of the melting-pot ideal for the promise of American life.

We cannot Americanize America worthily by sentimentalizing and moralizing history. When the best schools are expressly renouncing the questionable duty of teaching patriotism by means of history, it is not the time to force shibboleth upon the immigrant. This form of Americanization has been heard because it appealed to the vestiges of our old sentimentalized and moralized patriotism. This has so far held the field as the expression of the new American's new devotion. The inflections of other voices have been drowned. They must be heard. We must see if the lesson of the war has not been for hundreds of these later Americans a vivid realization of their trans-nationality, a new consciousness of what America meant to them as a citizenship in the world. It is the vague historic idealisms which have provided the fuel for the European flame.

Our American ideal can make no progress until we do away with this romantic gilding of the past.

All our idealisms must be those of future social goals in which all can participate, the good life of personality lived in the environment of the Beloved Community. No mere doubtful triumphs of the past, which redound to the glory of only one of our trans-nationalities, can satisfy us. It must be a future America, on which all can unite, which pulls us irresistibly toward it, as we understand each other more warmly.

To make real this striving amid dangers and apathies is work for a younger *intelligentsia* of America. Here is an enterprise of integration into which we can all pour ourselves, of a spiritual welding which should make us, if the final menace ever came, not weaker, but infinitely strong.

The Atlantic Monthly, July 1916

QUESTION 2

Equality: How Can It Be Achieved?

★ ★ ★

Nothing strikes so deep a chord in the American psyche as the idea that here, more than anywhere else in the world, anybody can rise from any place in the social order to the loftiest heights. When Abraham Lincoln greeted the 166th Ohio Regiment at the White House in 1864, he was the latest in a series of Presidents to have been born in a log cabin, so it was entirely plausible for him to tell the Union soldiers that any one of their children might grow up to occupy his office. (An element of the plausibility of Lincoln's remark was that all the soldiers were white.) To Lincoln, this possibility wasn't just an interesting happenstance. It was "an inestimable jewel," the heart of the rationale for the Union's decision to endure the nearly unbearable pain of the Civil War, against an adversary presumed to be less committed to a core principle of the United States. Our country would give everyone who was willing to work hard "equal privileges in the race of life."

American history is full of celebrated examples of eminent people who came from very modest backgrounds, and not just in politics. When the country started producing business tycoons, some of them, too, started out as penniless immigrants, farm boys, and so on: Andrew Carnegie, John D. Rockefeller, Henry Ford, Thomas Edison. Do spectacular individual stories like these suffice as justification for the entire national project? What is the test the country has to meet in order to fulfill Lincoln's version of America's promise, in which "industry,

enterprise, and intelligence" enjoyed "an open field and a fair
chance"? Can there be a systematic way of achieving it that is
embedded in our system of governance?

In 1893, the historian Frederick Jackson Turner gave a lec-
ture drawing attention to the end of the frontier as a signal event
in American society. In Turner's view, open land had provided
opportunity to all Americans—specifically, the opportunity to
become a small independent farmer—through the first century
of the United States. But if opportunity was all-important, and
the frontier was closed, then what? Historians have questioned
Turner's premise, but that doesn't mean it wasn't influential: it
made the need for a replacement for the frontier imperative.
Turner himself, like many prominent Americans after him,
settled on public education as the only plausible national guarantor of opportunity in the post-frontier era.

The Constitution doesn't mention education. That is not
only because the Framers believed that education should be a
state or local responsibility; it was also before the idea of universal public education had caught on, here or anywhere else.
In *Notes on the State of Virginia*, Thomas Jefferson criticized the
Virginia legislature for its failure to adopt his plan for creating a
free school system for boys in the primary grades. Horace Mann,
the nineteenth century's leading crusader for public education,
had to convince a skeptical public, even in the reform-minded
state of Massachusetts, where he was commissioner of education in the 1830s and '40s, to pay for education through its
taxes. As educators still do today, Mann paraded a number of
arguments before his audience. Education would generate business prosperity for the state. It would awaken a love of pure
learning in students. It would make them into better citizens.

Mann's key argument sounds like an anticipation of Lincoln's—education opens to every individual the chance to
rise—but it actually entails making a more expansive promise,
one that might make its effects felt across the board rather than
to a few lucky people. The way to create a better society here
than in class-bound Europe, he wrote, was to give everyone

"an equal chance for earning," which could be done only through education. It "is the great equalizer of the conditions of men—the balance-wheel of the social machinery." The result of equal educational opportunity would be a system that "tends to equality of condition." Economic redistribution by government would be unnecessary because so many people would be doing so well. It's a sign of the success of Mann and education advocates like him that Lincoln himself, two years before he greeted the soldiers of the 166th Ohio Regiment in the White House, signed into law the Morrill Act, which gave large tracts of federal land to the states so they could create colleges that taught "agriculture and the mechanic arts" to members of "the industrial classes." This put the country on a path to extending the opportunity for public education from lower-grade common schools into college.

It's one thing for the United States to be a country where any child can grow up to be President, quite another to be one where all adults are functionally equal, thanks to education. Mann could see, in 1848, that feudalism and early-stage industrial capitalism both generate inequality, but universal education was a new and untested idea. Today, more than 150 years later, it is clear how problematic its promise can be. Education mostly takes place early in life, when students are living at home with their parents, and it remains mainly a local government function. Is it really plausible that the education system could give every American child an equal start in the race of life? And, even if it could, what if the equal start produced extremely unequal results? What Mann didn't see, and we see clearly now, is that educational systems can enhance, rather than inhibit, inequality. And that raises one of the most pressing matters of the present moment: What should be our primary goal, equality of opportunity, or some version of Mann's goal of moving in the direction of greater equality overall?

For Americans that is an uncomfortable question, which is why we keep returning to the hope that education can provide some form of equality that the country can agree upon. By

the late nineteenth century, it had become clear that notional
access to education did not erase the disadvantages of being
poor. Schools for the poor were ill-funded, and children of
uneducated parents didn't start on the same footing as children
of educated ones. The settlement house movement, which
spread in big-city slums in the late nineteenth century, aimed
to help the urban poor, mainly immigrants, to have better
results in the race of life, by offering them guidance on adapting to America, including tutoring that was meant to help their
children in school. Jane Addams was the settlement house
movement's leading figure and one of the country's preemi-
nent intellectuals. In her 1899 article "The Subtle Problems of
Charity," excerpted in this section, she addressed the uncomfortable social fit between the mainly middle-class women
who worked in the settlement houses and their slum-dwelling
clients. Addams worried that the settlement houses, though
well-intentioned, were not actually promoting equality or even
democracy, because their work entailed members of a better-off
class trying to improve their economic inferiors by asking them
to abandon their own cultural values. Settlement house clients, Addams reported, put a premium on simple generosity and
group solidarity; settlement house officials preached an ethic of
individual improvement, thrift, temperance, and "the industrial
view of life." Although the heyday of settlement houses is far in
the past, the same attitudes still infuse the operations of many
efforts to improve the poor that are funded by the prosperous,
such as charter schools.

Of all the exceptions to the American ethos of opportunity
for all, the most obvious has been the status of African Americans: first enslaved, then, after a few years of Reconstruction,
subjected to legal segregation in the South, then segregated and
disadvantaged in fact if not in law. Throughout, black Americans have been systematically denied the right to a decent education. When the Supreme Court declared segregated schools
to be unconstitutional in its 1954 *Brown v. Board of Education*
decision, Chief Justice Earl Warren wrote that education was

"perhaps the most important function of state and local governments." That was an acknowledgment of the idea that education equals opportunity and opportunity is the essence of what
it means to be an American—so it was necessary for the federal
government to assert its power over the states. But not much
more than a decade later, after having passed legislation that
knocked down the main pillars of legal segregation, President
Lyndon Johnson gave a speech at Howard University in which
he significantly amended the metaphor of opportunity as a race
that Lincoln had used. "You do not take a person who, for years,
has been hobbled by chains and liberate him, bring him up to
the starting line of a race and then say, 'you are free to compete
with all the others,' and still justly believe that you have been
completely fair," Johnson declared.

Johnson was laying the groundwork for compensatory
programs, like affirmative action, that would try to undo the
deficiencies in American opportunity on account of race—but
it's significant that his administration often used the word
"opportunity" in the titles of these initiatives, because that was
the way to get public support for them. He named the agency
charged with enforcing affirmative action the Equal Employment Opportunity Commission, and the one that carried out
his War on Poverty, the Office of Economic Opportunity.
Opportunity for all doesn't immediately sound as if it would
require government action, but in this case, and many others
in the past, it has. In *Black Reconstruction*, written at a time
when he was a lonely voice in defense of the brief provision of
civil and voting rights to freed people in the 1870s, W.E.B. Du
Bois was eloquent on the subject of black people being barred
from taking part in the American ethos. "Ambition was not
for Negroes," he wrote. Unlike many writers on this subject,
though, Du Bois understood the problem of equality in broad
political and economic terms. During Reconstruction, black
people in the South had the right to vote; this gave them political power, which they used to create an educational system that
greatly increased literacy among African Americans in just a

few years. When they lost political power, this was taken away. Poor whites, who were attracted to the "public and psychological wage" (as Du Bois put it) that white supremacy conferred on them, oriented themselves politically along racial rather than economic lines, and the result was a conservative and highly unequal society.

For the last forty years, economic inequality in the United States has been steadily rising. One result is that, for the first time in decades, inequality is a major topic of conversation, even among politicians who are running for President. It's not clear where that will lead, but it's significant that the conversation is substantially about inequality per se, not the more tightly framed question of equality of opportunity for individuals. The country doesn't have—has never had—perfect equality of opportunity, but even if it did, some combination of luck and skill could make life turn out far better for some than for others. Is that something we'd be comfortable with? If it isn't, then it would be unavoidable to think about more equal results, as well as opportunities, as something the country should provide.

★ ★ ★

Horace Mann: from Twelfth Annual Report to the Massachusetts Board of Education

Intellectual Education, as a Means of Removing Poverty, and Securing Abundance.

Another cardinal object which the government of Massachusetts, and all the influential men in the State should propose to themselves, is the physical well-being of all the people,—the sufficiency, comfort, competence, of every individual, in regard to food, raiment, and shelter. And these necessaries and conveniences of life should be obtained by each individual for himself, or by each family for themselves, rather than accepted from the hand of charity, or extorted by poor-laws. It is not averred that this most desirable result can, in all instances, be obtained; but it is, nevertheless, the end to be aimed at. True statesmanship and true political economy, not less than true philanthropy, present this perfect theory as the goal, to be more and more closely approximated by our imperfect practice. The desire to achieve such a result cannot be regarded as an unreasonable ambition; for, though all mankind were well-fed, well-clothed, and well-housed, they might still be but half-civilized.

Poverty is a public as well as a private evil. There is no physical law necessitating its existence. The earth contains abundant resources for ten times,—doubtless for twenty times,—its present inhabitants. Cold, hunger, and nakedness, are not, like death, an inevitable lot. There are many single States in this Union which could supply an abundance of edible products for the inhabitants of the thirty States that compose it. There are single States, capable of raising a sufficient quantity of cotton to clothe the whole nation; and there are other

States having sufficient factories and machinery to manufacture it. The coal fields of Pennsylvania are sufficiently abundant to keep every house in the land, at the temperature of 65°, for centuries to come. Were there to be a competition, on the one hand, to supply wool for every conceivable fabric; and, on the other hand, to wear out these fabrics as fast as possible, the single State of New York would beat the whole country. There is, indeed, no assignable limit to the capacities of the earth for producing whatever is necessary for the sustenance, comfort, and improvement of the race. Indigence, therefore, and the miseries and degradations incident to indigence, seem to be no part of the eternal ordinances of Heaven. The bounty of God is not brought into question, or suspicion, by its existence; for man who suffers it might have avoided it. Even the wealth which the world now has on hand is more than sufficient to supply all the rational wants of every individual in it. Privations and sufferings exist, not from the smallness of its sum, but from the inequality of its distribution. Poverty is set over against profusion. In some, all healthy appetite is cloyed and sickened by repletion; while in others, the stomach seems to be a supernumerary organ in the system; or, like the human eye or human lungs before birth, is waiting to be transferred to some other region, where its functions may come into use. One gorgeous palace absorbs all the labor and expense that might have made a thousand hovels comfortable. That one man may ride in carriages of oriental luxury, hundreds of other men are turned into beasts of burden. To supply a superfluous wardrobe for the gratification of one man's pride, a thousand women and children shiver with cold; and for every flash of the diamonds that royalty wears, there is a tear of distress in the poor man's dwelling. Not one Lazarus, but a hundred, sit at the gate of Dives. Tantalus is no fiction. The ancient one might have been fabulous; but the modern ones are terrible realities. Millions are perishing in the midst of superfluities.

According to the European theory, men are divided into classes,—some to toil and earn, others to seize and enjoy.

According to the Massachusetts theory, all are to have an equal chance for earning, and equal security in the enjoyment of what they earn. The latter tends to equality of condition; the former to the grossest inequalities. Tried by any Christian standard of morals, or even by any of the better sort of heathen standards, can any one hesitate, for a moment, in declaring which of the two will produce the greater amount of human welfare; and which, therefore, is the more conformable to the Divine will? The European theory is blind to what constitutes the highest glory, as well as the highest duty, of a State. Its advocates and admirers are forgetful of that which should be their highest ambition, and proud of that which constitutes their shame. How can any one, possessed of the attributes of humanity, look with satisfaction upon the splendid treasures, the golden regalia, deposited in the Tower of London, or in Windsor Palace, each "an India in itself," while thousands around are dying of starvation; or have been made criminals by the combined forces of temptation and neglect? The present condition of Ireland cancels all the glories of the British crown. The brilliant conception which symbolizes the nationality of Great Britain as a superb temple, whose massive and grand proportions are upheld and adorned by the four hundred and thirty Corinthian columns of the aristocracy, is turned into a loathing and a scorn, when we behold the five millions of paupers that cower and shiver at its base. The galleries and fountains of Versailles, the Louvre of Paris, her Notre Dame, and her Madeleine, though multiplied by thousands in number and in brilliancy, would be no atonement for the hundred thousand Parisian *ouvriers*, without bread and without work. The galleries of painting and of sculpture, at Rome, at Munich, or at Dresden, which body forth the divinest ideals ever executed or ever conceived, are but an abomination in the sight of Heaven and of all good men, while actual, living beings,—beings that have hearts to palpitate, and nerves to agonize, and affections to be crushed or corrupted,— are experimenting, all around them, upon the capacities of human nature for suffering and for sin. Where standards like these exist, and are upheld by council and by court, by fashion and by law, *Christianity is yet to be discovered*. At least, it is yet to be applied in practice to the social condition of men.

Our ambition, as a State, should trace itself to a different origin, and propose to itself a different object. Its flame should be lighted at the skies. Its radiance and its warmth should reach the darkest and the coldest abodes of men. It should seek the solution of such problems as these: To what extent can competence displace pauperism? How nearly can we free ourselves from the low-minded and the vicious; not by their expatriation, but by their elevation? To what extent can the resources and powers of nature be converted into human welfare; the peaceful arts of life be advanced, and the vast treasures of human talent and genius be developed? How much of suffering, in all its forms, can be relieved; or, what is better than relief, how much can be prevented? Cannot the classes of crimes be lessened, and the number of criminals, in each class, be diminished? Our exemplars, both for public and for private imitation, should be the parables of the lost sheep and of the lost piece of silver. When we have spread competence through all the abodes of poverty; when we have substituted knowledge for ignorance, in the minds of the whole people; when we have reformed the vicious and reclaimed the criminal; then may we invite all neighboring nations to behold the spectacle, and say to them, in the conscious elation of virtue, "Rejoice with me," for I have found that which was lost. Until that day shall arrive, our duties will not be wholly fulfilled, and our ambition will have new honors to win.

But, is it not true, that Massachusetts, in some respects, instead of adhering more and more closely to her own theory, is becoming emulous of the baneful examples of Europe? The distance between the two extremes of society is lengthening, instead of being abridged. With every generation, fortunes increase, on the one hand, and some new privation is added to poverty, on the other. We are verging towards those extremes of opulence and of penury, each of which unhumanizes the human mind. A perpetual struggle for the bare necessaries of life, without the ability to obtain them, makes men wolfish. Avarice, on the other hand, sees, in all the victims of misery around it,—not objects for pity and succor,—but only crude materials to be worked up into more money.

I suppose it to be the universal sentiment of all those who mingle any ingredient of benevolence with their notions on Political Economy, that vast and overshadowing private fortunes are among the greatest dangers to which the happiness of the people in a republic can be subjected. Such fortunes would create a feudalism of a new kind; but one more oppressive and unrelenting than that of the Middle Ages. The feudal lords in England, and on the continent, never held their retainers in a more abject condition of servitude, than the great majority of foreign manufacturers and capitalists hold their operatives and laborers at the present day. The means employed are different, but the similarity in results is striking. What force did then, money does now. The villein of the Middle Ages had no spot of earth on which he could live, unless one were granted to him by his lord. The operative or laborer of the present day has no employment, and therefore no bread, unless the capitalist will accept his services. The vassal had no shelter but such as his master provided for him. Not one in five thousand of English operatives, or farm laborers, is able to build or own even a hovel; and therefore they must accept such shelter as Capital offers them. The baron prescribed his own terms to his retainers; those terms were peremptory, and the serf must submit or perish. The British manufacturer or farmer prescribes the rate of wages he will give to his work-people; he reduces these wages under whatever pretext he pleases; and they too have no alternative but submission or starvation. In some respects, indeed, the condition of the modern dependant is more forlorn than that of the corresponding serf class in former times. Some attributes of the patriarchal relation did spring up between the lord and his lieges, to soften the harsh relations subsisting between them. Hence came some oversight of the condition of

children, some relief in sickness, some protection and support
in the decrepitude of age. But only in instances comparatively
few, have kindly offices smoothed the rugged relation between
British Capital and British Labor. The children of the work-
people are abandoned to their fate; and, notwithstanding the
privations they suffer, and the dangers they threaten, no power
in the realm has yet been able to secure them an education; and
when the adult laborer is prostrated by sickness, or eventually
worn out by toil and age, the poorhouse, which has all along
been his destination, becomes his destiny.

Now two or three things will doubtless be admitted to be
true, beyond all controversy, in regard to Massachusetts. By its
industrial condition, and its business operations, it is exposed,
far beyond any other state in the Union, to the fatal extremes
of overgrown wealth and desperate poverty. Its population is
far more dense than that of any other state. It is four or five
times more dense than the average of all the other states, taken
together; and density of population has always been one of the
proximate causes of social inequality. According to population
and territorial extent, there is far more capital in Massachusetts,—capital which is movable, and instantaneously available,—than in any other state in the Union; and probably both
these qualifications respecting population and territory could
be omitted without endangering the truth of the assertion. It
has been recently stated, in a very respectable public journal,
on the authority of a writer conversant with the subject, that,
from the last of June, 1846, to the 1st of August, 1848, the
amount of money invested, by the citizens of Massachusetts,
"in manufacturing cities, railroads, and other improvements,"
is "fifty-seven millions of dollars, of which more than fifty has
been paid in and expended." The dividends to be received by
citizens of Massachusetts from June, 1848, to April, 1849, are
estimated, by the same writer, at ten millions, and the annual
increase of capital at "little short of twenty-two millions." If
this be so, are we not in danger of naturalizing and domesti-
cating among ourselves those hideous evils which are always

engendered between Capital and Labor, when all the capital is in the hands of one class, and all the labor is thrown upon another?

Now, surely, nothing but Universal Education can counterwork this tendency to the domination of capital and the servility of labor. If one class possesses all the wealth and the education, while the residue of society is ignorant and poor, it matters not by what name the relation between them may be called; the latter, in fact and in truth, will be the servile dependants and subjects of the former. But if education be equably diffused, it will draw property after it, by the strongest of all attractions; for such a thing never did happen, and never can happen, as that an intelligent and practical body of men should be permanently poor. Property and labor, in different classes, are essentially antagonistic; but property and labor, in the same class, are essentially fraternal. The people of Massachusetts have, in some degree, appreciated the truth, that the unexampled prosperity of the State,—its comfort, its competence, its general intelligence and virtue,—is attributable to the education, more or less perfect, which all its people have received; but are they sensible of a fact equally important?—namely, that it is to this same education that two thirds of the people are indebted for not being, to-day, the vassals of as severe a tyranny, in the form of capital, as the lower classes of Europe are bound to in the form of brute force.

Education, then, beyond all other devices of human origin, is the great equalizer of the conditions of men—the balance-wheel of the social machinery. I do not here mean that it so elevates the moral nature as to make men disdain and abhor the oppression of their fellow-men. This idea pertains to another of its attributes. But I mean that it gives each man the independence and the means, by which he can resist the selfishness of other men. It does better than to disarm the poor of their hostility towards the rich; it prevents being poor. Agrarianism is the revenge of poverty against wealth. The wanton destruction of the property of others,—the burning of hay-ricks and corn-ricks, the demolition of machinery, because it supersedes hand-labor, the sprinkling of vitriol on rich dresses,—is only agrarianism run mad. Education prevents both the revenge and the madness. On the other hand, a fellow-feeling for one's class or caste is the common instinct of hearts not wholly sunk in selfish regards for person, or for family. The spread of education, by enlarging the cultivated class or caste, will open a wider area over which the social feelings will expand; and, if this education should be universal and complete, it would do more than all things else to obliterate factitious distinctions in society.

The main idea set forth in the creeds of some political reformers, or revolutionizers, is, that some people are poor *because* others are rich. This idea supposes a fixed amount of property in the community, which, by fraud or force, or arbitrary law, is unequally divided among men; and the problem presented for solution is, how to transfer a portion of this property from those who are supposed to have too much, to those who feel and know that they have too little. At this point, both their theory and their expectation of reform stop. But the beneficent power of education would not be exhausted, even though it should peaceably abolish all the miseries that spring from the coëxistence, side by side, of enormous wealth and squalid want. It has a higher function. Beyond the power of diffusing old wealth, it has the prerogative of creating new. It is a thousand times more lucrative than fraud; and adds a thousand fold more to a nation's resources than the most successful conquests. Knaves and robbers can obtain only what was before possessed by others. But education creates or develops new treasures,— treasures not before possessed or dreamed of by any one.

November 24, 1848

* * *

Abraham Lincoln: Speech to the 166th Ohio Regiment

I suppose you are going home to see your families and friends. For the service you have done in this great struggle in which we are engaged I present you sincere thanks for myself and the country. I almost always feel inclined, when I happen to say anything to soldiers, to impress upon them in a few brief remarks the importance of success in this contest. It is not merely for to-day, but for all time to come that we should perpetuate for our children's children this great and free government, which we have enjoyed all our lives. I beg you to remember this, not merely for my sake, but for yours. I happen temporarily to occupy this big White House. I am a living witness that any one of your children may look to come here as my father's child has. It is in order that each of you may have through this free government which we have enjoyed, an open field and a fair chance for your industry, enterprise and intelligence; that you may all have equal privileges in the race of life, with all its desirable human aspirations. It is for this the struggle should be maintained, that we may not lose our birthright—not only for one, but for two or three years. The nation is worth fighting for, to secure such an inestimable jewel.

August 22, 1864

Jane Addams: from The Subtle Problems of Charity

PROBABLY there is no relation in life which our democracy is changing more rapidly than the charitable relation,—that relation which obtains between benefactor and beneficiary; at the same time, there is no point of contact in our modern experience which reveals more clearly the lack of that equality which democracy implies. We have reached the moment when democracy has made such inroads upon this relationship that the complacency of the old-fashioned charitable man is gone forever; while the very need and existence of charity deny us the consolation and freedom which democracy will at last give.

We find in ourselves the longing for a wider union than that of family or class, and we say that we have come to include all men in our hopes; but we fail to realize that all men are hoping, and are part of the same movement of which we are a part. Many of the difficulties in philanthropy come from an unconscious division of the world into the philanthropists and those to be helped. It is an assumption of two classes, and against this class assumption our democratic training revolts as soon as we begin to act upon it.

The trouble is that the ethics of none of us are clearly defined, and we are continually obliged to act in circles of habit based upon convictions which we no longer hold. Thus, our estimate of the effect of environment and social conditions has doubtless shifted faster than our methods of administering charity have changed. Formerly when it was believed that poverty was synonymous with vice and laziness, and that the prosperous man was the righteous man, charity was administered harshly with a good conscience; for the charitable agent really blamed the individual for his poverty, and the very fact of his own superior prosperity gave him a certain consciousness of superior morality. Since then we have learned to measure by other standards, and the money-earning capacity, while still rewarded out of all proportion to any other, is not respected as exclusively as it was; and its possession is by no means assumed to imply the possession of the highest moral qualities. We have learned to judge men in general by their social virtues as well as by their business capacity, by their devotion to intellectual and disinterested aims, and by their public spirit, and we naturally resent being obliged to judge certain individuals solely upon the industrial side for no other reason than that they are poor. Our democratic instinct constantly takes alarm at this consciousness of two standards.

Of the various struggles which a decade of residence in a settlement implies, none have made a more definite impression on my mind than the incredibly painful difficulties which involve both giver and recipient when one person asks charitable aid of another.

An attempt is made in this paper to show what are some of the perplexities which harass the mind of the charity worker; to trace them to ethical survivals which are held not only by the benefactor, but by the recipients of charity as well; and to suggest wherein these very perplexities may possibly be prophetic.

It is easy to see that one of the root difficulties in the charitable relationship lies in the fact that the only families who apply for aid to the charitable agencies are those who have come to grief on the industrial side; it may be through sickness, through loss of work, or for other guiltless and inevitable reasons, but the fact remains that they are industrially ailing, and must be bolstered and helped into industrial health. The charity visitor, let us assume, is a young college woman, well-bred and open-minded. When she visits the family assigned to her, she is embarrassed to find herself obliged to lay all the stress of her teaching and advice upon the industrial virtues, and to treat the members of the family almost exclusively as factors in the industrial system. She insists that they must work and be self-supporting; that the most dangerous of all situations is idleness; that seeking one's own pleasure, while ignoring claims and responsibilities, is the most ignoble of actions. The members of her assigned family may have charms and virtues,—they may possibly be kind and affectionate and considerate of one another, generous to their friends; but it is her business to stick to the industrial side. As she daily holds up these standards, it often occurs to the mind of the sensitive visitor, whose conscience has been made tender by much talk of brotherhood and equality which she has heard at college, that she has no right to say these things; that she herself has never been self-supporting; that, whatever her virtues may be, they are not the industrial virtues; that her untrained hands are no more fitted to cope with actual conditions than are those of her broken-down family.

The grandmother of the charity visitor could have done the industrial preaching very well, because she did have the industrial virtues; if not skillful in weaving and spinning, she was yet mistress of other housewifely accomplishments. In a generation our experiences have changed—our views with them; while we still keep on in the old methods, which could be applied when our consciences were in line with them, but which are daily becoming more difficult as we divide up into people who work with their hands and those who do not; and the charity visitor, belonging to the latter class, is perplexed by recognitions and suggestions which the situation forces upon her. Our democracy has taught us to apply our moral teaching all around, and the moralist is rapidly becoming so sensitive that when his life does not exemplify his ethical convictions, he finds it difficult to preach.

Added to this is a consciousness in the mind of the visitor of a genuine misunderstanding of her motives by the recipients of her charity and by their neighbors. Let us take a neighborhood of poor people, and test their ethical standards by those of the charity visitor, who comes with the best desire in the world to help them out of their distresses. A most striking incongruity, at once apparent, is the difference between the emotional kindness with which relief is given by one poor neighbor to another poor neighbor, and the guarded care with which relief is given by a charity visitor to a charity recipient. The neighborhood mind is immediately confronted not only by the difference of method, but also by an absolute clashing of two ethical standards.

A very little familiarity with the poor districts of any city is sufficient to show how primitive and frontier-like are the neighborly relations. There is the greatest willingness to lend or borrow anything, and each resident of a given tenement house knows the most intimate family affairs of all the others. The fact that the economic condition of all alike is on a most precarious level makes the ready outflow of sympathy and material assistance the most natural thing in the world. There are numberless instances of heroic self-sacrifice quite unknown in the circles where greater economic advantages make that kind of intimate knowledge of one's neighbors impossible. An Irish family, in which the man has lost his place, and the woman is struggling to eke out the scanty savings by day work, will take in a widow and her five children who have been turned into the street, without a moment's reflection upon the physical discomforts involved. The most maligned landlady is usually ready to lend a scuttleful of coal to a suffering tenant, or to share her supper. A woman for whom the writer had long tried in vain to find work failed to appear at the appointed time when a situation was found at last. Upon investigation it transpired that a neighbor further down the street was taken ill; that the children ran for the family friend, who went, of course; saying simply, when reasons for her failure to come to work were demanded, "It broke me heart to leave the place, but what could I do?"

Another woman, whose husband was sent up to the city prison for the maximum term, just three months before the birth of her child, having gradually sold her supply of household furniture, found herself penniless. She sought refuge with a friend whom she supposed to be living in three rooms in another part of the town. When she arrived, however, she discovered that her friend's husband had been out of work so long that they had been reduced to living in one room. The friend at once took her in, and the friend's husband was obliged to sleep upon a bench in the park every night for a week; which he did uncomplainingly, if not cheerfully. Fortunately it was summer, "and it only rained one night." The writer could not discover from the young mother that she had any special claim upon the "friend" beyond the fact that they had formerly worked together in the same factory. The husband she had never seen until the night of her arrival, when he at once went forth in search of a midwife who would consent to come upon his promise of future payment.

The evolutionists tell us that the instinct to pity, the impulse to aid his fellows, served man at a very early period as a rude rule of right and wrong. There is no doubt that this rude rule still holds among many people with whom charitable agencies are brought into contact, and that their ideas of right and wrong are quite honestly outraged by the methods of these agencies. When they see the delay and caution with which relief is given, these do not appear to them conscientious scruples, but the cold and calculating action of the selfish man. This is not the aid that they are accustomed to receive from their neighbors, and they do not understand why the impulse which drives people to be good to the poor should be so severely supervised. They feel, remotely, that the charity visitor is moved by motives that are alien and unreal; they may be superior motives, but they are "ag'in' nature." They cannot comprehend why a person whose intellectual perceptions are stronger than his natural impulses should go into charity work at all. The only man they are accustomed to see whose intellectual perceptions are stronger than his tenderness of heart is the selfish and avaricious man, who is frankly "on the make." If the charity visitor is such a person, why does she pretend to like the poor? Why does she not go into business at once? We may say, of course, that it is a primitive view of life which thus confuses intellectuality and business ability, but it is a view quite honestly held by many poor people who are obliged to receive charity from time to time. In moments of indignation they have been known to say, "What do you want, anyway? If you have nothing to give us, why not let us alone, and stop your questionings and investigations?" This indignation, which is for the most part taciturn, and a certain kindly contempt for her abilities often puzzle the charity visitor. The latter may be explained by the standard of worldly success which the visited families hold. In the minds of the poor success does not ordinarily go with charity and kind-heartedness, but rather with the opposite qualities. The rich landlord is he who collects with sternness; who accepts no excuse, and will have his own. There are moments of irritation and of real bitterness against him, but there is admiration, because he is rich and successful. The good-natured landlord, he who pities and spares his poverty-pressed tenants, is seldom rich. He often lives in the back of his house, which he has owned for a long time, perhaps has inherited; but he has been able to accumulate little. He commands the genuine love and devotion of many a poor soul, but he is treated with a certain lack of respect. In one sense he is a failure, so long have we all been accustomed to estimate success by material returns. The charity visitor, just because she is a person who concerns herself with the poor, receives a touch of this good-natured and kindly contempt, sometimes real affection, but little genuine respect. The poor are accustomed to help one another, and to respond according to their kindliness; but when it comes to worldly judgment, they are still in that stage where they use industrial success as the sole standard. In the case of the charity visitor, they are deprived of both standards; she has neither natural kindness nor dazzling riches; and they find it of course utterly impossible to judge of the motive of organized charity.

Doubtless we all find something distasteful in the juxtaposition of the two words "organized" and "charity." The idea of organizing an emotion is in itself repelling, even to those of us who feel most sorely the need of more order in altruistic effort and see the end to be desired. We say in defense that we are striving to turn this emotion into a motive: that pity is capricious, and not to be depended on; that we mean to give it the dignity of conscious duty. But at bottom we distrust a little a scheme which substitutes a theory of social conduct for the natural promptings of the heart, and we ourselves feel the complexity of the situation. The poor man who has fallen into distress, when he first asks aid, instinctively expects tenderness, consideration, and forgiveness. If it is the first time, it has taken him long to make up his mind to the step. He comes somewhat bruised and battered, and instead of being met by warmth of heart and sympathy he is at once chilled by an investigation and an intimation that he ought to work. He does not see that he is being dealt with as a child of defective will is cared for by a stern parent. There have been no years of previous intercourse and established relation, as between parents and children. He feels only the postponement or refusal, which he considers harsh. He does not "live to thank his parents for it," as the disciplined child is reported to do, but cherishes a hardness of heart to his grave. The only really popular charity is that of visiting nurses, who carry about with them a professional training, which may easily be interpreted into sympathy and kindness, in their ministration to obvious needs without investigation.

The state of mind which an investigation arouses on both sides is most unfortunate; but the perplexity and clashing of different standards, with the consequent misunderstandings, are not so bad as the moral deterioration which is almost sure to follow.

When the agent or visitor appears among the poor, and they discover that under certain conditions food and rent and medical aid are dispensed from some unknown source, every man, woman, and child is quick to learn what the conditions may be, and to follow them. Though in their eyes a glass of beer is quite right and proper when taken as any self-respecting man should take it; though they know that cleanliness is an expensive virtue which can be expected of few; though they realize that saving is well-nigh impossible when but a few cents can be laid by at a time; though their feeling for the church may be something quite elusive of definition and quite apart from daily living,—to the visitor they gravely laud temperance and cleanliness and thrift and religious observance. The deception doubtless arises from a wondering inability to understand the ethical ideals which can require such impossible virtues, combined with a tradition that charity visitors do require them, and from an innocent desire to please. It is easy to trace the development of the mental suggestions thus received.

The most serious effect upon the individual comes when dependence upon the charitable society is substituted for the natural outgoing of human love and sympathy, which, happily, we all possess in some degree. The spontaneous impulse to sit up all night with a neighbor's sick child is turned into righteous indignation against the district nurse because she goes home at six o'clock. Or the kindness which would have prompted a quick purchase of much needed medicine is transformed into a voluble scoring of the dispensary, because it gives prescriptions, and not drugs; and "who can get well on a piece of paper?"

If a poor woman knows that her neighbor next door has no shoes, she is quite willing to lend her own, that her neighbor may go decently to mass or to work; for she knows the smallest item about the scanty wardrobe, and cheerfully helps out. When the charity visitor comes in, all the neighbors are baffled as to what her circumstances may be. They know she does not need a new pair of shoes, and rather suspect that she has a dozen pairs at home; which indeed she sometimes has. They imagine untold stores which they may call upon, and her most generous gift is considered niggardly, compared with what she might do. She ought to get new shoes for the family all round; "she sees well enough that they need them." It is no more than the neighbor herself would do. The charity visitor has broken through the natural rule of giving, which, in a primitive society, is bounded only by the need of the recipient and the resources of the giver; and she gets herself into untold trouble when she is judged by the ethics of that primitive society.

The neighborhood understands the selfish rich people who stay in their own part of the town, where all their associates have shoes and other things. Such people do not bother themselves about the poor; they are like the rich landlords of the neighborhood experience. But this lady visitor, who pretends to be good to the poor, and certainly does talk as though she were kind-hearted, what does she come for, if she does not intend to give them things which so plainly are needed? The visitor says, sometimes, that in holding her poor family so hard to a standard of thrift she is really breaking down a rule of higher living which they formerly possessed; that saving, which seems quite commendable in a comfortable part of the town, appears almost criminal in a poorer quarter, where the next-door neighbor needs food, even if the children of the family do not. She feels the sordidness of constantly being obliged to urge the industrial view of life. The benevolent individual of fifty years ago honestly believed that industry and self-denial in youth would result in comfortable possessions for old age. It was, indeed, the method he had practiced in his own youth, and by which he had probably obtained whatever fortune he possessed. He therefore reproved the poor family for indulging their children, urged them to work long hours, and was utterly untouched by many scruples which afflict the contemporary charity visitor. She says sometimes: "Why must I talk always on getting work and saving money, the things I know nothing about? If it were anything else I had to urge, I could do it; anything like Latin prose, which I had worried through myself, would not be so hard." But she finds it difficult to connect the experiences of her youth with the experiences of the visited family.

Because of this diversity in experience the visitor is continually surprised to find that the safest platitudes may be challenged. She refers quite naturally to the "horrors of the saloon," and discovers that the head of her visited family, who knows the saloons very well, does not connect them with "horrors" at all. He remembers all the kindnesses he has received there, the free lunch and treating which go on, even when a man is out of work and not able to pay up; the poor fellows who are allowed to sit in their warmth when every other door is closed to them; the loan of five dollars he got there, when the charity visitor was miles away, and he was threatened with eviction. He may listen politely to her reference to horrors, but considers it only "temperance talk."

The same thing happens when she urges upon him a spirit of independence, and is perhaps foolish enough to say that "every American man can find work and is bound to support his family." She soon discovers that the workingman, in the city at least, is utterly dependent for the tenure of his position upon the good will of his foreman, upon the business prosperity of the firm, or the good health of the head of it; and that, once work is lost, it may take months to secure another place. There is no use in talking independence to a man when he is going to stand in a row, hat in hand, before an office desk, in the hope of getting a position. The visitor is shocked when she finds herself recommending to the head of her visited family, whom she has sent to a business friend of hers to find work, not to be too outspoken when he goes to the place, and not to tell that he has had no experience in that line unless he is asked. She has in fact come around to the view which has long been his.

The charity visitor may blame the women for lack of gentleness toward their children, for being hasty and rude to them, until she learns to reflect that the standard of breeding is not that of gentleness toward the children so much as the observance of certain conventions, such as the punctilious wearing of mourning garments after the death of a child. The standard of gentleness each mother has to work out largely by herself, assisted only by the occasional shamefaced remark of a neighbor, that "they do better when you are not too hard on them;" but the wearing of mourning garments is sustained by the definitely expressed sentiment of every woman in the street. The mother would have to bear social blame, a certain social ostracism, if she failed to comply with that requirement. It is not comfortable to outrage the conventions of those among whom we live, and if our social life be a narrow one, it is still more difficult. The visitor may choke a little when she sees the lessened supply of food and the scanty clothing provided for the remaining children, in order that one may be conventionally mourned. But she does not talk so strongly against it as she would have done during her first month of experience with the family since bereaved.

The subject of clothes, indeed, perplexes the visitor constantly, and the result of her reflections may be summed up something in this wise: The girl who has a definite social standing, who has been to a fashionable school or to a college, whose family live in a house seen and known by all her friends and associates, can afford to be very simple or even shabby as to her clothes, if she likes. But the working girl, whose family lives in a tenement or moves from one small apartment to another, who has little social standing, and has to make her own place, knows full well how much habit and style of dress have to do with her position. Her income goes into her clothing out of all proportion to that which she spends upon other things. But if social advancement is her aim, it is the most sensible thing which she can do. She is judged largely by her clothes. Her house-furnishing with its pitiful little decorations, her scanty supply of books, are never seen by the people whose social opinions she most values. Her clothes are her background, and from them she is largely judged. It is due to this fact that girls' clubs succeed best in the business part of a town, where "working girls" and "young ladies" meet upon an equal footing, and where the clothes superficially look very much alike. Bright and ambitious girls will come to these down-town clubs to eat lunch and rest at noon, to study all sorts of subjects and listen to lectures, when they might hesitate a long time about joining a club identified with their own neighborhood, where they would be judged not solely on their personal merits and the unconscious social standing afforded to good clothes, but by other surroundings

which are not nearly up to these. For the same reason, girls'
clubs are infinitely more difficult to organize in little towns and
villages, where every one knows every one else, just how the
front parlor is furnished, and the amount of mortgage there
is upon the house. These facts get in the way of a clear and
unbiased judgment; they impede the democratic relationship,
and add to the self-consciousness of all concerned. Every one
who has had to do with down-town girls' clubs has had the
experience of going into the home of some bright, well-dressed
girl, to discover it uncomfortable and perhaps wretched, and to
find the girl afterwards carefully avoiding her, although she may
not have been at home when the call was made, and the visitor
may have carried herself with the utmost courtesy throughout.
In some very successful down-town clubs the home address is
not given at all, and only the "business address" is required.
Have we worked out our democracy in regard to clothes farther
than in regard to anything else?

The charity visitor has been rightly brought up to consider
it vulgar to spend much money upon clothes, to care so much
for "appearances." She realizes dimly that the care for personal
decoration over that for one's home or habitat is in some way
primitive and undeveloped; but she is silenced by its obvious
need. She also catches a hint of the fact that the disproportionate expenditure of the poor in the matter of clothes is largely
due to the exclusiveness of the rich, who hide from them the
interior of their houses and their more subtle pleasures, while
of necessity exhibiting their street clothes and their street manners. Every one who goes shopping at the same time with the
richest woman in town may see her clothes, but only those
invited to her receptions see the Corot on her walls or the bind-
ings in her library. The poor naturally try to bridge the difference by reproducing the street clothes which they have seen;
they therefore imitate, sometimes in more showy and often in
more trying colors, in cheap and flimsy material, in poor shoes
and flippant hats, the extreme fashion of the well-to-do. They
are striving to conform to a common standard which their

democratic training presupposes belongs to us all. The charity visitor may regret that the Italian peasant woman has laid aside her picturesque kerchief, and substituted a cheap street hat. But it is easy to recognize the first attempt toward democratic expression.

The Atlantic Monthly, February 1899

★ ★ ★

W.E.B. Du Bois: from *Black Reconstruction*

The political success of the doctrine of racial separation, which overthrew Reconstruction by uniting the planter and the poor white, was far exceeded by its astonishing economic results. The theory of laboring class unity rests upon the assumption that laborers, despite internal jealousies, will unite because of their opposition to exploitation by the capitalists. According to this, even after a part of the poor white laboring class became identified with the planters, and eventually displaced them, their interests would be diametrically opposed to those of the mass of white labor, and of course to those of the black laborers. This would throw white and black labor into one class, and precipitate a united fight for higher wage and better working conditions.

Most persons do not realize how far this failed to work in the South, and it failed to work because the theory of race was supplemented by a carefully planned and slowly evolved method, which drove such a wedge between the white and black workers that there probably are not today in the world two groups of workers with practically identical interests who hate and fear each other so deeply and persistently and who are kept so far apart that neither sees anything of common interest.

It must be remembered that the white group of laborers, while they received a low wage, were compensated in part by a sort of public and psychological wage. They were given public deference and titles of courtesy because they were white. They were admitted freely with all classes of white people to public functions, public parks, and the best schools. The police were drawn from their ranks, and the courts, dependent upon their votes, treated them with such leniency as to encourage lawlessness. Their vote selected public officials, and while this had small effect upon the economic situation, it had great effect upon their personal treatment and the deference shown them. White schoolhouses were the best in the community, and conspicuously placed, and they cost anywhere from twice to ten times as much per capita as the colored schools. The newspapers specialized on news that flattered the poor whites and almost utterly ignored the Negro except in crime and ridicule.

On the other hand, in the same way, the Negro was subject to public insult; was afraid of mobs; was liable to the jibes of children and the unreasoning fears of white women; and was compelled almost continuously to submit to various badges of inferiority. The result of this was that the wages of both classes could be kept low, the whites fearing to be supplanted by Negro labor, the Negroes always being threatened by the substitution of white labor.

Mob violence and lynching were the inevitable result of the attitude of these two classes and for a time were a sort of permissible Roman holiday for the entertainment of vicious whites. One can see for these reasons why labor organizers and labor agitators made such small headway in the South. They were, for the most part, appealing to laborers who would rather have low wages upon which they could eke out an existence than see colored labor with a decent wage. White labor saw in every advance of Negroes a threat to their racial prerogatives, so that in many districts Negroes were afraid to build decent homes or dress well, or own carriages, bicycles or automobiles, because of possible retaliation on the part of the whites.

Thus every problem of labor advance in the South was skillfully turned by demagogues into a matter of inter-racial jealousy. Perhaps the most conspicuous proof of this was the Atlanta riot in 1906, which followed Hoke Smith's vicious attempt to become United States Senator on a platform which first attacked corporations and then was suddenly twisted into scandalous traducing of the Negro race.

To this day no casual and unsophisticated reader of the white Southern press could possibly gather that the American Negro masses were anything but degraded, ignorant, inefficient examples of an incurably inferior race.

The result of all this had to be unfortunate for the Negro. He was a caged human being, driven into a curious mental provincialism. An inferiority complex dominated him. He did not believe himself a man like other men. He could not teach his children self-respect. The Negro as a group gradually lost his manners, his courtesy, his lighthearted kindliness. Large numbers sank into apathy and fatalism! There was no chance for the black man; there was no use in striving; ambition was not for Negroes.

The effect of caste on the moral integrity of the Negro race in America has thus been widely disastrous; servility and fawning, gross flattery of white folk and lying to appease and cajole them; failure to achieve dignity and self-respect and moral self-assertion, personal cowardliness and submission to insult and aggression; exaggerated and despicable humility; lack of faith of Negroes in themselves and in other Negroes and in all colored folk; inordinate admiration for the stigmata of success among white folk: wealth and arrogance, cunning dishonesty and assumptions of superiority; the exaltation of laziness and indifference as just as successful as the industry and striving which invites taxation and oppression; dull apathy and cynicism; faith in no future and the habit of moving and wandering in search of justice; a religion of prayer and submission to replace determination and effort.

These are not universal results or else the Negro long since would have dwindled and died in crime and disease. But they are so widespread as to bring inner conflict as baffling as the problems of interracial relations, and they hold back the moral grit and organized effort which are the only hope of survival.

On this and in spite of this comes an extraordinary record of accomplishment, a record so contradictory of what one might easily expect that many people and even the Negroes themselves are deceived by it. The real question is not so much what the Negro has done in spite of caste, as what he might have accomplished with reasonable encouragement. He has cut down his illiteracy more than two-thirds in fifty years, but with decent schools it ought to have been cut down 99 per cent. He has accumulated land and property, but has not been able to hold one-tenth of that which he has rightly earned. He has achieved success in many lines, as an inventor, scientist, scholar and writer. But most of his ability has been choked in chain-gangs and by open deliberate discrimination and conspiracies of silence. He has made a place for himself in literature and art, but the great deeps of his artistic gifts have never yet been plumbed. And yet, for all that he has accomplished, not only the nation but the South itself claims credit and actually points to it as proof of the wisdom or at least the innocuousness of organized suppression!

It is but human experience to find that the complete suppression of a race is impossible. Despite inner discouragement and submission to the oppression of others there persisted the mighty spirit, the emotional rebound that kept a vast number struggling for its rights, for self-expression, and for social uplift. Such men, in many cases, became targets for the white race. They were denounced as trouble makers. They were denied opportunity. They were driven from their homes. They were lynched.

It is doubtful if there is another group of twelve million people in the midst of a modern cultured land who are so widely inhibited and mentally confined as the American Negro. Within the colored race the philosophy of salvation has by the pressure of caste been curiously twisted and distorted. Shall they use the torch and dynamite? Shall they go North, or fight it out in the South? Shall they segregate themselves even more than they are now, in states, towns, cities or sections? Shall they leave the country? Are they Americans or foreigners? Shall they stand and sing "My Country 'Tis of Thee"? Shall they marry and rear children and save and buy homes, or deliberately commit race suicide?

Ordinarily such questions within a group settle themselves by laboratory experiment. It is shown that violence does not pay, that quiet persistent effort wins; bitterness and pessimism prove a handicap. And yet in the case of the Negro it is almost impossible to obtain such definite laboratory results. Failure cannot be attributed to individual neglect, and success does not necessarily follow individual effort. It is impossible to disentangle the results of caste and the results of work and striving. Ordinarily a group experiments—tries now this, now that, measures results and eliminates bad advice and unwise action by achieving success. But here success is so curtailed and frustrated that guiding wisdom fails. Why should we save? What good does it do to be upstanding, with self-respect? Who gains by thrift, or rises by education?

Such mental frustration cannot indefinitely continue. Some day it may burst in fire and blood. Who will be to blame? And where the greater cost? Black folk, after all, have little to lose, but Civilization has all.

This the American black man knows: his fight here is a fight to the finish. Either he dies or wins. If he wins it will be by no subterfuge or evasion of amalgamation. He will enter modern civilization here in America as a black man on terms of perfect and unlimited equality with any white man, or he will enter not at all. Either extermination root and branch, or absolute equality. There can be no compromise. This is the last great battle of the West.

Evil results of the revolution of 1876 have not been confined to Negroes. The reaction on the whites was just as significant. The white people of the South are essentially a fine kindly breed, the same sort of human beings that one finds the world over. Perhaps their early and fatal mistake was when they refused long before the Civil War to allow in the South differences of opinion. They would not let honest white Southerners continue to talk against slavery. They drove out the noncon-formist; they would not listen to the radical. The result was that there has been built up in the South an intolerance fatal to human culture. Men act as they do in the South, they murder, they lynch, they insult, because they listen to but one side of a question. They seldom know by real human contact Negroes who are men. They read books that laud the South and the "Lost Cause," but they are childish and furious when criticized, and interpret all criticism as personal attack.

The result is that the South in the main is ranged against liberalism. No liberal movement in the United States or in the world has been able to make advance among Southerners. They are militaristic and will have nothing to do with a peace movement. Young Southerners eagerly crowd West Point and Annapolis. The South is not interested in freedom for dark India. It has no sympathy with the oppressed of Africa or of Asia. It is for the most part against unions and the labor move-ment, because there can be no real labor movement in the South; their laboring class is cut in two and the white laborers must be ranged upon the side of their own exploiters by persis-tent propaganda and police force. Labor can gain in the South no class-consciousness. Strikes cannot be effective because the white striker can be threatened with the colored "scab" and the colored striker can be clapped in jail.

The result of the disfranchisement of the Negro on the political life of the South has been pitiful. Southerners argued that if the Negro was disfranchised, normal political life would be possible for the South. They did not realize that a living working class can never lose its political power and that all they did in 1876 was to transfer that political power from the hands of labor to the hands of capital, where it has been concentrated ever since. Moreover, after that transfer the forms of republican government became a continuing farce.

As Chamberlain said: "Every present citizen of South Caro-lina knows, and those who are truthful and frank will confess that the ballot debauched in 1876 remains debauched; the violence taught them remains now, if not in the same, in other forms; the defiance of law learned then in what was called a good cause survives in the horrid orgies of degradation and of lynchings."[1]

There can be no doubt that the revolution of 1876 established fraud and oligarchy in the South and the remains of that régime are still with us. Local government in the South to this day is handicapped and frustrated by caste and by the use of the color line to divide the electorate and dominate the Negro. As late as 1931, the Atlanta *Constitution* said of the Georgia legislature: "Never in its history has Georgia been inflicted with so incompetent a legislature as the one just adjourned."

George W. Cable said in 1885: "The vote, after all, was a secondary point, and the robbery and bribery on one side, and whipping and killing on the other were but huge accidents of the situation. The two main questions were really these: on the freedman's side, how to establish republican state government under the same recognition of his rights that the rest of Christendom accorded him; and on the former master's side, how to get back to the old semblance of republican state government, and—allowing that the freedman was de facto a voter—still to maintain a purely arbitrary superiority of all whites over all blacks, and a purely arbitrary equality of all blacks among themselves as an alien, menial and dangerous class.

"Exceptionally here and there someone in the master caste did throw off the old and accept the new ideas, and, if he would allow it, was instantly claimed as a leader by the newly liberated thousands around him. But just as promptly the old master race branded him also an alien reprobate, and in ninety-nine cases out of a hundred, if he had not already done so, he soon began to confirm by his actions the brand of his cheek."

The paradox of this whole muddle is that what the South started to do in 1876 was never accomplished and never will be.

---

[1] *Atlantic Monthly*, LXXXVII, p. 483.

The Negro cannot be disfranchised. He votes in every policy and the only result of disfranchisement is to bind the white South hand and foot and deliver it to its own worst self. Stevens and Sumner stand eternally vindicated.

Particularly has the South suffered spiritually by the effort to use propaganda and enforce belief. This always results in deliberate lying. Not that all white Southerners deliberately lie about the Negro, but to an astonishing degree the honest South allows known lies to stand uncontradicted.

The wide distortion of facts which became prevalent in the white South during and after Reconstruction as a measure of self-defense has never been wholly crushed since. For years Southerners denied that there was any fraud and cheating in elections. Henry Grady stood in Boston and told New England that the Negro was as free to vote in the South as the white laborer was in the North. Booker T. Washington repeatedly testified as to the good will and essential honesty of purpose of Southerners and put the whole burden of responsibility for advance upon the Negro himself. "The Southern white man is the Negro's best friend," scream all the Southern papers, even today. And this in the face of the open record of five thousand lynchings, jails bursting with black prisoners incarcerated on trivial and trumped-up charges, and caste staring from every train and street car.

This whole phantasmagoria has been built on the most miserable of human fictions: that in addition to the manifest differences between men there is a deep, awful and ineradicable cleft which condemns most men to eternal degradation. It is a cheap inheritance of the world's infancy, unworthy of grown folk. My rise does not involve your fall. No superior has interest in inferiority. Humanity is one and its vast variety is its glory and not its condemnation. If all men make the best of themselves, if all men have the chance to meet and know each other, the result is the love born of knowledge and not the hate based on ignorance.

The result of this upon the higher life in the South is extraordinary. Fundamentalism rules in religion because men hesitate openly to reason about the Golden Rule. Literature, art and music are curiously dominated by the Negro. The only literature the South has had for years is based largely upon the Negro. Southern music is Negro music. Yet Negroes themselves are seldom recognized as interpreters of art, and white artists must work under severe social limitations and at second hand; they thus lack necessary sincerity, depth and frankness.

Democracy in the South and in the United States is hampered by the Southern attitude. The Southerner, by winning the victory which the Fourteenth Amendment tried to deny, uses the Negro population as a basis of his political representation and allows few Negroes to vote; so that the white Southerner marches to the polls with many times as much voting power in his hand as the voter in the North.

The South does and must vote for reaction. There can be, therefore, neither in the South nor in the nation a successful third party movement. This was proven in the case of Theodore Roosevelt and LaFollette. A solid bloc of reaction in the South can always be depended upon to unite with Northern conservatism to elect a president.

One can only say to all this that whatever the South gained through its victory in the revolution of 1876 has been paid for at a price which literally staggers humanity. Imperialism, the exploitation of colored labor throughout the world, thrives upon the approval of the United States, and the United States gives that approval because of the South. World war waits on and supports imperial aggression and international jealousy. This was too great a price to pay for anything which the South gained.

The chief obstacle in this rich realm of the United States, endowed with every natural resource and with the abilities of a hundred different peoples—the chief and only obstacle to the coming of that kingdom of economic equality which is the only logical end of work is the determination of the white world to keep the black world poor and themselves rich. A clear vision of a world without inordinate individual wealth, of capital without profit and of income based on work alone, is the path out, not only for America but for all men. Across this path stands the South with flaming sword.

Of course, it would be humanly impossible for any such régime to be completely successful anywhere without protest and reaction from within. Alms-giving to Negroes in the South has always been almost universal. Even petty pilfering has been winked at. Beyond this, and of far greater social significance, have been the personal friendships between blacks and whites with aid and advice, even at great pecuniary and spiritual costs. Large-hearted Southern white men and women have in unnumbered cases quietly and without advertisement done enormous work to make life bearable and success possible for thousands of Negroes.

Most of the benevolence of this sort, however, has been of a personal and individual matter. In only a minority of cases have such Southern white people been willing to stand on principle and demand for all Negroes rights as men and treatment according to desert. When in some cases such opinion and clear advocacy has been made and has consequently evoked the usual social punishment, it is singular and almost peculiar to the South how seldom Southern whites have had the courage to stand up and suffer for righteousness' sake against the mass terror of public opinion.

In the South the iconoclast, the martyr, not only on the Negro question, but on other moral matters, have been conspicuously absent; and where they have arisen, they have soon either subsided into silence or retreated to the more tolerant atmosphere of the North, leaving the South all the poorer and all the more easily hammered into conformity with the mob.

If white and black in the South were free and intelligent there would be friendship and some intermarriage and there ought to be; but none would marry where he did not wish to, and there could be no greater intermingling in the future than in the shameful past, unless this union of races proved successful and attractive.

The revolution of 1876 was, in fine, a victory for which the South has every right to hang its head. After enslaving the Negro for two and one-half centuries, it turned on his emancipation to beat a beaten man, to trade in slaves, and to kill the defenseless; to break the spirit of the black man and humiliate him into hopelessness; to establish a new dictatorship of property in the South through the color line. It was a triumph of men who in their effort to replace equality with caste and to build inordinate wealth on a foundation of abject poverty have succeeded in killing democracy, art and religion.

And yet, despite this, and despite the long step backward toward slavery that black folk have been pushed, they have made withal a brave and fine fight; a fight against ridicule and monstrous caricature, against every refinement of cruelty and gross insult, against starvation, disease and murder in every form. It has left in their soul its scars, its deep scars; but when all is said, through it all has gone a thread of brave and splendid friendship from those few and rare men and women of white skins, North and South, who have dared to know and help and love black folk.

The unending tragedy of Reconstruction is the utter inability of the American mind to grasp its real significance, its national and worldwide implications. It was vain for Sumner and Stevens to hammer in the ears of the people that this problem involved the very foundations of American democracy, both political and economic. We are still too blind and infatuated to conceive of the emancipation of the laboring class in half the nation as a revolution comparable to the upheavals in France in the past, and in Russia, Spain, India and China today. We were worried when the beginnings of this experiment cost Eighteen Millions of Dollars, and quite aghast when a debt of Two Hundred and Twenty-Five Millions was involved, including waste and theft. We apparently expected that this social upheaval was going to be accomplished with peace, honesty and efficiency, and that the planters were going quietly to surrender the right to live on the labor of black folk, after two hundred and fifty years of habitual exploitation. And it seems to America a proof of inherent race inferiority that four million slaves did not completely emancipate themselves in eighty years, in the midst of nine million bitter enemies, and indifferent public opinion of the whole nation. If the Reconstruction of the Southern states, from slavery to free labor, and from aristocracy to industrial democracy, had been conceived as a major national program of America, whose accomplishment at any price was well worth the effort, we should be living today in a different world.

The attempt to make black men American citizens was in a certain sense all a failure, but a splendid failure. It did not fail where it was expected to fail. It was Athanasius contra mundum, with back to the wall, outnumbered ten to one, with all the wealth and all the opportunity, and all the world against him. And only in his hands and heart the consciousness of a great and just cause; fighting the battle of all the oppressed and despised humanity of every race and color, against the massed hirelings of Religion, Science, Education, Law, and brute force.

Black Reconstruction (*1935*)

QUESTION 3

A More Perfect Union: What Is the Government For?

★ ★ ★

The government of the world's most powerful nation was designed at a time when its people regarded centralized government with great suspicion, if not outright fear. That foundational caution, at this moment, feels anything but anachronistic. We have all too many examples from around the world, historically and today, of governments that oppress their people in every possible way, including by murdering them. At home and in the present, it is hardly inconceivable that the American government would be capable of starting wars without democratic consent, or of designating pariah categories of citizens and denying them their basic rights, or of unilaterally granting unwarranted favors to the rich and powerful. Our Constitution was written to replace the Articles of Confederation, which limited the national government's powers so severely that it could not function. The American government's powers have increased over time, but tensions over the proper scope of government power, between threatening excess and crippling limitation, have never gone away.

We can understand the Framers' suspicion of government as a reaction against the experience of colonial rule by a faraway king and parliament, but it surely went deeper than that. The Constitution is filled with proscriptions; all ten amendments in the Bill of Rights are devoted to preventing the government from doing things. The Federalist Papers represented the views of Alexander Hamilton, John Jay, and James Madison, who sought to persuade a skeptical public to ratify the Constitution by frequently assuring their readers that the new government would not subject them to tyranny. The name of the new nation itself communicated decentralized government power.

It helps us to understand what the Framers had in mind, as well as what is frustrating about the structure of the government today, to think about two other fears of theirs, in addition to the fundamental fear of a too powerful central government. One was a fear that one person, or body, within the government would have too much power to control what the entire government did. The other was a fear of what we'd now call democracy—a system of government designed to be directly responsive to the passions of a majority of its citizens. Somehow we have wound up with a government that has set aside many of the embedded protections against empowering the state overall, and the President in particular, but maintained some of the protections against directly empowering the people.

Madison's enduringly elegant Federalist Number 51 is an attempt to allay those foundational fears. The essential technique is what Madison calls "the necessary partition of power." Not only will governance be divided between the individual states and the nation; it will also be divided among three separate branches. What the Framers imagined to be the most powerful branch of the national government, the Congress, will be split into two bodies, each able to check the excesses of the other; the states, too, would use this power-limiting legislative structure; and Congress itself will share power with the courts and with the government departments under the control of the President. The Constitution spells out the intricately cautious design of the relationship between the executive and legislative branches of the government: vetoes, legislative confirmation of executive appointees, bill-signing, and of course the power of Congress to remove the President from office through impeachment.

Madison's mistrust of democracy is deeply embedded in the argument of Federalist Number 51, and in the Constitution itself. The structure of the Senate gives low-population states like Wyoming and Vermont far more political power than they would naturally have. House districts are tendentiously drawn by partisan state legislatures (whose members, rather than voters, also selected U.S. senators for more than a century). The presidency is decided by the electoral college, not by direct election. None of this is an accident. The best-remembered passage in Federalist Number 51 is "If men were angels, no government would be necessary. If angels were to govern men, neither external nor internal controuls on government would be necessary. In framing a government which is to be administered by men over men, the great difficulty lies in this: You must first enable the government to controul the governed; and in the next place, oblige it to controul itself." This communicates a profound mistrust of human nature; although government itself must be constantly checked, it must exist because people's natural behavior is so incipiently malign that it, too, urgently requires limitation, and government is the most reliable instrument at hand for that. Just as government itself could be set up as a balance-of-powers system among its branches, politics could be a never-ending competition among regions and interest groups so numerous "that the rights of individuals or the minority, will be in little danger from interested combinations of the majority." Part of the appeal of creating a geographically large nation was that it would have so many interests that no one of them could predominate.

Madison's defense of the rights of individuals and minorities was based on quite different definitions of these terms than we would use today. Wealthy property holders like him thought of themselves as a minority group vulnerable to being overwhelmed by the propertyless mob, or by commercial interests in the more populated parts of the country, and they did not think the Constitution protected women and African Americans against unequal treatment. That the language of Federalist Number 51 still resonates is a demonstration that governing principles and systems can transcend the specific circumstances in which they originated. People's views on the powers of the government of the United States tend to vary according to how comfortable they are with who is in charge. I am writing at a time when many Americans are intensely uncomfortable.

One can see, through the texts included here, the developing forces that brought us to the situation we are in now: a very powerful national government, with an overwhelmingly powerful chief executive, that remains relatively unresponsive to the majority.

The landmark Supreme Court case of *McCulloch v. Maryland*, in 1819, was a milestone on the way to understanding the American political compact as one in which the state governments were clearly subordinate to the federal government. Congress had chartered the Second Bank of the United States in 1816. In 1818, the state of Maryland imposed a tax on the bank, which James McCulloch, the bank's cashier, refused to pay. The court ruled unanimously that the state's tax was unconstitutional. The *McCulloch* case came down to whether the government could take on new powers that, unlike the power to tax or the power to regulate interstate commerce, hadn't been specifically enumerated in the Constitution. Writing for the court, Chief Justice John Marshall ruled that under the Constitution's broad grant to the federal government of the authority "to make all Laws which shall be necessary and proper," the federal government could charter a national bank that a state government could not tax. Marshall in effect was rejecting the late twentieth century conservative idea that the Supreme Court's interpretation of the Constitution should be determined by the Framer's original intent. He knew the Framers personally—in particular, he knew that Madison and Alexander Hamilton had disagreed about whether the establishment of the First Bank of the United States in 1791 violated the country's founding principles—and he concluded that the Constitution should be continually reinterpreted to make it possible for the government to meet new needs. That doctrine opened the way for an expansion of the federal government's powers.

Over the course of the nineteenth century, the United States established its domain as extending from the Atlantic to the Pacific. It fought a terrible Civil War to preserve the Union. It began to establish itself as a world power. But the federal government remained rather small. By 1900 there were still only eight federal departments, and only one regulatory agency, the Interstate Commerce Commission. Federal government spending represented only 3 percent of the American economy, as against 20 percent today. There was no income tax. What made the government take on so many new powers in the early decades of the twentieth century was not just that the country had become so large, populous, and prosperous. It was also that the old fear of excessive centralized power had reawakened in a different form. Now it wasn't Great Britain, or the national government, or the "tyranny of the majority" that set off public alarm, it was the advent of very large business organizations and great fortunes, far beyond a scale that would have occurred to the Framers as they were drafting their central power-limiting document. Just as today the giant technology companies—Google, Facebook, Amazon, Apple—seem to have come out of nowhere to dominate many aspects of the life of the country, including politics, so it seemed to many Americans at the beginning of the twentieth century as they contemplated Standard Oil, U.S. Steel, and the Southern Pacific Railroad.

At the outset of the twentieth century the government established the Department of Commerce, the Federal Trade Commission, the Food and Drug Administration, the Federal Reserve Board, and the income tax, all of which gave it an enhanced role in the economic life of the country. But liberals, at least, still felt that the government was too small and powerless relative to the giant new trusts and corporations. In 1932, when Franklin Roosevelt ran for President for the first time, there was the additional problem that the country was in a severe economic crisis, with 25 percent unemployment and the banking system unable to function, that private business institutions seemed incapable of solving. Who but an enhanced federal government could help?

During the campaign Roosevelt was not yet crisply defined as the father of the New Deal. In the summer of 1932 a member of his "brain trust" of academic advisors, Adolf Berle of Columbia Law School, wrote Roosevelt complaining that he had no widely understood plan for how he proposed to govern. Roosevelt replied by asking Berle to provide one, and the result was Roosevelt's Commonwealth Club address, written by Berle and his wife Beatrice and delivered in San Francisco in September 1932. The fundamental principle of the United States, Roosevelt asserted, was Jeffersonian "individualism" and limited government. But the Industrial Revolution had brought into the country's life "a group of financial Titans." They had been given their head so that railroads, factories, and cities could be built, but now they "had become great uncontrolled and irresponsible units of power within the State"—collectively, "the despot of the twentieth century." The only way to restrain their power was through government, and therefore government would, must, accept new responsibilities.

Back in the 1830s, Alexis de Tocqueville, the French aristocrat who was the most astute observer of the early American republic and who shared the Framers' deep mistrust of majoritarian democracy, worried, in the chapter from *Democracy in America* included here, about a new kind of "despotism" coming to the United States. What he feared seems to foreshadow what we would now call a welfare state—the term didn't exist then. Tocqueville believed it would turn the American people into "a flock of timid and industrious animals, with the government as its shepherd." Roosevelt's creation of federal programs, like

Social Security, that helped many millions of ordinary people to meet their basic needs would have horrified Tocqueville, but it created a political constituency for a greatly enhanced federal government. Curtailing the power of business was a popular cause during the first decades of the twentieth century, and it is becoming one again now, but providing a measure of personal economic security is surely even more popular. During Roosevelt's presidency, the number of federal employees, and the government's spending and its share of the economy, more than doubled even before the beginning of the Second World War, during which it more than doubled again. Another generation of federal agencies was born: the Securities and Exchange Commission, the Federal Housing Administration, the Federal Communications Commission, and many others. All this clearly expanded the size, scope, and influence of the federal government.

Even so, the United States has never created a national health service, a national telecommunications company, or a national airline, and many social functions that government performed elsewhere rested with private business, though substantially because of government prodding. The part of our government that became, and remains, outstandingly large compared to other countries is the military. The alliance that won the Second World War included the Soviet Union, which bore by far the worst of the human cost of the fighting. The price the United States paid for the Soviets' essential role in defeating Germany was that it acquiesced to control of all of Eastern Europe by what had become the only other major world power. Fearful of the Soviets' expansionist ambitions, especially after the first Soviet test of a nuclear weapon, in late 1949, the United States declined to restore its armed forces to their prewar scope. Instead it maintained a peacetime military establishment of unprecedented power and global reach.

The dully titled but vividly written "NSC-68: United States Objectives and Programs for National Security," from

1950, is a blueprint for the country's defense posture, produced by a committee headed by the hawkish banker-statesman Paul Nitze, who was a high-ranking official of the State Department at the time. Nitze's language is strikingly alarmed and martial. The Soviet leaders were "evil men," animated by a "fanatic faith." They had created a "grim oligarchy," a "slave state." The future of civilization was at stake. It would be necessary to enhance the country's military power greatly, and also its economic and political power. We should be prepared to fight more wars, in faraway locations. Mere containment of the Soviets' ambitions was not enough. In the long run our relentless pressure would cause the balance of power to shift decisively in our favor. Nitze and his colleagues clearly thought of themselves as steering a middle course, between those who did not sufficiently appreciate the gravity of the threat from the Soviet Union and those who wanted to put the country back on a wartime footing, with the goal of defeating the Soviets militarily and suspending peacetime liberties in the meantime. They placed themselves on the side of domestic freedom, justice, and toleration—principles that our rival did not honor.

Even after the end of the four long decades of the Cold War, the United States has maintained the principle that it should be by far the most militarily powerful country in the world, though somewhat less expensively. It isn't just that the country maintains an enormous permanent military with global reach; it's also that the national security establishment is far more powerful, and more under the personal control of the President, than the Framers could have imagined. At one person's command, the United States has overthrown governments halfway around the world, spied on its own citizens, started wars, and threatened to use nuclear weapons even though we were not at war. That is a far cry from the founding idea of a government constrained from doing very much, with each of its elements severely constrained by the others.

American politicians of all ideologies are fond of proclaiming that the United States is the greatest nation on earth. It's hard to accept greatness as a goal without implicitly accepting the idea of a very large and powerful national government. If that is what we now want, we should at least hold tight to the tradition of hyperawareness of the danger that putting too much political power in too few hands entails.

★ ★ ★

James Madison: The Federalist No. 51

To the People of the State of New-York.

To what expedient then shall we finally resort for maintaining in practice the necessary partition of power among the several departments, as laid down in the constitution? The only answer that can be given is, that as all these exterior provisions are found to be inadequate, the defect must be supplied, by so contriving the interior structure of the government, as that its several constituent parts may, by their mutual relations, be the means of keeping each other in their proper places. Without presuming to undertake a full development of this important idea, I will hazard a few general observations, which may perhaps place it in a clearer light, and enable us to form a more correct judgment of the principles and structure of the government planned by the convention.

In order to lay a due foundation for that separate and distinct exercise of the different powers of government, which to a certain extent, is admitted on all hands to be essential to the preservation of liberty, it is evident that each department should have a will of its own; and consequently should be so constituted, that the members of each should have as little agency as possible in the appointment of the members of the others. Were this principle rigorously adhered to, it would require that all the appointments for the supreme executive, legislative, and judiciary magistracies, should be drawn from the same fountain of authority, the people, through channels, having no communication whatever with one another. Perhaps such a plan of constructing the several departments would be less difficult in practice than it may in contemplation appear. Some difficulties however, and some additional expence, would attend the execution of it. Some deviations therefore from the principle must be admitted. In the constitution of the judiciary department in particular, it might be inexpedient to insist rigorously on the principle; first, because peculiar qualifications being essential in the members, the primary consideration ought to be to select that mode of choice, which best secures these qualifications; secondly, because the permanent tenure by which the appointments are held in that department, must soon destroy all sense of dependence on the authority conferring them.

It is equally evident that the members of each department should be as little dependent as possible on those of the others, for the emoluments annexed to their offices. Were the executive magistrate, or the judges, not independent of the legislature in this particular, their independence in every other would be merely nominal.

But the great security against a gradual concentration of the several powers in the same department, consists in giving to those who administer each department, the necessary constitutional means, and personal motives, to resist encroachments of the others. The provision for defence must in this, as in all other cases, be made commensurate to the danger of attack. Ambition must be made to counteract ambition. The interest of the man must be connected with the constitutional rights of the place. It may be a reflection on human nature, that such devices should be necessary to controul the abuses of government. But what is government itself but the greatest of all reflections on human nature? If men were angels, no government would be necessary. If angels were to govern men, neither external nor internal controuls on government would be necessary. In framing a government which is to be administered by men over men, the great difficulty lies in this: You must first enable the government to controul the governed; and in the next place, oblige it to controul itself. A dependence on the people is no doubt the primary controul on the government; but experience has taught mankind the necessity of auxiliary precautions.

This policy of supplying by opposite and rival interests, the defect of better motives, might be traced through the whole system of human affairs, private as well as public. We see it particularly displayed in all the subordinate distributions of power; where the constant aim is to divide and arrange the several offices in such a manner as that each may be a check on the other; that the private interest of every individual, may be a centinel over the public rights. These inventions of prudence cannot be less requisite in the distribution of the supreme powers of the state.

But it is not possible to give to each department an equal power of self defence. In republican government the legislative authority, necessarily, predominates. The remedy for this inconveniency is, to divide the legislature into different branches; and to render them by different modes of election, and different principles of action, as little connected with each other, as the nature of their common functions, and their common dependence on the society, will admit. It may even be necessary to guard against dangerous encroachments by still further precautions. As the weight of the legislative authority requires that it should be thus divided, the weakness of the executive may require, on the other hand, that it should be fortified. An absolute negative, on the legislature, appears at first view to be the natural defence with which the executive magistrate should be armed. But perhaps it would be neither altogether safe, nor alone sufficient. On ordinary occasions, it might not be exerted with the requisite firmness; and on extraordinary occasions, it might be perfidiously abused. May not this defect of an absolute negative be supplied, by some qualified connection between this weaker department, and the weaker branch of the stronger department, by which the latter may be led to support the constitutional rights of the former, without being too much detached from the rights of its own department?

If the principles on which these observations are founded be just, as I persuade myself they are, and they be applied as a criterion, to the several state constitutions, and to the federal constitution, it will be found, that if the latter does not perfectly correspond with them, the former are infinitely less able to bear such a test.

There are moreover two considerations particularly applicable to the federal system of America, which place that system in a very interesting point of view.

First. In a single republic, all the power surrendered by the people, is submitted to the administration of a single government; and usurpations are guarded against by a division of the government into distinct and separate departments. In the compound republic of America, the power surrendered by the people, is first divided between two distinct governments, and then the portion allotted to each, subdivided among distinct and separate departments. Hence a double security arises to the rights of the people. The different governments will controul each other; at the same time that each will be controuled by itself.

Second. It is of great importance in a republic, not only to guard the society against the oppression of its rulers; but to guard one part of the society against the injustice of the other part. Different interests necessarily exist in different classes of citizens. If a majority be united by a common interest, the rights of the minority will be insecure. There are but two methods of providing against this evil: The one by creating a will in the community independent of the majority, that is, of the society itself; the other by comprehending in the society so many separate descriptions of citizens, as will render an unjust combination of a majority of the whole, very improbable, if not impracticable. The first method prevails in all governments possessing an hereditary or self appointed authority. This at best is but a precarious security; because a power independent of the society may as well espouse the unjust views of the major, as the rightful interests, of the minor party, and may possibly be turned against both parties. The second method will be exemplified in the federal republic of the United States. Whilst all authority in it will be derived from and dependent on the society, the society itself will be broken into so many parts, interests and classes of citizens, that the rights of individuals or of the minority, will be in little danger from interested combinations of the majority. In a free government, the security for civil rights must be the same as for religious rights. It consists in the one case in the multiplicity of interests, and in the other, in the multiplicity of sects. The degree of security in both cases will depend on the number of interests and sects; and this may be presumed to depend on the extent of country and number of people comprehended under the same government. This view of the subject must particularly recommend a proper federal system to all the sincere and considerate friends of republican government: Since it shews that in exact proportion as the territory of the union may be formed into more circumscribed confederacies or states, oppressive combinations of a majority will be facilitated, the best security under the republican form, for the rights of every class of citizens, will be diminished; and consequently, the stability and independence of some member of the government, the only other security, must be proportionally increased. Justice is the end of government. It is the end of civil society. It ever has been, and ever will be pursued, until it be obtained, or until liberty be lost in the pursuit. In a society under the forms of which the stronger faction can readily unite and oppress the weaker, anarchy may as truly be said to reign, as in a state of nature where the weaker individual is not secured against the violence of the stronger: And as in the latter state even the stronger individuals are prompted by the uncertainty of their condition, to submit to a government which may protect the weak as well as themselves: So in the former state, will the more powerful factions or parties be gradually induced by a like motive, to wish for a government which will protect all parties, the weaker as well as the more powerful. It can be little doubted, that if the state of Rhode Island was separated from the confederacy, and left to itself, the insecurity of rights under the popular form of government within such narrow limits, would be displayed by such reiterated oppressions of factious majorities, that some power altogether independent of the people would soon be called for by the voice of the very factions whose misrule had proved the necessity of it. In the extended republic of the United States, and among the great variety of interests, parties and sects which it embraces, a coalition of a majority of the whole society could seldom take place on any other principles than those of justice and the general good; and there being thus less danger to a minor from the will of the major party, there must be less pretext also, to provide for the security of the former, by introducing into the government a will not dependent on the latter; or in other words, a will independent of the society itself. It is no less certain than it is important, notwithstanding the contrary opinions which have been entertained, that the larger the society, provided it lie within a practicable sphere, the more duly capable it will be of self government. And happily for the *republican cause*, the practicable sphere may be carried to a very great extent, by a judicious modification and mixture of the *federal principle*.

PUBLIUS.

The Independent Journal, February 6, 1788

★ ★ ★

John Marshall: from Opinion for the Court in *McCulloch v. Maryland*

This government is acknowledged by all to be one of enumerated powers. The principle, that it can exercise only the powers granted to it, would seem too apparent to have required to be enforced by all those arguments which its enlightened friends, while it was depending before the people, found it necessary to urge. That principle is now universally admitted. But the question respecting the extent of the powers actually granted, is perpetually arising, and will probably continue to arise, as long as our system shall exist.

In discussing these questions, the conflicting powers of the general and State governments must be brought into view, and the supremacy of their respective laws, when they are in opposition, must be settled.

If any one proposition could command the universal assent of mankind, we might expect it would be this—that the government of the Union, though limited in its powers, is supreme within its sphere of action. This would seem to result necessarily from its nature. It is the government of all; its powers are delegated by all; it represents all, and acts for all. Though any one State may be willing to control its operations, no State is willing to allow others to control them. The nation, on those subjects on which it can act, must necessarily bind its component parts. But this question is not left to mere reason: the people have, in express terms, decided it, by saying, "this constitution, and the laws of the United States, which shall be made in pursuance thereof," "shall be the supreme law of the land," and by requiring that the members of the State legislatures, and the officers of the executive and judicial departments of the States, shall take the oath of fidelity to it.

The government of the United States, then, though limited in its powers, is supreme; and its laws, when made in pursuance of the constitution, form the supreme law of the land, "any thing in the constitution or laws of any State to the contrary notwithstanding."

Among the enumerated powers, we do not find that of establishing a bank or creating a corporation. But there is no phrase in the instrument which, like the articles of confederation, excludes incidental or implied powers; and which requires that every thing granted shall be expressly and minutely described. Even the 10th amendment, which was framed for the purpose of quieting the excessive jealousies which had been excited, omits the word "expressly," and declares only that the powers "not delegated to the United States, nor prohibited to the States, are reserved to the States or to the people;" thus leaving the question, whether the particular power which may become the subject of contest has been delegated to the one government, or prohibited to the other, to depend on a fair construction of the whole instrument. The men who drew and adopted this amendment had experienced the embarrassments resulting from the insertion of this word in the articles of confederation, and probably omitted it to avoid those embarrassments. A constitution, to contain an accurate detail of all the subdivisions of which its great powers will admit, and of all the means by which they may be carried into execution, would partake of the prolixity of a legal code, and could scarcely be embraced by the human mind. It would probably never be understood by the public. Its nature, therefore, requires, that only its great outlines should be marked, its important objects designated, and the minor ingredients which compose those objects be deduced from the nature of the objects themselves. That this idea was entertained by the framers of the American constitution, is not only to be inferred from the nature of the instrument, but from the language. Why else were some of the limitations, found in the ninth section of the 1st article, introduced? It is also, in some degree, warranted by their having omitted to use any restrictive term which might prevent its receiving a fair and just interpretation. In considering this question, then, we must never forget, that it is a *constitution* we are expounding.

But the argument on which most reliance is placed, is drawn from the peculiar language of this clause. Congress is not empowered by it to make all laws, which may have relation to the powers conferred on the government, but such only as may be *"necessary and proper"* for carrying them into execution. The word *"necessary,"* is considered as controlling the whole sentence, and as limiting the right to pass laws for the execution of the granted powers, to such as are indispensable, and without which the power would be nugatory. That it excludes the choice of means, and leaves to Congress, in each case, that only which is most direct and simple.

Is it true, that this is the sense in which the word "necessary" is always used? Does it always import an absolute physical necessity, so strong, that one thing, to which another may be termed necessary, cannot exist without that other? We think it does not. If reference be had to its use, in the common affairs of the world, or in approved authors, we find that it frequently imports no more than that one thing is convenient, or useful, or essential to another. To employ the means necessary to an end, is generally understood as employing any means calculated to produce the end, and not as being confined to those single means, without which the end would be entirely unattainable. Such is the character of human language, that no word conveys to the mind, in all situations, one single definite idea; and nothing is more common than to use words in a figurative sense. Almost all compositions contain words, which, taken in their rigorous sense, would convey a meaning different from that which is obviously intended. It is essential to just construction, that many words which import something excessive, should be understood in a more mitigated sense—in that sense which common usage justifies. The word "necessary" is of this description. It has not a fixed character peculiar to itself. It admits of all degrees of comparison; and is often connected with other words, which increase or diminish the impression the mind receives of the urgency it imports. A thing may be necessary, very necessary, absolutely or indispensably necessary. To no mind would the same idea be conveyed, by these several phrases. This comment on the word is well illustrated, by the passage cited at the bar, from the 10th section of the 1st article of the constitution. It is, we think, impossible to compare the sentence which prohibits a State from laying "imposts, or duties on imports or exports, except what may be *absolutely* necessary for executing its inspection laws," with that which authorizes Congress "to make all laws which shall be necessary and proper for carrying into execution" the powers of the general government, without feeling a conviction that the convention understood itself to change materially the meaning of the word "necessary," by prefixing the word "absolutely." This word, then, like others, is used in various senses; and, in its construction, the subject, the context, the intention of the person using them, are all to be taken into view.

Let this be done in the case under consideration. The subject is the execution of those great powers on which the welfare of a nation essentially depends. It must have been the intention of those who gave these powers, to insure, as far as human prudence could insure, their beneficial execution. This could not be done by confiding the choice of means to such narrow limits as not to leave it in the power of Congress to adopt any which might be appropriate, and which were conducive to the end. This provision is made in a constitution intended to endure for ages to come, and, consequently, to be adapted to the various *crises* of human affairs. To have prescribed the means by which government should, in all future time, execute its powers, would have been to change, entirely, the character of the instrument, and give it the properties of a legal code. It would have been an unwise attempt to provide, by immutable rules, for exigencies which, if foreseen at all, must have been seen dimly, and which can be best provided for as they occur. To have declared that the best means shall not be used, but those alone without which the power given would be nugatory, would have been to deprive the legislature of the capacity to avail itself of experience, to exercise its reason, and to accommodate its legislation to circumstances. If we apply this principle of construction to any of the powers of the government, we shall find it so pernicious in its operation that we shall be compelled to discard it. The powers vested in Congress may certainly be carried into execution, without prescribing an oath of office. The power to exact this security for the faithful performance of duty, is not given, nor is it indispensably necessary. The different departments may be established; taxes may be imposed and collected; armies and navies may be raised and maintained; and money may be borrowed, without requiring an oath of office. It might be argued, with as much plausibility as other incidental powers have been assailed, that the Convention was not unmindful of this subject. The oath which might be exacted—that of fidelity to the constitution—is prescribed, and no other can be required. Yet, he would be charged with insanity who should contend, that the legislature might not superadd, to the oath directed by the constitution, such other oath of office as its wisdom might suggest.

So, with respect to the whole penal code of the United States: whence arises the power to punish in cases not prescribed by the constitution? All admit that the government may, legitimately, punish any violation of its laws; and yet, this is not among the enumerated powers of Congress. The right to enforce the observance of law, by punishing its infraction, might be denied with the more plausibility, because it is expressly given in some cases. Congress is empowered "to provide for the punishment of counterfeiting the securities and current coin of the United States," and "to define and punish piracies and felonies committed on the high seas, and offences against the law of nations." The several powers of Congress may exist, in a very imperfect state to be sure, but they may exist and be carried into execution, although no punishment should be inflicted in cases where the right to punish is not expressly given.

Take, for example, the power "to establish post offices and post roads." This power is executed by the single act of making the establishment. But, from this has been inferred the power and duty of carrying the mail along the post road, from one post office to another. And, from this implied power, has again been inferred the right to punish those who steal letters from the post office, or rob the mail. It may be said, with some plausibility, that the right to carry the mail, and to punish those who rob it, is not indispensably necessary to the establishment of a post office and post road. This right is indeed essential to the beneficial exercise of the power, but not indispenably necessary to its existence. So, of the punishment of the crimes of stealing or falsifying a record or process of a Court of the United States, or of perjury in such Court. To punish these offences is certainly conducive to the due administration of justice. But courts may exist, and may decide the causes brought before them, though such crimes escape punishment.

The baneful influence of this narrow construction on all the operations of the government, and the absolute impracticability of maintaining it without rendering the government incompetent to its great objects, might be illustrated by numerous examples drawn from the constitution, and from our laws. The good sense of the public has pronounced, without hesitation, that the power of punishment appertains to sovereignty, and may be exercised whenever the sovereign has a right to act, as incidental to his constitutional powers. It is a means for carrying into execution all sovereign powers, and may be used, although not indispensably necessary. It is a right incidental to the power, and conducive to its beneficial exercise.

If this limited construction of the word "necessary" must be abandoned in order to punish, whence is derived the rule which would reinstate it, when the government would carry its powers into execution by means not vindictive in their nature? If the word "necessary" means "needful," "requisite," "essential," "conducive to," in order to let in the power of punishment for the infraction of law; why is it not equally comprehensive when required to authorize the use of means which facilitate the execution of the powers of government without the infliction of punishment?

In ascertaining the sense in which the word "necessary" is used in this clause of the constitution, we may derive some aid from that with which it is associated. Congress shall have power "to make all laws which shall be necessary and *proper* to carry into execution" the powers of the government. If the word "necessary" was used in that strict and rigorous sense for which the counsel for the State of Maryland contend, it would be an extraordinary departure from the usual course of the human mind, as exhibited in composition, to add a word, the only possible effect of which is to qualify that strict and rigorous meaning; to present to the mind the idea of some choice of means of legislation not straitened and compressed within the narrow limits for which gentlemen contend.

But the argument which most conclusively demonstrates the error of the construction contended for by the counsel for the State of Maryland, is founded on the intention of the Convention, as manifested in the whole clause. To waste time and argument in proving that, without it, Congress might carry its powers into execution, would be not much less idle than to hold a lighted taper to the sun. As little can it be required to prove, that in the absence of this clause, Congress would have some choice of means. That it might employ those which, in its judgment, would most advantageously effect the object to be accomplished. That any means adapted to the end, any means which tended directly to the execution of the constitutional powers of the government, were in themselves constitutional. This clause, as construed by the State of Maryland, would abridge, and almost annihilate this useful and necessary right

of the legislature to select its means. That this could not be
intended, is, we should think, had it not been already contro-
verted, too apparent for controversy. We think so for the following reasons:

1st. The clause is placed among the powers of Congress, not
among the limitations on those powers.

2nd. Its terms purport to enlarge, not to diminish the powers
vested in the government. It purports to be an additional power,
not a restriction on those already granted. No reason has been,
or can be assigned for thus concealing an intention to narrow
the discretion of the national legislature under words which
purport to enlarge it. The framers of the constitution wished
its adoption, and well knew that it would be endangered by
its strength, not by its weakness. Had they been capable of
using language which would convey to the eye one idea, and,
after deep reflection, impress on the mind another, they would
rather have disguised the grant of power, than its limitation. If,
then, their intention had been, by this clause, to restrain the
free use of means which might otherwise have been implied,
that intention would have been inserted in another place, and
would have been expressed in terms resembling these. "In carrying into execution the foregoing powers, and all others," &c.
"no laws shall be passed but such as are necessary and proper."
Had the intention been to make this clause restrictive, it would
unquestionably have been so in form as well as in effect.

The result of the most careful and attentive consideration
bestowed upon this clause is, that if it does not enlarge, it
cannot be construed to restrain the powers of Congress, or to
impair the right of the legislature to exercise its best judgment
in the selection of measures to carry into execution the constitutional powers of the government. If no other motive for
its insertion can be suggested, a sufficient one is found in the
desire to remove all doubts respecting the right to legislate on
that vast mass of incidental powers which must be involved in
the constitution, if that instrument be not a splendid bauble.

We admit, as all must admit, that the powers of the government are limited, and that its limits are not to be transcended. But we think the sound construction of the constitution must allow to the national legislature that discretion, with respect to the means by which the powers it confers are to be carried into execution, which will enable that body to perform the high duties assigned to it, in the manner most beneficial to the people. Let the end be legitimate, let it be within the scope of the constitution, and all means which are appropriate, which are plainly adapted to that end, which are not prohibited, but consist with the letter and spirit of the constitution, are constitutional.

March 6, 1819

★ ★ ★

Alexis de Tocqueville: from *Democracy in America*

What Kind of Despotism Democratic Nations Have to Fear

DURING my stay in the United States I had observed that a democratic social state similar to that of the Americans might make it unusually easy to establish despotism, and on my return to Europe I saw how many of our princes had already made use of ideas, sentiments, and needs engendered by that same social state in order to enlarge their sphere of power.

This led me to the thought that Christian nations might ultimately fall victim to oppression similar to that which once weighed on a number of peoples of Antiquity.

A more detailed examination of the subject and five years of new meditations have not diminished my fears but have changed their focus.

In centuries past, no sovereign was ever so absolute and so powerful as to undertake to administer by himself, and without the assistance of secondary powers, all the parts of a great empire. No ruler ever attempted to subject all his people indiscriminately to the minute details of a uniform code, or descended to their level to dictate and manage the lives of each and every one of them. The idea of such an undertaking never occurred to the mind of man, and had anyone conceived of such a thing, the want of enlightenment, the imperfection of administrative procedures, and above all the natural obstacles created by the inequality of conditions would soon have halted the execution of such a vast design.

When the power of the Caesars was at its height, the various peoples that inhabited the Roman world preserved their diverse customs and mores: though subject to the same monarch, most of the provinces were separately administered. Powerful and active municipalities were everywhere, and even though all the government of the empire was concentrated in the hands of the emperor alone, and he remained, when necessary, the arbiter of all things, the details of social life and of individual existence ordinarily escaped his control.

To be sure, the emperors wielded vast power without any counterweight, which enabled them to freely indulge their most bizarre penchants and to use the entire force of the state to gratify them. Often they abused this power to deprive a citizen arbitrarily of his property or his life. Their tyranny weighed mightily on a few, but it did not extend to a large number. It fastened on certain great objectives as primary and neglected the rest; it was violent and limited.

If despotism were to establish itself in today's democratic nations, it would probably have a different character. It would be more extensive and more mild, and it would degrade men without tormenting them.[1]

I have no doubt that in centuries of enlightenment and equality like our own, it will be easier for sovereigns to gather all public powers into their hands alone and to penetrate the sphere of private interests more deeply and regularly than any sovereign of Antiquity was ever able to do. But the same equality that facilitates despotism also tempers it. As men become increasingly similar and more and more equal, we have seen how public mores become milder and more humane. When no citizen has great power or wealth, tyranny in a sense lacks both opportunity and a stage. Since all fortunes are modest, passions are naturally contained, the imagination is limited, and pleasures are simple. This universal moderation moderates the sovereign himself and confines the erratic impulses of his desire within certain limits.

Quite apart from these reasons, which derive from the very nature of the social state, I could add many others, but to do so

---

[1] See Note I, page 140.

would take me far afield, and I prefer to remain within the limit that I have set for myself.

Democratic governments may become violent and even cruel in certain moments of great effervescence and great peril, but such crises will be rare and temporary.

When I think of the petty passions of men today, of the softness of their mores, the extent of their enlightenment, the purity of their religion, and the mildness of their morality, of their laborious and orderly habits, and of the restraint that nearly all of them maintain in vice as well as in virtue, what I fear is not that they will find tyrants among their leaders but rather that they will find protectors.

I therefore believe that the kind of oppression that threatens democratic peoples is unlike any the world has seen before. Our contemporaries will find no image of it in their memories. I search in vain for an expression that exactly reproduces my idea of it and captures it fully. The old words "despotism" and "tyranny" will not do. The thing is new, hence I must try to define it, since I cannot give it a name.

I am trying to imagine what new features despotism might have in today's world: I see an innumerable host of men, all alike and equal, endlessly hastening after petty and vulgar pleasures with which they fill their souls. Each of them, withdrawn into himself, is virtually a stranger to the fate of all the others. For him, his children and personal friends comprise the entire human race. As for the remainder of his fellow citizens, he lives alongside them but does not see them. He touches them but does not feel them. He exists only in himself and for himself, and if he still has a family, he no longer has a country.

Over these men stands an immense tutelary power, which assumes sole responsibility for securing their pleasure and watching over their fate. It is absolute, meticulous, regular, provident, and mild. It would resemble paternal authority if only its purpose were the same, namely, to prepare men for manhood. But on the contrary, it seeks only to keep them in childhood irrevocably. It likes citizens to rejoice, provided they think only of rejoicing. It works willingly for their happiness but wants to be the sole agent and only arbiter of that happiness. It provides for their security, foresees and takes care of their needs, facilitates their pleasures, manages their most important affairs, directs their industry, regulates their successions, and divides their inheritances. Why not relieve them entirely of the trouble of thinking and the difficulty of living?

Every day it thus makes man's use of his free will rarer and more futile. It circumscribes the action of the will more narrowly, and little by little robs each citizen of the use of his own faculties. Equality paved the way for all these things by preparing men to put up with them and even to look upon them as a boon.

The sovereign, after taking individuals one by one in his powerful hands and kneading them to his liking, reaches out to embrace society as a whole. Over it he spreads a fine mesh of uniform, minute, and complex rules, through which not even the most original minds and most vigorous souls can poke their heads above the crowd. He does not break men's wills but softens, bends, and guides them. He seldom forces anyone to act but consistently opposes action. He does not destroy things but prevents them from coming into being. Rather than tyrannize, he inhibits, represses, saps, stifles, and stultifies, and in the end he reduces each nation to nothing but a flock of timid and industrious animals, with the government as its shepherd.

I have always believed that this kind of servitude—the regulated, mild, peaceful servitude that I have just described—could be combined more easily than one might imagine with some of the external forms of liberty, and that it would not be impossible for it to establish itself in the shadow of popular sovereignty itself.

Our contemporaries are constantly wracked by two warring passions: they feel the need to be led and the desire to remain free. Unable to destroy either of these contrary instincts, they seek to satisfy both at once. They imagine a single, omnipotent, tutelary power, but one that is elected by the citizens. They combine centralization with popular sovereignty. This gives them some respite. They console themselves for being treated as wards by imagining that they have chosen their own protectors. Each individual allows himself to be clapped in chains because he sees that the other end of the chain is held not by a man or a class but by the people themselves.

In this system citizens emerge from dependence for a moment to indicate their master and then return to it.

There are many people nowadays who adjust quite easily to a compromise of this kind between administrative despotism and popular sovereignty and who believe that they have done enough to guarantee the liberty of individuals when in fact they have surrendered that liberty to the national government. That is not enough for me. The nature of the master matters far less to me than the fact of obedience.

I will not deny, however, that a constitution of this kind is infinitely preferable to one that concentrates all powers and then deposits them in the hands of an irresponsible man or body. Of all the various forms that democratic despotism might take, that would surely be the worst.

When the sovereign is elected or closely supervised by a truly elective and independent legislature, he may in some cases subject individuals to greater oppression, but that oppression is always less degrading because each citizen, hobbled and reduced to impotence though he may be, can still imagine that in obeying he is only submitting to himself, and that it is to one of his wills that he is sacrificing all the others.

I also understand that when the sovereign represents the nation and is dependent on it, the forces and rights that are taken from each citizen not only serve the head of state but profit the state itself, and that private individuals derive some fruit from the sacrifice of their independence to the public.

To create a national representation in a highly centralized country is therefore to diminish but not to destroy the harm that extreme centralization may do.

Clearly, individual intervention in the most important matters can be preserved in this way, but it is no less ruthlessly expunged in smaller and private matters. What people forget is that it is above all in matters of detail that the subjugation of men becomes dangerous. I, for one, should be inclined to believe that liberty is less necessary in great things than in lesser ones if I thought that one could ever be assured of one without possessing the other.

Subjection in lesser affairs manifests itself daily and is felt by all citizens indiscriminately. It does not make them desperate, but it does constantly thwart their will and lead them to give up on expressing it. In this way it gradually smothers their spirit and saps their soul, whereas obedience, which is required only in a limited number of very serious but very rare circumstances, only occasionally points up the existence of servitude, whose weight only certain men must bear. In vain will you ask the same citizens whom you have made so dependent on the central government to choose the representatives of that government from time to time. This use of their freedom to choose—so important yet so brief and so rare—will not prevent them from slowly losing the ability to think, feel, and act on their own and thus from sinking gradually beneath the level of humanity.

Furthermore, they will soon become incapable of exercising the one great privilege they have left. The democratic peoples that have introduced liberty in the political sphere while increasing despotism in the administrative sphere have been led into some very peculiar kinds of behavior. When it is necessary to deal with minor affairs in which simple common sense would suffice, they deem their citizens incapable of it, but when it is a matter of governing the entire state, they grant those same citizens vast prerogatives. They treat them alternately as play-things of the sovereign and as his masters, as more than kings yet less than men. After trying out all the various systems of election without finding one that suits them, they are surprised and keep on looking, as if the ills they see did not have far more to do with the constitution of the country than with that of the electoral body.

It is indeed difficult to imagine how men who have entirely renounced the habit of managing their own affairs could be successful in choosing those who ought to lead them. It is impossible to believe that a liberal, energetic, and wise government can ever emerge from the ballots of a nation of servants.

The possibility of a constitution's being republican in its head and ultramonarchical in all of its other parts has always struck me as an ephemeral monster. The vices of those who govern and the imbecility of the governed would quickly bring about its ruin, and the people, tired of their representatives and of themselves, would either create freer institutions or soon return to prostrating themselves at the feet of a single master.[2]

I

I have often wondered what would happen if, given the mildness of democratic mores and the restless spirit of the army, a military government were ever established in some of today's nations.

I think that the government itself would not differ much from the portrait I have indicated in the chapter to which this note refers, and that it would not reproduce the fierce characteristics of military oligarchy.

I am convinced that what would happen in this case would be a sort of fusion of the habits of the clerk with those of the soldier. The administration would take on something of the military spirit and the military some of the customs of the civil administration. The result would be a regular, clear, precise, absolute chain of command. The people would reflect an image of the army, and society would be regimented like a barracks.

---

[2] See Note II, page 141.

II

One cannot say in an absolute and general way whether the greatest danger today is license or tyranny, anarchy or despotism. Both are equally to be feared, and both can arise equally easily out of one and the same cause, which is *general apathy*, the fruit of individualism. Because of this apathy, the executive power is in a position to oppress as soon as it assembles a moderate array of forces, and the day after, if a party can put thirty men in the field, it acquires a similar ability to oppress. Neither one is capable of founding anything that will last, so that what makes for easy success prevents lasting success. They rise because nothing resists them and fall because nothing supports them.

What is important to combat is therefore not so much anarchy or despotism as apathy, which can create either one almost indifferently.

Democracy in America, volume II (1840)

* ★ ★

Franklin D. Roosevelt: Address to the Commonwealth Club of California

My friends:

I COUNT it a privilege to be invited to address the Common-wealth Club. It has stood in the life of this city and State, and it is perhaps accurate to add, the Nation, as a group of citizen lead-ers interested in fundamental problems of Government, and chiefly concerned with achievement of progress in Government through non-partisan means. The privilege of addressing you, therefore, in the heat of a political campaign, is great. I want to respond to your courtesy in terms consistent with your policy.

I want to speak not of politics but of Government. I want to speak not of parties, but of universal principles. They are not political, except in that larger sense in which a great American once expressed a definition of politics, that nothing in all of human life is foreign to the science of politics.

I do want to give you, however, a recollection of a long life spent for a large part in public office. Some of my conclusions and observations have been deeply accentuated in these past few weeks. I have traveled far—from Albany to the Golden Gate. I have seen many people, and heard many things, and today, when in a sense my journey has reached the half-way mark, I am glad of the opportunity to discuss with you what it all means to me.

Sometimes, my friends, particularly in years such as these, the hand of discouragement falls upon us. It seems that things are in a rut, fixed, settled, that the world has grown old and tired and very much out of joint. This is the mood of depression, of dire and weary depression.

But then we look around us in America, and everything tells us that we are wrong. America is new. It is in the process of change and development. It has the great potentialities of youth, and particularly is this true of the great West, and of this coast, and of California.

I would not have you feel that I regard this as in any sense a new community. I have traveled in many parts of the world, but never have I felt the arresting thought of the change and development more than here, where the old, mystic East would seem to be near to us, where the currents of life and thought and commerce of the whole world meet us. This factor alone is sufficient to cause man to stop and think of the deeper meaning of things, when he stands in this community.

But more than that, I appreciate that the membership of this club consists of men who are thinking in terms beyond the immediate present, beyond their own immediate tasks, beyond their own individual interests. I want to invite you, therefore, to consider with me in the large, some of the relationships of Government and economic life that go deeply into our daily lives, our happiness, our future and our security.

The issue of Government has always been whether individual men and women will have to serve some system of Government or economics, or whether a system of Government and economics exists to serve individual men and women. This question has persistently dominated the discussion of Government for many generations. On questions relating to these things men have differed, and for time immemorial it is probable that honest men will continue to differ.

The final word belongs to no man; yet we can still believe in change and in progress. Democracy, as a dear old friend of mine in Indiana, Meredith Nicholson, has called it, is a quest, a never-ending seeking for better things, and in the seeking for these things and the striving for them, there are many roads to follow. But, if we map the course of these roads, we find that there are only two general directions.

When we look about us, we are likely to forget how hard people have worked to win the privilege of Government. The growth of the national Governments of Europe was a struggle for the development of a centralized force in the Nation, strong enough to impose peace upon ruling barons. In many instances the victory of the central Government, the creation of a strong central Government, was a haven of refuge to the individual. The people preferred the master far away to the exploitation and cruelty of the smaller master near at hand.

But the creators of national Government were perforce ruthless men. They were often cruel in their methods, but they did strive steadily toward something that society needed and very much wanted, a strong central State able to keep the peace, to stamp out civil war, to put the unruly nobleman in his place, and to permit the bulk of individuals to live safely. The man of ruthless force had his place in developing a pioneer country, just as he did in fixing the power of the central Government in the development of Nations. Society paid him well for his services and its development. When the development among the Nations of Europe, however, had been completed, ambition and ruthlessness, having served their term, tended to overstep their mark.

There came a growing feeling that Government was conducted for the benefit of a few who thrived unduly at the expense of all. The people sought a balancing—a limiting force. There came gradually, through town councils, trade guilds, national parliaments, by constitution and by popular participation and control, limitations on arbitrary power.

Another factor that tended to limit the power of those who ruled, was the rise of the ethical conception that a ruler bore a responsibility for the welfare of his subjects.

The American colonies were born in this struggle. The American Revolution was a turning point in it. After the Revolution the struggle continued and shaped itself in the public life of the country. There were those who because they had seen the confusion which attended the years of war for

American independence surrendered to the belief that popular Government was essentially dangerous and essentially unworkable. They were honest people, my friends, and we cannot deny that their experience had warranted some measure of fear. The most brilliant, honest and able exponent of this point of view was Hamilton. He was too impatient of slow-moving methods. Fundamentally he believed that the safety of the republic lay in the autocratic strength of its Government, that the destiny of individuals was to serve that Government, and that fundamentally a great and strong group of central institutions, guided by a small group of able and public spirited citizens, could best direct all Government.

But Mr. Jefferson, in the summer of 1776, after drafting the Declaration of Independence turned his mind to the same problem and took a different view. He did not deceive himself with outward forms. Government to him was a means to an end, not an end in itself; it might be either a refuge and a help or a threat and a danger, depending on the circumstances. We find him carefully analyzing the society for which he was to organize a Government. "We have no paupers. The great mass of our population is of laborers, our rich who cannot live without labor, either manual or professional, being few and of moderate wealth. Most of the laboring class possess property, cultivate their own lands, have families and from the demand for their labor, are enabled to exact from the rich and the competent such prices as enable them to feed abundantly, clothe above mere decency, to labor moderately and raise their families."

These people, he considered, had two sets of rights, those of "personal competency" and those involved in acquiring and possessing property. By "personal competency" he meant the right of free thinking, freedom of forming and expressing opinions, and freedom of personal living, each man according to his own lights. To insure the first set of rights, a Government must so order its functions as not to interfere with the individual. But even Jefferson realized that the exercise of the property rights might so interfere with the rights of the individual that the Government, without whose assistance the property rights could not exist, must intervene, not to destroy individualism, but to protect it.

You are familiar with the great political duel which followed; and how Hamilton, and his friends, building toward a dominant centralized power were at length defeated in the great election of 1800, by Mr. Jefferson's party. Out of that duel came the two parties, Republican and Democratic, as we know them today.

So began, in American political life, the new day, the day of the individual against the system, the day in which individualism was made the great watchword of American life. The happiest of economic conditions made that day long and splendid. On the Western frontier, land was substantially free. No one, who did not shirk the task of earning a living, was entirely without opportunity to do so. Depressions could, and did, come and go; but they could not alter the fundamental fact that most of the people lived partly by selling their labor and partly by extracting their livelihood from the soil, so that starvation and dislocation were practically impossible. At the very worst there was always the possibility of climbing into a covered wagon and moving west where the untilled prairies afforded a haven for men to whom the East did not provide a place. So great were our natural resources that we could offer this relief not only to our own people, but to the distressed of all the world; we could invite immigration from Europe, and welcome it with open arms. Traditionally, when a depression came a new section of land was opened in the West; and even our temporary misfortune served our manifest destiny.

It was in the middle of the nineteenth century that a new force was released and a new dream created. The force was what is called the industrial revolution, the advance of steam and machinery and the rise of the forerunners of the modern industrial plant. The dream was the dream of an economic machine, able to raise the standard of living for everyone; to bring luxury within the reach of the humblest; to annihilate distance by steam power and later by electricity, and to release everyone from the drudgery of the heaviest manual toil. It was to be expected that this would necessarily affect Government. Heretofore, Government had merely been called upon to produce conditions within which people could live happily, labor peacefully, and rest secure. Now it was called upon to aid in the consummation of this new dream. There was, however, a shadow over the dream. To be made real, it required use of the talents of men of tremendous will and tremendous ambition, since by no other force could the problems of financing and engineering and new developments be brought to a consummation.

So manifest were the advantages of the machine age, however, that the United States fearlessly, cheerfully, and, I think, rightly, accepted the bitter with the sweet. It was thought that no price was too high to pay for the advantages which we could draw from a finished industrial system. The history of the last half century is accordingly in large measure a history of a group of financial Titans, whose methods were not scrutinized with too much care, and who were honored in proportion as they produced the results, irrespective of the means they used. The financiers who pushed the railroads to the Pacific were always ruthless, often wasteful, and frequently corrupt; but they did build railroads, and we have them today. It has been estimated that the American investor paid for the American railway system more than three times over in the process; but despite this fact the net advantage was to the United States. As long as we had free land; as long as population was growing by leaps and bounds; as long as our industrial plants were insufficient to supply our own needs, society chose to give the ambitious man free play and unlimited reward provided only that he produced the economic plant so much desired.

During this period of expansion, there was equal opportunity for all and the business of Government was not to interfere but to assist in the development of industry. This was done at the request of business men themselves. The tariff was originally imposed for the purpose of "fostering our infant industry," a phrase I think the older among you will remember as a political issue not so long ago. The railroads were subsidized, sometimes by grants of money, oftener by grants of land; some of the most valuable oil lands in the United States were granted to assist the financing of the railroad which pushed through the Southwest. A nascent merchant marine was assisted by grants of money, or by mail subsidies, so that our steam shipping might ply the seven seas. Some of my friends tell me that they do not want the Government in business. With this I agree; but I wonder whether they realize the implications of the past. For while it has been American doctrine that the Government must not go into business in competition with private enterprises, still it has been traditional, particularly in Republican administrations, for business urgently to ask the Government to put at private disposal all kinds of Government assistance. The same man who tells you that he does not want to see the Government interfere in business—and he means it, and has plenty of good reasons for saying so—is the first to go to Washington and ask the Government for a prohibitory tariff on his product. When things get just bad enough, as they did two years ago, he will go with equal speed to the United States Government and ask for a loan; and the Reconstruction Finance Corporation is the outcome of it. Each group has sought protection from the Government for its own special interests, without realizing that the function of Government must be to favor no small group at the expense of its duty to protect the rights of personal freedom and of private property of all its citizens.

In retrospect we can now see that the turn of the tide came with the turn of the century. We were reaching our last frontier; there was no more free land and our industrial combinations had become great uncontrolled and irresponsible units of power within the State. Clear-sighted men saw with fear the danger that opportunity would no longer be equal; that the growing corporation, like the feudal baron of old, might threaten the economic freedom of individuals to earn a living. In that hour, our antitrust laws were born. The cry was raised against the great corporations. Theodore Roosevelt, the first great Republican Progressive, fought a Presidential campaign on the issue of "trust busting" and talked freely about malefactors of great wealth. If the Government had a policy it was rather to turn the clock back, to destroy the large combinations and to return to the time when every man owned his individual small business.

This was impossible; Theodore Roosevelt, abandoning the idea of "trust busting," was forced to work out a difference between "good" trusts and "bad" trusts. The Supreme Court set forth the famous "rule of reason" by which it seems to have meant that a concentration of industrial power was permissible if the method by which it got its power, and the use it made of that power, were reasonable.

Woodrow Wilson, elected in 1912, saw the situation more clearly. Where Jefferson had feared the encroachment of political power on the lives of individuals, Wilson knew that the new power was financial. He saw, in the highly centralized economic system, the despot of the twentieth century, on whom great masses of individuals relied for their safety and their livelihood, and whose irresponsibility and greed (if they were not controlled) would reduce them to starvation and penury. The concentration of financial power had not proceeded so far in 1912 as it has today; but it had grown far enough for Mr. Wilson to realize fully its implications. It is interesting, now, to read his speeches. What is called "radical" today (and I have reason to know whereof I speak) is mild compared to the campaign of Mr. Wilson. "No man can deny," he said, "that the lines of endeavor have more and more narrowed and stiffened; no man who knows anything about the development of industry in this country can have failed to observe that the larger kinds of credit are more and more difficult to obtain unless you obtain them upon terms of uniting your efforts with those who already control the industry of the country, and nobody can fail to observe that every man who tries to set himself up in competition with any process of manufacture which has taken place under the control of large combinations of capital will presently find

himself either squeezed out or obliged to sell and allow himself to be absorbed." Had there been no World War—had Mr.
Wilson been able to devote eight years to domestic instead of
to international affairs—we might have had a wholly different
situation at the present time. However, the then distant roar of
European cannon, growing ever louder, forced him to abandon
the study of this issue. The problem he saw so clearly is left with
us as a legacy; and no one of us on either side of the political
controversy can deny that it is a matter of grave concern to the
Government.

A glance at the situation today only too clearly indicates
that equality of opportunity as we have known it no longer
exists. Our industrial plant is built; the problem just now is
whether under existing conditions it is not overbuilt. Our last
frontier has long since been reached, and there is practically
no more free land. More than half of our people do not live on
the farms or on lands and cannot derive a living by cultivating their own property. There is no safety valve in the form of
a Western prairie to which those thrown out of work by the
Eastern economic machines can go for a new start. We are not
able to invite the immigration from Europe to share our endless
plenty. We are now providing a drab living for our own people.

Our system of constantly rising tariffs has at last reacted
against us to the point of closing our Canadian frontier on the
north, our European markets on the east, many of our Latin-
American markets to the south, and a goodly proportion of
our Pacific markets on the west, through the retaliatory tariffs
of those countries. It has forced many of our great industrial
institutions which exported their surplus production to such
countries, to establish plants in such countries, within the tariff
walls. This has resulted in the reduction of the operation of
their American plants, and opportunity for employment.

Just as freedom to farm has ceased, so also the opportunity
in business has narrowed. It still is true that men can start small
enterprises, trusting to native shrewdness and ability to keep
abreast of competitors; but area after area has been preempted

altogether by the great corporations, and even in the fields which still have no great concerns, the small man starts under a handicap. The unfeeling statistics of the past three decades show that the independent business man is running a losing race. Perhaps he is forced to the wall; perhaps he cannot command credit; perhaps he is "squeezed out," in Mr. Wilson's words, by highly organized corporate competitors, as your corner grocery man can tell you. Recently a careful study was made of the concentration of business in the United States. It showed that our economic life was dominated by some six hundred odd corporations who controlled two-thirds of American industry. Ten million small business men divided the other third. More striking still, it appeared that if the process of concentration goes on at the same rate, at the end of another century we shall have all American industry controlled by a dozen corporations, and run by perhaps a hundred men. Put plainly, we are steering a steady course toward economic oligarchy, if we are not there already.

Clearly, all this calls for a re-appraisal of values. A mere builder of more industrial plants, a creator of more railroad systems, an organizer of more corporations, is as likely to be a danger as a help. The day of the great promoter or the financial Titan, to whom we granted anything if only he would build, or develop, is over. Our task now is not discovery or exploitation of natural resources, or necessarily producing more goods. It is the soberer, less dramatic business of administering resources and plants already in hand, of seeking to reestablish foreign markets for our surplus production, of meeting the problem of underconsumption, of adjusting production to consumption, of distributing wealth and products more equitably, of adapting existing economic organizations to the service of the people. The day of enlightened administration has come.

Just as in older times the central Government was first a haven of refuge, and then a threat, so now in a closer economic system the central and ambitious financial unit is no longer a servant of national desire, but a danger. I would draw the parallel one step farther. We did not think because national Government had become a threat in the 18th century that therefore we should abandon the principle of national Government. Nor today should we abandon the principle of strong economic units called corporations, merely because their power is susceptible of easy abuse. In other times we dealt with the problem of an unduly ambitious central Government by modifying it gradually into a constitutional democratic Government. So today we are modifying and controlling our economic units.

As I see it, the task of Government in its relation to business is to assist the development of an economic declaration of rights, an economic constitutional order. This is the common task of statesman and business man. It is the minimum requirement of a more permanently safe order of things.

Happily, the times indicate that to create such an order not only is the proper policy of Government, but it is the only line of safety for our economic structures as well. We know, now, that these economic units cannot exist unless prosperity is uniform, that is, unless purchasing power is well distributed throughout every group in the Nation. That is why even the most selfish of corporations for its own interest would be glad to see wages restored and unemployment ended and to bring the Western farmer back to his accustomed level of prosperity and to assure a permanent safety to both groups. That is why some enlightened industries themselves endeavor to limit the freedom of action of each man and business group within the industry in the common interest of all; why business men everywhere are asking a form of organization which will bring the scheme of things into balance, even though it may in some measure qualify the freedom of action of individual units within the business.

The exposition need not further be elaborated. It is brief and incomplete, but you will be able to expand it in terms of your own business or occupation without difficulty. I think everyone who has actually entered the economic struggle—which means everyone who was not born to safe wealth—knows in his own experience and his own life that we have now to apply the earlier concepts of American Government to the conditions of today.

The Declaration of Independence discusses the problem of Government in terms of a contract. Government is a relation of give and take, a contract, perforce, if we would follow the thinking out of which it grew. Under such a contract rulers were accorded power, and the people consented to that power on consideration that they be accorded certain rights. The task of statesmanship has always been the re-definition of these rights in terms of a changing and growing social order. New conditions impose new requirements upon Government and those who conduct Government.

I held, for example, in proceedings before me as Governor, the purpose of which was the removal of the Sheriff of New York, that under modern conditions it was not enough for a public official merely to evade the legal terms of official wrongdoing. He owed a positive duty as well. I said in substance that if he had acquired large sums of money, he was when accused required to explain the sources of such wealth. To that extent this wealth was colored with a public interest. I said that in financial matters, public servants should, even beyond private citizens, be held to a stern and uncompromising rectitude.

I feel that we are coming to a view through the drift of our legislation and our public thinking in the past quarter century that private economic power is, to enlarge an old phrase, a public trust as well. I hold that continued enjoyment of that power by any individual or group must depend upon the fulfillment of that trust. The men who have reached the summit of American business life know this best; happily, many of these urge the binding quality of this greater social contract.

The terms of that contract are as old as the Republic, and as new as the new economic order.

Every man has a right to life; and this means that he has also a right to make a comfortable living. He may by sloth or crime decline to exercise that right; but it may not be denied him. We have no actual famine or dearth; our industrial and agricultural mechanism can produce enough and to spare. Our Government formal and informal, political and economic, owes to everyone an avenue to possess himself of a portion of that plenty sufficient for his needs, through his own work.

Every man has a right to his own property; which means a right to be assured, to the fullest extent attainable, in the safety of his savings. By no other means can men carry the burdens of those parts of life which, in the nature of things, afford no chance of labor; childhood, sickness, old age. In all thought of property, this right is paramount; all other property rights must yield to it. If, in accord with this principle, we must restrict the operations of the speculator, the manipulator, even the financier, I believe we must accept the restriction as needful, not to hamper individualism but to protect it.

These two requirements must be satisfied, in the main, by the individuals who claim and hold control of the great industrial and financial combinations which dominate so large a part of our industrial life. They have undertaken to be, not business men, but princes of property. I am not prepared to say that the system which produces them is wrong. I am very clear that they must fearlessly and competently assume the responsibility which goes with the power. So many enlightened business men know this that the statement would be little more than a platitude, were it not for an added implication.

This implication is, briefly, that the responsible heads of finance and industry instead of acting each for himself, must work together to achieve the common end. They must, where necessary, sacrifice this or that private advantage; and in reciprocal self-denial must seek a general advantage. It is here that formal Government—political Government, if you choose—comes in. Whenever in the pursuit of this objective the lone wolf, the unethical competitor, the reckless promoter, the Ishmael or Insull whose hand is against every man's, declines to join in achieving an end recognized as being for the public welfare, and threatens to drag the industry back to a state of anarchy, the Government may properly be asked to apply restraint. Likewise, should the group ever use its collective power contrary to the public welfare, the Government must be swift to enter and protect the public interest.

The Government should assume the function of economic regulation only as a last resort, to be tried only when private initiative, inspired by high responsibility, with such assistance and balance as Government can give, has finally failed. As yet there has been no final failure, because there has been no attempt; and I decline to assume that this Nation is unable to meet the situation.

The final term of the high contract was for liberty and the pursuit of happiness. We have learned a great deal of both in the past century. We know that individual liberty and individual happiness mean nothing unless both are ordered in the sense that one man's meat is not another man's poison. We know that the old "rights of personal competency," the right to read, to think, to speak, to choose and live a mode of life, must be respected at all hazards. We know that liberty to do anything which deprives others of those elemental rights is outside the protection of any compact; and that Government in this regard is the maintenance of a balance, within which every individual may have a place if he will take it; in which every individual may find safety if he wishes it; in which every individual may attain such power as his ability permits, consistent with his assuming the accompanying responsibility.

All this is a long, slow talk. Nothing is more striking than the simple innocence of the men who insist, whenever an objective is present, on the prompt production of a patent scheme guaranteed to produce a result. Human endeavor is not so simple as that. Government includes the art of formulating a policy, and using the political technique to attain so much of that policy as will receive general support; persuading, leading, sacrificing, teaching always, because the greatest duty of a statesman is to educate. But in the matters of which I have spoken, we are learning rapidly, in a severe school. The lessons so learned must not be forgotten, even in the mental lethargy of a speculative upturn. We must build toward the time when a major depression cannot occur again; and if this means sacrificing the easy profits of inflationist booms, then let them go; and good riddance.

Faith in America, faith in our tradition of personal responsibility, faith in our institutions, faith in ourselves demand that we recognize the new terms of the old social contract. We shall fulfill them, as we fulfilled the obligation of the apparent Utopia which Jefferson imagined for us in 1776, and which Jefferson, Roosevelt and Wilson sought to bring to realization. We must do so, lest a rising tide of misery, engendered by our common failure, engulf us all. But failure is not an American habit; and in the strength of great hope we must all shoulder our common load.

September 23, 1932

★ ★ ★

Paul Nitze et al.: from NSC-68: United States Objectives and Programs for National Security

I. Background of the Present Crisis

Within the past thirty-five years the world has experienced two global wars of tremendous violence. It has witnessed two revolutions—the Russian and the Chinese—of extreme scope and intensity. It has also seen the collapse of five empires—the Ottoman, the Austro-Hungarian, German, Italian and Japanese—and the drastic decline of two major imperial systems, the British and the French. During the span of one generation, the international distribution of power has been fundamentally altered. For several centuries it had proved impossible for any one nation to gain such preponderant strength that a coalition of other nations could not in time face it with greater strength. The international scene was marked by recurring periods of violence and war, but a system of sovereign and independent states was maintained, over which no state was able to achieve hegemony.

Two complex sets of factors have now basically altered this historical distribution of power. First, the defeat of Germany and Japan and the decline of the British and French Empires have interacted with the development of the United States and the Soviet Union in such a way that power has increasingly gravitated to these two centers. Second, the Soviet Union, unlike previous aspirants to hegemony, is animated by a new fanatic faith, antithetical to our own, and seeks to impose its absolute authority over the rest of the world. Conflict has, therefore, become endemic and is waged, on the part of the Soviet Union, by violent or non-violent methods in accordance with the dictates of expediency. With the development of increasingly terrifying weapons of mass destruction, every individual faces the ever-present possibility of annihilation should the conflict enter the phase of total war.

On the one hand, the people of the world yearn for relief from the anxiety arising from the risk of atomic war. On the other hand, any substantial further extension of the area under the domination of the Kremlin would raise the possibility that no coalition adequate to confront the Kremlin with greater strength could be assembled. It is in this context that this Republic and its citizens in the ascendancy of their strength stand in their deepest peril.

The issues that face us are momentous, involving the fulfillment or destruction not only of this Republic but of civilization itself. They are issues which will not await our deliberations. With conscience and resolution this Government and the people it represents must now take new and fateful decisions.

II. Fundamental Purpose of the United States

The fundamental purpose of the United States is laid down in the Preamble to the Constitution: ". . . to form a more perfect Union, establish Justice, insure domestic Tranquility, provide for the common defence, promote the general Welfare, and secure the Blessings of Liberty to ourselves and our Posterity." In essence, the fundamental purpose is to assure the integrity and vitality of our free society, which is founded upon the dignity and worth of the individual.

Three realities emerge as a consequence of this purpose: Our determination to maintain the essential elements of individual freedom, as set forth in the Constitution and Bill of Rights; our determination to create conditions under which our free and democratic system can live and prosper; and our determination to fight if necessary to defend our way of life, for which as in the Declaration of Independence, "with a firm reliance on the protection of Divine Providence, we mutually pledge to each other our lives, our Fortunes and our sacred Honor."

III. Fundamental Design of the Kremlin

The fundamental design of those who control the Soviet Union and the international communist movement is to retain and solidify their absolute power, first in the Soviet Union and second in the areas now under their control. In the minds of the Soviet leaders, however, achievement of this design requires the dynamic extension of their authority and the ultimate elimination of any effective opposition to their authority.

The design, therefore, calls for the complete subversion or forcible destruction of the machinery of government and structure of society in the countries of the non-Soviet world and their replacement by an apparatus and structure subservient to and controlled from the Kremlin. To that end Soviet efforts are now directed toward the domination of the Eurasian land mass. The United States, as the principal center of power in the non-Soviet world and the bulwark of opposition to Soviet expansion, is the principal enemy whose integrity and vitality must be subverted or destroyed by one means or another if the Kremlin is to achieve its fundamental design.

IV. The Underlying Conflict in the Realm of Ideas and Values Between the U.S. Purpose and the Kremlin Design

A. *Nature of conflict*:

The Kremlin regards the United States as the only major threat to the achievement of its fundamental design. There is a basic conflict between the idea of freedom under a government of laws, and the idea of slavery under the grim oligarchy of the Kremlin, which has come to a crisis with the polarization of power described in Section I, and the exclusive possession of atomic weapons by the two protagonists. The idea of freedom, moreover, is peculiarly and intolerably subversive of the idea of slavery. But the converse is not true. The implacable purpose of the slave state to eliminate the challenge of freedom has placed the two great powers at opposite poles. It is this fact which gives the present polarization of power the quality of crisis.

The free society values the individual as an end in himself, requiring of him only that measure of self discipline and self restraint which make the rights of each individual compatible with the rights of every other individual. The freedom of the individual has as its counterpart, therefore, the negative responsibility of the individual not to exercise his freedom in ways inconsistent with the freedom of other individuals and the positive responsibility to make constructive use of his freedom in the building of a just society.

From this idea of freedom with responsibility derives the marvelous diversity, the deep tolerance, the lawfulness of the free society. This is the explanation of the strength of free men. It constitutes the integrity and the vitality of a free and democratic system. The free society attempts to create and maintain an environment in which every individual has the opportunity to realize his creative powers. It also explains why the free society tolerates those within it who would use their freedom to destroy it. By the same token, in relations between nations, the prime reliance of the free society is on the strength and appeal of its idea, and it feels no compulsion sooner or later to bring all societies into conformity with it.

For the free society does not fear, it welcomes, diversity. It derives its strength from its hospitality even to antipathetic ideas. It is a market for free trade in ideas, secure in its faith that free men will take the best wares, and grow to a fuller and better realization of their powers in exercising their choice.

The idea of freedom is the most contagious idea in history, more contagious than the idea of submission to authority. For the breadth of freedom cannot be tolerated in a society which has come under the domination of an individual or group of individuals with a will to absolute power. Where the despot holds absolute power—the absolute power of the absolutely powerful will—all other wills must be subjugated in an act of willing submission, a degradation willed by the individual upon himself under the compulsion of a perverted faith. It is the first article of this faith that he finds and can only find the meaning of his existence in serving the ends of the system. The system becomes God, and submission to the will of God becomes submission to the will of the system. It is not enough to yield outwardly to the system—even Ghandian non-violence is not acceptable—for the spirit of resistance and the devotion to a higher authority might then remain, and the individual would not be wholly submissive.

The same compulsion which demands total power over all men within the Soviet state without a single exception, demands total power over all Communist Parties and all states under Soviet domination. Thus Stalin has said that the theory and tactics of Leninism as expounded by the Bolshevik party are mandatory for the proletarian parties of all countries. A true internationalist is defined as one who unhesitatingly upholds the position of the Soviet Union and in the satellite states true patriotism is love of the Soviet Union. By the same token the "peace policy" of the Soviet Union, described at a Party Congress as "a more advantageous form of fighting capitalism," is a device to divide and immobilize the non-Communist world, and the peace the Soviet Union seeks is the peace of total conformity to Soviet policy.

The antipathy of slavery to freedom explains the iron curtain; the isolation, the autarchy of the society whose end is absolute power. The existence and persistence of the idea of freedom is a permanent and continuous threat to the foundation of the slave society; and it therefore regards as intolerable the long-continued existence of freedom in the world. What is new, what makes the continuing crisis, is the polarization of power which now inescapably confronts the slave society with the free.

The assault on free institutions is world-wide now, and in the context of the present polarization of power a defeat of free institutions anywhere is a defeat everywhere. The shock we sustained in the destruction of Czechoslovakia was not in the measure of Czechoslovakia's material importance to us. In a material sense, her capabilities were already at Soviet disposal. But when the integrity of Czechoslovak institutions was destroyed, it was in the intangible scale of values that we registered a loss more damaging than the material loss we had already suffered.

Thus unwillingly our free society finds itself mortally challenged by the Soviet system. No other value system is so wholly irreconcilable with ours, so implacable in its purpose to destroy ours, so capable of turning to its own uses the most dangerous and divisive trends in our own society, no other so skillfully and powerfully evokes the elements of irrationality in human nature everywhere, and no other has the support of a great and growing center of military power.

B. *Objectives*:

The objectives of a free society are determined by its fundamental values and by the necessity for maintaining the material environment in which they flourish. Logically and in fact, therefore, the Kremlin's challenge to the United States is directed not only to our values but to our physical capacity to protect their environment. It is a challenge which encompasses both peace and war and our objectives in peace and war must take account of it.

1. Thus we must make ourselves strong, both in the way in which we affirm our values in the conduct of our national life, and in the development of our military and economic strength.

2. We must lead in building a successfully functioning political and economic system in the free world. It is only by practical affirmation, abroad as well as at home, of our essential values, that we can preserve our own integrity, in which lies the real frustration of the Kremlin design.

3. But beyond thus affirming our values our policy and actions must be such as to foster a fundamental change in

the nature of the Soviet system, a change toward which the frustration of the design is the first and perhaps the most important step. Clearly it will not only be less costly but more effective if this change occurs to a maximum extent as a result of internal forces in Soviet society.

In a shrinking world, which now faces the threat of atomic warfare, it is not an adequate objective merely to seek to check the Kremlin design, for the absence of order among nations is becoming less and less tolerable. This fact imposes on us, in our own interests, the responsibility of world leadership. It demands that we make the attempt, and accept the risks inherent in it, to bring about order and justice by means consistent with the principles of freedom and democracy. We should limit our requirement of the Soviet Union to its participation with other nations on the basis of equality and respect for the rights of others. Subject to this requirement, we must with our allies and the former subject peoples seek to create a world society based on the principle of consent. Its framework cannot be inflexible. It will consist of many national communities of great and varying abilities and resources, and hence of war potential. The seeds of conflicts will inevitably exist or will come into being. To acknowledge this is only to acknowledge the impossibility of a final solution. Not to acknowledge it can be fatally dangerous in a world in which there are no final solutions.

All these objectives of a free society are equally valid and necessary in peace and war. But every consideration of devotion to our fundamental values and to our national security demands that we seek to achieve them by the strategy of the cold war. It is only by developing the moral and material strength of the free world that the Soviet regime will become convinced of the falsity of its assumptions and that the pre-conditions for workable agreements can be created. By practically demonstrating the integrity and vitality of our system the free world widens the area of possible agreement and thus can hope gradually to bring about a Soviet acknowledgement of realities which in sum will eventually constitute a frustration of the Soviet design. Short of this, however, it might be possible to create a situation which will induce the Soviet Union to accommodate itself, with or without the conscious abandonment of its design, to coexistence on tolerable terms with the non-Soviet world. Such a development would be a triumph for the idea of freedom and democracy. It must be an immediate objective of United States policy.

There is no reason, in the event of war, for us to alter our over-all objectives. They do not include unconditional surrender, the subjugation of the Russian peoples or a Russia shorn of its economic potential. Such a course would irrevocably unite the Russian people behind the regime which enslaves them. Rather these objectives contemplate Soviet acceptance of the specific and limited conditions requisite to an international environment in which free institutions can flourish, and in which the Russian people will have a new chance to work out their own destiny. If we can make the Russian people our allies in the enterprise we will obviously have made our task easier and victory more certain.

The objectives outlined in NSC 20/4 (November 23, 1948) and quoted in Chapter X, are fully consistent with the objectives stated in this paper, and they remain valid. The growing intensity of the conflict which has been imposed upon us, however, requires the changes of emphasis and the additions that are apparent. Coupled with the probable fission bomb capability and possible thermonuclear bomb capability of the Soviet Union, the intensifying struggle requires us to face the fact that we can expect no lasting abatement of the crisis unless and until a change occurs in the nature of the Soviet system.

C. *Means*:

The free society is limited in its choice of means to achieve its ends.

Compulsion is the negation of freedom, except when it is used to enforce the rights common to all. The resort to force, internally or externally, is therefore a last resort for a free society. The act is permissible only when one individual or groups of individuals within it threaten the basic rights of other individuals or when another society seeks to impose its will upon it. The free society cherishes and protects as fundamental the rights of the minority against the will of a majority, beeause these rights are the inalienable rights of each and every individual.

The resort to force, to compulsion, to the imposition of its will is therefore a difficult and dangerous act for a free society, which is warranted only in the face of even greater dangers. The necessity of the act must be clear and compelling; the act must commend itself to the overwhelming majority as an inescapable exception to the basic idea of freedom; or the regenerative capacity of free men after the act has been performed will be endangered.

The Kremlin is able to select whatever means are expedient in seeking to carry out its fundamental design. Thus it can make the best of several possible worlds, conducting the struggle on those levels where it considers it profitable and enjoying the benefits of a pseudo-peace on those levels where it is not ready for a contest. At the ideological or psychological level, in the struggle for men's minds, the conflict is world-wide. At the political and economic level, within states and in the relations between states, the struggle for power is being intensified. And at the military level, the Kremlin has thus far been careful not to commit a technical breach of the peace, although using its vast forces to intimidate its neighbors, and to support an aggressive foreign policy, and not hesitating through its agents to resort to arms in favorable circumstances. The attempt to carry out its fundamental design is being pressed, therefore, with all means which are believed expedient in the present situation, and the Kremlin has inextricably engaged us in the conflict between its design and our purpose.

We have no such freedom of choice, and least of all in the use of force. Resort to war is not only a last resort for a free society, but it is also an act which cannot definitively end the fundamental conflict in the realm of ideas. The idea of slavery can only be overcome by the timely and persistent demonstration of the superiority of the idea of freedom. Military victory alone would only partially and perhaps only temporarily affect the fundamental conflict, for although the ability of the Kremlin to threaten our security might be for a time destroyed, the resurgence of totalitarian forces and the re-establishment of the Soviet system or its equivalent would not be long delayed unless great progress were made in the fundamental conflict.

Practical and ideological considerations therefore both impel us to the conclusion that we have no choice but to demonstrate the superiority of the idea of freedom by its constructive application, and to attempt to change the world situation by means short of war in such a way as to frustrate the Kremlin design and hasten the decay of the Soviet system.

For us the role of military power is to serve the national purpose by deterring an attack upon us while we seek by other means to create an environment in which our free society can flourish, and by fighting, if necessary, to defend the integrity and vitality of our free society and to defeat any aggressor. The Kremlin uses Soviet military power to back up and serve the Kremlin design. It does not hesitate to use military force aggressively if that course is expedient in the achievement of its design. The differences between our fundamental purpose and the Kremlin design, therefore, are reflected in our respective attitudes toward and use of military force.

Our free society, confronted by a threat to its basic values, naturally will take such action, including the use of military force, as may be required to protect those values. The integrity of our system will not be jeopardized by any measures, covert or overt, violent or non-violent, which serve the purposes of frustrating the Kremlin design, nor does the necessity for conducting ourselves so as to affirm our values in actions as well as words forbid such measures, provided only they are appropriately calculated to that end and are not so excessive or misdirected as to make us enemies of the people instead of the evil men who have enslaved them.

But if war comes, what is the role of force? Unless we so use it that the Russian people can perceive that our effort is directed against the regime and its power for aggression, and not against their own interests, we will unite the regime and the people in the kind of last ditch fight in which no underlying problems are solved, new ones are created, and where our basic principles are obscured and compromised. If we do not in the application of force demonstrate the nature of our objectives we will, in fact, have compromised from the outset our fundamental purpose. In the words of the Federalist (No. 28) "The means to be employed must be proportioned to the extent of the mischief." The mischief may be a global war or it may be a Soviet campaign for limited objectives. In either case we should take no avoidable initiative which would cause it to become a war of annihilation, and if we have the forces to defeat a Soviet drive for limited objectives it may well be to our interest not to let it become a global war. Our aim in applying force must be to compel the acceptance of terms consistent with our objectives, and our capabilities for the application of force should, therefore, within the limits of what we can sustain over the long pull, be congruent to the range of tasks which we may encounter.

April 7, 1950

The Power of Money: How to Control It?

★ ★ ★

The tension between money and democracy is fundamental in the United States. While the U.S. Constitution displays an exquisite awareness of the dangers of concentrated political power, it does not address the dangers of concentrated economic power. That's understandable. In the late eighteenth century the United States was an agricultural nation, whose industries often were so new that they needed special help from government in order to survive. Economic power was concentrated, but less spectacularly than it is today. As the country prospered with the passage of time, and the people at the top of the economic order became richer, the question of whether money conferred too much political power became more pressing. It has never gone away.

In the early decades of the nineteenth century, the power of money and an expanded concept of democracy grew together. Andrew Jackson, the first humbly born President, and his successor, Martin Van Buren, oversaw a significant expansion of voting rights, to white males without significant means, and the growth of political parties—unmentioned in the Constitution—into large, elaborately organized, highly significant and durable institutions. The Federal Reserve was not established until the early twentieth century; in the young republic, central-bank functions were performed by government-chartered, privately owned banks, such as the First Bank of the United States, founded in 1791 by Alexander Hamilton, the initial secretary of the treasury. Jackson made opposition to the Second Bank of the United States, chartered in 1816, a central theme of his political career. His 1832 message vetoing the renewal of its charter, excerpted here, is a display of pure populism. It accuses the bank of being a scheme "to make the rich richer and the potent more powerful," at the expense of "the humble members of society—the farmers, mechanics, and laborers."

The tensions expressed in Jackson's message are still with us, but the way they play out in contemporary politics is not so simple. President Barack Obama was a public admirer of a popular play celebrating Alexander Hamilton, while his administration planned to remove the portrait of Andrew Jackson, a slaveholder and a bloody Indian fighter, from the front of the $20 bill. President Donald Trump put the $20 bill plan on hold and installed Jackson's portrait in a prominent place in the Oval Office, because he wanted to position himself as the tribune of the perceived Jacksonian constituency of white males who are struggling against cosmopolitan moneyed interests. Today both parties have access to, and influence from, big money.

Through the middle decades of the nineteenth century, the party system that Jackson strengthened kept growing, to the point that it controlled politics with a completeness that would seem jarring today. Political bosses proliferated, especially in the big cities with large immigrant populations. Their power came from a straightforward pecuniary trade-off of votes for government jobs, contracts, and services—and sometimes for cash as well. Even in the federal government, the winning party would sweep all employees out of office and replace them with loyalists who had performed campaign services. Historians often look back approvingly on the party machines because their heyday coincided with very high levels of voter participation, and, on the whole, they helped people who had no resources, but the spectacle of their exercise of power horrified educated, reform-minded people.

One of these was Carl Schurz, one of the leading statesmen of the late nineteenth century. A political refugee from
Germany, Schurz was a Civil War general, a newspaper editor,
a United States senator who later served as secretary of the
interior, and a leading figure in the early Republican Party.
Like Andrew Jackson, he doesn't fit neatly into the political
categories of the present. Schurz was a crusader against slavery
who then became a crusader against the political empowerment of freed people in the former Confederacy. He broke with
President Ulysses Grant, his wartime commander in the Union
Army, over this issue. To Schurz, black Republican voters in
the South were like white Democratic machine voters in the
North—pawns of the political bosses. If this was a problem,
then the solution was to professionalize government through
the establishment of a civil service removed from political
influence, a cause for which Schurz advocated passionately
throughout his career, as the 1894 speech excerpted here shows.

Schurz thought of himself as a reformer, someone who was
fighting against political corruption and the idea of government
as a mechanism for doling out rewards to whoever had won
the last election. He was more closely attuned to the political
misdeeds of bosses and machines than of big businesses, but
his dream was to create a less political form of governance, in
which disinterested officials would make decisions impartially.
Schurz's dream has persisted down to the present; it represents
one often-proposed solution to the problem of money in politics. But at the moment he was delivering his speech, political
money was everywhere, so much so that it wasn't all pushing
in the same direction. The Jackson-descended machines were
mostly Democratic. The Republicans, emerging after the Civil
War as the party of business and finance, had their machines
too, funded primarily by the rising class of business tycoons.
Money bought votes on election day, decisions by government
officials, and the passage of bills in Congress. When labor
unions emerged as a political force, they pumped money into
politics too.

In 1910, Theodore Roosevelt had become unhappy with the administration of his friend and chosen successor, William Howard Taft. Roosevelt's dissatisfaction culminated in his failed attempt to win a third term in 1912. Denied the Republican nomination, he ran as a third-party candidate, which split the Republican vote and gave the White House to Woodrow Wilson, the first Democratic President of the twentieth century. A significant milestone on the way to Roosevelt's decision to run was the speech included here, which he delivered in the summer of 1910 at the dedication ceremony of a memorial to the radical abolitionist John Brown in Osawatomie, Kansas, where Brown had fought proslavery raiders before the Civil War.

Roosevelt squarely, unsparingly blamed big business for threatening the core precepts of American democracy, and called for a dramatic limiting of the power of corporations and the rich. One aspect of this great project would be getting the corporations' and trusts' money out of politics, but that amounted to an almost minor, subordinate note in Roosevelt's speech. The heart of what Roosevelt called "the New Nationalism" would be an enhancement of the power of the federal government, so that it could establish control over the power of money. There would be new taxes on income and inheritance, new government agencies, new regulations, and new social legislation to help ordinary people, all adding up to a "far more active governmental interference with social and economic conditions in this country than we have yet had." Roosevelt was openly impatient with "the impotence which springs from overdivision of governmental powers" in the constitutional scheme of government; just as he wanted government's power to be enhanced in society, he wanted the executive branch's power to be enhanced within government. Only a future President, perhaps himself, could amass the new governmental capabilities that would be required to defeat the dominance of big business and the rich.

In the long history of attempts to limit the influence of money in politics and government, one dimension is the balance of power between the market and the state. There, Roosevelt was placing himself firmly on the side of the state. Another dimension is the balance between centralized and decentralized power. American populism has usually associated itself with suspicion of concentrated power, no less in government than in business. Roosevelt had no such suspicion; he was far more in the tradition of Alexander Hamilton than of Thomas Jefferson and Andrew Jackson. It's important to notice the line in the New Nationalism speech where he declares, "Combinations in industry are the result of an imperative economic law which cannot be repealed by political legislation." Though he has a reputation as a trustbuster, Roosevelt did not run for President in 1912 as an advocate of antitrust actions; that was the role of Wilson, who was advised by the future Supreme Court justice Louis Brandeis. Roosevelt liked the idea of a clash of the titans—government being granted superpowers so that it could control superpowered business.

There is a political problem with Roosevelt's approach, which he can be forgiven for not seeing in advance. If the country moved in a generally Rooseveltian direction, with the federal government establishing greater control over ever larger business enterprises, then the value of influence over government would keep increasing. And that meant business would keep trying to find ways, including but not limited to spending money, to bend government and politics to its will. Highly concentrated government power presents an attractive target to its opponents, and also to corporations that stand to gain enormously from government decisions. During the second half of the twentieth century, partly because of the success of the civil service movement at reducing patronage hiring in government, the influence of the old political bosses and their machines radically decreased. So, thanks substantially to successful lobbying by business, did the political power of labor unions. That left fewer countervailing forces to the power of big business. Could government withstand a relatively unified tidal wave of corporate spending and lobbying?

Those who think of government today as utterly corrupt should remind themselves that, although the influence of money in politics is enormous, the form it takes is probably more benign and more publicly visible than it used to be: mainly reported political contributions that are used substantially to fund massive media and organizing campaigns. The dream of reformers in the late twentieth and early twenty-first centuries—the equivalent of civil service a century earlier—has been instituting strict limits on campaign contributions, especially by business interests. These limits have generally not worked, partly because the people being limited have been energetic about finding loopholes in the laws, and partly because the form political spending takes today makes available the argument that the First Amendment protects unlimited political spending as a form of free speech.

The Supreme Court's decision in the 2010 *Citizens United v. Federal Election Commission* case undid both a previous Supreme Court decision and one of the most important pieces of campaign reform legislation, by declaring that independent corporate and union spending on political advertising could not be legally prohibited. A hundred years earlier, Theodore Roosevelt had declared that the Constitution "does not give the right of suffrage to any corporation." The *Citizens United* decision interpreted the Constitution as giving corporations the same First Amendment rights as people. Justice John Paul Stevens's outraged ninety-page dissent, excerpted here, rightly accused his colleagues in the majority of betraying Roosevelt's legacy. A few days after the decision, President Obama, in his State of the Union address, looked right at the Supreme Court justices who were sitting a few feet away from him in the House of Representative chamber and predicted that *Citizens United* "will open the floodgates for special interests, including foreign corporations, to spend without limit in our elections."

In tone, that sounds a lot like Andrew Jackson's veto message back in 1832. Are we doomed forever to struggle unsuccessfully against the power of money in politics? Let's hope not. The Supreme Court is unlikely to change its mind about extending First Amendment protections to corporations anytime soon. It may be helpful, though, to think of the problem less in in terms of getting the money out of politics and more in terms of changing the ecology of money in politics, so that smaller players and different interests are more empowered and there is therefore a more equitable balance of power among political funders. There, we can be cautiously optimistic. Post–*Citizens United* organizing, in particular the growth of small-donor online contributions into a major element in the world of money and politics, represents a real improvement. In an imperfectible world, movement in a better direction deserves our applause.

★ ★ ★

Andrew Jackson: from Veto of the Bank Charter

A bank of the United States is in many respects convenient for the Government and useful to the people. Entertaining this opinion, and deeply impressed with the belief that some of the powers and privileges possessed by the existing bank are unauthorized by the Constitution, subversive of the rights of the States, and dangerous to the liberties of the people, I felt it my duty at an early period of my Administration to call the attention of Congress to the practicability of organizing an institution combining all its advantages and obviating these objections. I sincerely regret that in the act before me I can perceive none of those modifications of the bank charter which are necessary, in my opinion, to make it compatible with justice, with sound policy, or with the Constitution of our country.

The present corporate body, denominated the president, directors, and company of the Bank of the United States, will have existed at the time this act is intended to take effect twenty years. It enjoys an exclusive privilege of banking under the authority of the General Government, a monopoly of its favor and support, and, as a necessary consequence, almost a monopoly of the foreign and domestic exchange. The powers, privileges, and favors bestowed upon it in the original charter, by increasing the value of the stock far above its par value, operated as a gratuity of many millions to the stockholders.

An apology may be found for the failure to guard against this result in the consideration that the effect of the original act of incorporation could not be certainly foreseen at the time of its passage. The act before me proposes another gratuity to the holders of the same stock, and in many cases to the same men, of at least seven millions more. This donation finds no apology in any uncertainty as to the effect of the act. On all hands it is conceded that its passage will increase at least 20 or 30 per cent more the market price of the stock, subject to the payment of the annuity of $200,000 per year secured by the act, thus adding in a moment one-fourth to its par value. It is not our own citizens only who are to receive the bounty of our Government. More than eight millions of the stock of this bank are held by foreigners. By this act the American Republic proposes virtually to make them a present of some millions of dollars. For these gratuities to foreigners and to some of our own opulent citizens the act secures no equivalent whatever. They are the certain gains of the present stockholders under the operation of this act, after making full allowance for the payment of the bonus.

Every monopoly and all exclusive privileges are granted at the expense of the public, which ought to receive a fair equivalent. The many millions which this act proposes to bestow on the stockholders of the existing bank must come directly or indirectly out of the earnings of the American people. It is due to them, therefore, if their Government sell monopolies and exclusive privileges, that they should at least exact for them as much as they are worth in open market. The value of the monopoly in this case may be correctly ascertained. The twenty-eight millions of stock would probably be at an advance of 50 per cent, and command in market at least $42,000,000, subject to the payment of the present bonus. The present value of the monopoly, therefore, is $17,000,000, and this the act proposes to sell for three millions, payable in fifteen annual installments of $200,000 each.

It is not conceivable how the present stockholders can have any claim to the special favor of the Government. The present corporation has enjoyed its monopoly during the period stipulated in the original contract. If we must have such a corporation, why should not the Government sell out the whole stock and thus secure to the people the full market value of the privileges granted? Why should not Congress create and sell twenty-eight millions of stock, incorporating the purchasers with all the powers and privileges secured in this act and putting the premium upon the sales into the Treasury?

But this act does not permit competition in the purchase of this monopoly. It seems to be predicated on the erroneous idea that the present stockholders have a prescriptive right not only to the favor but to the bounty of Government. It appears that more than a fourth part of the stock is held by foreigners and the residue is held by a few hundred of our own citizens, chiefly of the richest class. For their benefit does this act exclude the whole American people from competition in the purchase of this monopoly and dispose of it for many millions less than it is worth. This seems the less excusable because some of our citizens not now stockholders petitioned that the door of competition might be opened, and offered to take a charter on terms much more favorable to the Government and country.

But this proposition, although made by men whose aggregate wealth is believed to be equal to all the private stock in the existing bank, has been set aside, and the bounty of our Government is proposed to be again bestowed on the few who have been fortunate enough to secure the stock and at this moment wield the power of the existing institution. I can not perceive the justice or policy of this course. If our Government must sell monopolies, it would seem to be its duty to take nothing less than their full value, and if gratuities must be made once in fifteen or twenty years let them not be bestowed on the subjects of a foreign government nor upon a designated and favored class of men in our own country. It is but justice and good policy, as far as the nature of the case will admit, to confine our favors to our own fellow-citizens, and let each in his turn enjoy an opportunity to profit by our bounty. In the bearings of the act before me upon these points I find ample reasons why it should not become a law.

It has been urged as an argument in favor of rechartering the present bank that the calling in its loans will produce great embarrassment and distress. The time allowed to close its concerns is ample, and if it has been well managed its pressure will be light, and heavy only in case its management has been bad. If, therefore, it shall produce distress, the fault will be its own, and it would furnish a reason against renewing a power which has been so obviously abused. But will there ever be a time when this reason will be less powerful? To acknowledge its force is to admit that the bank ought to be perpetual, and as a consequence the present stockholders and those inheriting their rights as successors be established a privileged order, clothed both with great political power and enjoying immense pecuniary advantages from their connection with the Government.

It is to be regretted that the rich and powerful too often bend the acts of government to their selfish purposes. Distinctions in society will always exist under every just government. Equality of talents, of education, or of wealth can not be produced by human institutions. In the full enjoyment of the gifts of Heaven and the fruits of superior industry, economy, and virtue, every man is equally entitled to protection by law; but when the laws undertake to add to these natural and just advantages artificial distinctions, to grant titles, gratuities, and exclusive privileges, to make the rich richer and the potent more powerful, the humble members of society—the farmers, mechanics, and laborers—who have neither the time nor the means of securing like favors to themselves, have a right to complain of the injustice of their Government. There are no necessary evils in government. Its evils exist only in its abuses. If it would confine itself to equal protection, and, as Heaven does its rains, shower its favors alike on the high and the low, the rich and the poor, it would be an unqualified blessing. In the act before me there seems to be a wide and unnecessary departure from these just principles.

Nor is our Government to be maintained or our Union preserved by invasions of the rights and powers of the several

States. In thus attempting to make our General Government strong we make it weak. Its true strength consists in leaving individuals and States as much as possible to themselves—in making itself felt, not in its power, but in its beneficence; not in its control, but in its protection; not in binding the States more closely to the center, but leaving each to move unobstructed in its proper orbit.

Experience should teach us wisdom. Most of the difficulties our Government now encounters and most of the dangers which impend over our Union have sprung from an abandonment of the legitimate objects of Government by our national legislation, and the adoption of such principles as are embodied in this act. Many of our rich men have not been content with equal protection and equal benefits, but have besought us to make them richer by act of Congress. By attempting to gratify their desires we have in the results of our legislation arrayed section against section, interest against interest, and man against man, in a fearful commotion which threatens to shake the foundations of our Union. It is time to pause in our career to review our principles, and if possible revive that devoted patriotism and spirit of compromise which distinguished the sages of the Revolution and the fathers of our Union. If we can not at once, in justice to interests vested under improvident legislation, make our Government what it ought to be, we can at least take a stand against all new grants of monopolies and exclusive privileges, against any prostitution of our Government to the advancement of the few at the expense of the many, and in favor of compromise and gradual reform in our code of laws and system of political economy.

July 10, 1832

Carl Schurz: from Address on Civil Service Reform

What Civil Service Reform demands, is simply that the business part of the Government shall be carried on in a sound, businesslike manner. This seems so obviously reasonable that among people of common sense there should be no two opinions about it. And the condition of things to be reformed is so obviously unreasonable, so flagrantly absurd and vicious, that we should not believe it could possibly exist among sensible people, had we not become accustomed to its existence among ourselves. In truth, we can hardly bring the whole exorbitance of that viciousness and absurdity home to our own minds unless we contemplate it as reflected in the mirror of a simile.

Imagine, then, a bank the stockholders of which, many in number, are divided into two factions—let us call them the Jones party and the Smith party—who quarrel about some question of business policy, as, for instance, whether the bank is to issue currency or not. The Jones party is in control, but the Smith men persuade over to their side a sufficient number of Jones men to give them—the Smith men—a majority at the next stockholders' meeting. Thus they succeed in getting the upper hand. They oust the old board of directors, and elect a new board consisting of Smith men. The new Smith board at once remove all the officers, president, cashier, tellers, bookkeepers, and clerks down to the messenger boys—the good and the bad alike—simply because they are Jones men, and fill their places forthwith with new persons who are selected, not on the ground that they have in any way proved their fitness for the positions so filled, but simply because they are Smith men; and those of the Smith men who have shown the greatest zeal and skill in getting a majority of votes for the Smith party are held to have the strongest claims for salaried places in the bank. The new men struggle painfully with the duties novel to them until they acquire some experience, but even then it needs in many instances two men or more to do the work of one.

In the course of events dissatisfaction spreads among the stockholders with the Smith management, partly shared by ambitious Smith men who thought themselves entitled to reward in the shape of places and salaries, but were "left out in the cold." Now the time for a new stockholders' meeting arrives. After a hot fight the Jones party carries the day. Its ticket of directors being elected, off go the heads of the Smith president, the Smith cashier, the Smith tellers, the Smith book-keepers and clerks, to be replaced by true-blue Jones men who have done the work of the campaign and are expected to do more of it when the next election comes. And so the career of the bank goes on with its periodical changes of party in power at longer or shorter intervals, and its corresponding clean sweeps of the bank service, with mismanagement and occasional fraud and peculation as inevitable incidents.

You might watch the proceedings of such a banking con-cern with intense curiosity and amusement. But I ask you, what prudent man among you would deposit his money in it or invest in its stock? And why would you not? Because you would think that this is not sensible men's business, but foolish boys' play; that such management would necessarily result in reckless waste and dishonesty, and tend to land many of the bank's officers in Canada, and not a few of its depositors or investors in the poorhouse. Such would be your judgment, and in pronouncing it you would at the same time pronounce judgment upon the manner in which the business part of our national Government, as well as of many if not most of our State and municipal governments, has been conducted for sev-eral generations. This is the spoils system. And I have by no means presented an exaggerated or even a complete picture of it; nay, rather a mild sketch, indicating only with faint touches the demoralizing influences exercised by that system with such baneful effect upon the whole political life of the nation.

The spoils system, that practice which turns public offices, high and low, from public trusts into objects of prey and booty for the victorious party, may without extravagance of language be called one of the greatest criminals in our history, if not the greatest. In the whole catalogue of our ills there is none more dangerous to the vitality of our free institutions.

It tends to divert our whole political life from its true aims. It teaches men to seek something else in politics than the public good. It puts mercenary selfishness as the motive power for political action in the place of public spirit, and organizes that selfishness into a dominant political force.

It attracts to active party politics the worst elements of our population, and with them crowds out the best. It transforms political parties from associations of patriotic citizens, formed to serve a public cause, into bands of mercenaries using a cause to serve them. It perverts party contests from contentions of opinion into scrambles for plunder. By stimulating the mercenary spirit it promotes the corrupt use of money in party contests and in elections.

It takes the leadership of political organizations out of the hands of men fit to be leaders of opinion and workers for high aims, and turns it over to the organizers and leaders of bands of political marauders. It creates the boss and the machine, putting the boss into the place of the statesman, and the despotism of the machine in the place of an organized public opinion.

It converts the public officeholder, who should be the servant of the people, into the servant of a party or of an influential politician, extorting from him time and work which should belong to the public, and money which he receives from the public for public service. It corrupts his sense of duty by making him understand that his obligation to his party or his political patron is equal if not superior to his obligation to the public interest, and that his continuance in office does not depend on his fidelity to duty. It debauches his honesty by seducing him to use the opportunities of his office to indemnify himself for the burdens forced upon him as a party slave. It undermines in all directions the discipline of the public service.

It falsifies our constitutional system. It leads to the usurpation, in a large measure, of the executive power of appointment by members of the legislative branch, substituting their irresponsible views of personal or party interest for the judgment as to the public good, and the sense of responsibility of the executive. It subjects those who exercise the appointing power, from the President of the United States down, to the intrusion of hordes of office-hunters and their patrons, who rob them of the time and strength they should devote to the public interest. It has already killed two of our Presidents, one, the first Harrison, by worry, and the other, Garfield, by murder; and more recently it has killed a mayor in Chicago and a judge in Tennessee.

It degrades our Senators and Representatives in Congress to the contemptible position of office-brokers, and even of mere agents of office-brokers, making the business of dickering about spoils as weighty to them as their duties as legislators. It introduces the patronage as an agency of corrupt influence between the executive and the legislature. It serves to obscure the criminal character of bribery by treating bribery with offices as a legitimate practice. It thus reconciles the popular mind to practices essentially corrupt, and thereby debauches the popular sense of right and wrong in politics.

It keeps in high political places, to the exclusion of better men, persons whose only ability consists in holding a personal following by adroit manipulation of the patronage. It has thus sadly lowered the standard of statesmanship in public position, compared with the high order of ability displayed in all other walks of life.

It does more than anything else to turn our large municipalities into sinks of corruption, to render Tammany Halls possible, and to make of the police force here and there a protector of crime and a terror to those whose safety it is to guard. It exposes us, by the scandalous spectacle of its periodical spoils carnivals, to the ridicule and contempt of civilized mankind, promoting among our own people the growth of serious doubts as to the practicability of democratic institutions on a great scale, and in an endless variety of ways it introduces into our political life more elements of demoralization, debasement and decadence than any other agency of evil I know of, aye, perhaps more than all other agencies of evil combined.

As to the general policy, I have had opportunities for observing events under no less than ten Administrations, and I have never known the patronage to be extensively used for the purpose of pushing a policy by winning votes in Congress, without giving the Administration concerned far more trouble than influence, and without making for it more enemies than friends. It may capture the support of a man here and there, but it will always in a larger circle stir up jealousy, heartburnings and bitterness, and it will so stimulate the mercenary spirit in Congress that at last the Administration can hardly obtain any support for anything without paying for it at the expense of its conscience and its honor.

The ordinary spoilsman cannot be permanently propiti-ated unless he gets everything he wishes. You try to please him by giving him the disposal of an ambassadorship, but he will become your enemy if you refuse him a small postoffice. And the appetite grows with the eating. No Administration can suf-ficiently satisfy that appetite to secure the reliable good will of the greedy without utter moral ruin and disgrace. This is the teaching of history.

Thus all the pretended political advantages ascribed to the spoils system dwindle into nothing; nay, on candid scrutiny they appear as added curses. It offers not the slightest compensation for the wasteful misrule, the sickening demoralization, and the appalling dangers to our free institutions which it brings in its train. It is so unmitigated an evil, so barbarous an anachronism, so utterly unfit for a civilized, self-respecting, and patriotic people, that we must wonder how it ever could throw root or be tolerated in this great and proud Republic.

And yet we have to face the fact that there are still strong and stubborn forces standing behind it. There is the *vis inertiæ* of habit which persuades slow-thinking people that what has been so long must continue to be. There is the multitude of those afflicted with an almost morbid desire for public office as a sort of distinction and an easy means of support, to be had as a present for the asking. There are the political speculators who see in spoils politics opportunities for pelf. There are the political wire-pullers who know no other politics than dicker and trade, and whom the abolition of the spoils system would deprive of their occupation. There are the members of legislatures, and of Congress, and the Governors and other officials who feel that they cannot sustain themselves in public life by their ability as statesmen; and fall back upon the tricks of the patronage jobber to continue their superfluous public existence. There is the cowardice of the politician in high place who prays to be delivered of the burden and annoyance of the patronage, but whose courage collapses as soon as a constituent asks him for an office. And last but not least, there is the power of the party organizations that have the prestige of regularity and that are almost exclusively controlled by spoils politicians.

All these elements combined surely make a strong force, and this force has for years desperately contested every inch of ground against the onward movement of Reform. But on the other hand the friends of Reform rejoice to know that on their side a power is rising up with constantly increasing strength, to which in a free country eventually everything must yield—the power of public opinion. And this power has never made itself felt as strongly as now. It is not the mere critical fault-finding of the political philosopher, not a mere sentimental cry for something ideal, that makes itself heard. It is the voice of the sober-minded citizen who may long have regarded the Civil Service Reformer as a visionary, but who now by stern experience has been made aware that something is essentially wrong in the practical working of our institutions, and that a remedy is urgently called for.

So we hear from all sides expressions of disgust at the scandalous spectacle of the spoils-carnival with every change of party in power, and the reckless distribution of public offices among political workers undeserving of honor and confidence. One public man in high station after another declares that the position of spoils-jobbers to which they are degraded puts upon them intolerable burdens, and that it must cease. In all parts of the country chambers of commerce, boards of trade and individual merchants protest that so many of our consulates abroad have long enough been held by incompetents, who merely wish to spend some time in foreign lands for their health or to get good music lessons for their daughters, that it is time we should cease to make such offices the laughing-stock and contempt of foreign nations, and that at last only men should be sent out known to be fit to serve the interests of our commerce as the consuls of our commercial competitors serve theirs. But, more significant than all this, where government comes nearest home to the individual citizen, its abuses have stirred up the strongest feeling. The people of some of our great municipalities are crying out that they have been scandalously misgoverned and robbed and oppressed by organized bands of mercenary politicians, who by hook or crook obtain complete possession of the municipal governments, or at least exercise a pernicious influence in them, and that there must be an end of this.

Nor are these complaints brought forth without the suggestion of a remedy. In every instance they are accompanied with the demand that the branch of the public service complained of—national, State, or municipal—must be "taken out of politics."

Never has the popular instinct hit the nail on the head more squarely than by this demand. For what does it mean to take a public function out of politics? It means simply that with regard to all the public offices and employments concerned, rules for appointment and promotion be introduced which rigidly exclude political and personal favoritism, and secure places and preferment only to those who in some prescribed manner establish the superiority of their mental and moral fitness for the work to be done.

For a place in the administrative part of the Government not the mere henchman of some party leader or committee, but he who proves himself better qualified for the duties of the office than his competitors; for the consular service, not a mere political drummer or a man who has put some member of Congress under political obligation, but he who proves himself especially well versed in commercial affairs and law, and in command of the other necessary equipments for the performance of consular duty; for the police force, not a mere graduate of a whiskey-shop whom some party boss or ward-heeler wishes to wield the police club, but he who is found in point of moral character, as well as mental and physical qualifications, to be a person of superior fitness for the duties of a policeman; and for promotion in the service, not the mere favorite of some political magnate or of his wife or daughter, but he who has shown that he deserves that promotion by superior capacity, efficiency, and fidelity to duty! This is what it means to take public functions out of politics. And this is the merit system. This is Civil Service Reform.

December 12, 1894

★ ★ ★

Theodore Roosevelt: The New Nationalism

WE come here to-day to commemorate one of the epoch-making events of the long struggle for the rights of man—the long struggle for the uplift of humanity. Our country—this great Republic—means nothing unless it means the triumph of a real democracy, the triumph of popular government, and, in the long run, of an economic system under which each man shall be guaranteed the opportunity to show the best that there is in him. That is why the history of America is now the central feature of the history of the world; for the world has set its face hopefully toward our democracy; and, O my fellow citizens, each one of you carries on your shoulders not only the burden of doing well for the sake of your own country, but the burden of doing well and of seeing that this nation does well for the sake of mankind.

There have been two great crises in our country's history: first, when it was formed, and then, again, when it was perpetuated; and, in the second of these great crises—in the time of stress and strain which culminated in the Civil War, on the outcome of which depended the justification of what had been done earlier, you men of the Grand Army, you men who fought through the Civil War, not only did you justify your generation, not only did you render life worth living for our generation, but you justified the wisdom of Washington and Washington's colleagues. If this Republic had been founded by them only to be split asunder into fragments when the strain came, then the judgment of the world would have been that Washington's work was not worth doing. It was you who crowned Washington's

work, as you carried to achievement the high purpose of Abraham Lincoln.

Now, with this second period of our history the name of
John Brown will be forever associated; and Kansas was the the-
atre upon which the first act of the second of our great national
life dramas was played. It was the result of the struggle in Kansas
which determined that our country should be in deed as well
as in name devoted to both union and freedom; that the great
experiment of democratic government on a national scale
should succeed and not fail. In name we had the Declaration
of Independence in 1776; but we gave the lie by our acts to
the words of the Declaration of Independence until 1865; and
words count for nothing except in so far as they represent acts.
This is true everywhere; but, O my friends, it should be truest of
all in political life. A broken promise is bad enough in private
life. It is worse in the field of politics. No man is worth his salt
in public life who makes on the stump a pledge which he does
not keep after election; and, if he makes such a pledge and does
not keep it, hunt him out of public life. I care for the great deeds
of the past chiefly as spurs to drive us onward in the present. I
speak of the men of the past partly that they may be honored
by our praise of them, but more that they may serve as examples
for the future.

It was a heroic struggle; and, as is inevitable with all such
struggles, it had also a dark and terrible side. Very much was
done of good, and much also of evil; and, as was inevitable in
such a period of revolution, often the same man did both good
and evil. For our great good fortune as a nation, we, the people
of the United States as a whole, can now afford to forget the
evil, or, at least, to remember it without bitterness, and to fix our
eyes with pride only on the good that was accomplished. Even
in ordinary times there are very few of us who do not see the
problems of life as through a glass, darkly; and when the glass
is clouded by the murk of furious popular passion, the vision of
the best and the bravest is dimmed. Looking back, we are all of

us now able to do justice to the valor and the disinterestedness and the love of the right, as to each it was given to see the right, shown both by the men of the North and the men of the South in that contest which was finally decided by the attitude of the West. We can admire the heroic valor, the sincerity, the self-devotion shown alike by the men who wore the blue and the men who wore the gray; and our sadness that such men should have had to fight one another is tempered by the glad knowledge that ever hereafter their descendants shall be found fighting side by side, struggling in peace as well as in war for the uplift of their common country, all alike resolute to raise to the highest pitch of honor and usefulness the nation to which they all belong. As for the veterans of the Grand Army of the Republic, they deserve honor and recognition such as is paid to no other citizens of the Republic; for to them the republic owes its all; for to them it owes its very existence. It is because of what you and your comrades did in the dark years that we of to-day walk, each of us, head erect, and proud that we belong, not to one of a dozen little squabbling contemptible commonwealths, but to the mightiest nation upon which the sun shines.

I do not speak of this struggle of the past merely from the historic standpoint. Our interest is primarily in the application to-day of the lessons taught by the contest of half a century ago. It is of little use for us to pay lip-loyalty to the mighty men of the past unless we sincerely endeavor to apply to the problems of the present precisely the qualities which in other crises enabled the men of that day to meet those crises. It is half melancholy and half amusing to see the way in which well-meaning people gather to do honor to the men who, in company with John Brown, and under the lead of Abraham Lincoln, faced and solved the great problems of the nineteenth century, while, at the same time, these same good people nervously shrink from, or frantically denounce, those who are trying to meet the problems of the twentieth century in the spirit which was accountable for the successful solution of the problems of Lincoln's time.

Of that generation of men to whom we owe so much, the man to whom we owe most is, of course, Lincoln. Part of our debt to him is because he forecast our present struggle and saw the way out. He said:

"I hold that while man exists it is his duty to improve not only his own condition, but to assist in ameliorating mankind."

And again:

"Labor is prior to, and independent of, capital. Capital is only the fruit of labor, and could never have existed if labor had not first existed. Labor is the superior of capital, and deserves much the higher consideration."

If that remark was original with me, I should be even more strongly denounced as a Communist agitator than I shall be anyhow. It is Lincoln's. I am only quoting it; and that is one side; that is the side the capitalist should hear. Now, let the working man hear his side.

"Capital has its rights, which are as worthy of protection as any other rights. . . . Nor should this lead to a war upon the owners of property. Property is the fruit of labor; . . . property is desirable; is a positive good in the world."

And then comes a thoroughly Lincolnlike sentence:

"Let not him who is houseless pull down the house of another, but let him work diligently and build one for himself, thus by example assuring that his own shall be safe from violence when built."

It seems to me that, in these words, Lincoln took substantially the attitude that we ought to take; he showed the proper sense of proportion in his relative estimates of capital and labor, of human rights and property rights. Above all, in this speech, as in many others, he taught a lesson in wise kindliness and charity; an indispensable lesson to us of to-day. But this wise kindliness and charity never weakened his arm or numbed his heart. We cannot afford weakly to blind ourselves to the actual conflict which faces us to-day. The issue is joined, and we must fight or fail.

In every wise struggle for human betterment one of the main objects, and often the only object, has been to achieve in large measure equality of opportunity. In the struggle for this great end, nations rise from barbarism to civilization, and through it people press forward from one stage of enlightenment to the next. One of the chief factors in progress is the destruction of special privilege. The essence of any struggle for healthy liberty has always been, and must always be, to take from some one man or class of men the right to enjoy power, or wealth, or position, or immunity, which has not been earned by service to his or their fellows. That is what you fought for in the Civil War, and that is what we strive for now.

At many stages in the advance of humanity, this conflict between the men who possess more than they have earned and the men who have earned more than they possess is the central condition of progress. In our day it appears as the struggle of freemen to gain and hold the right of self-government as against the special interests, who twist the methods of free government into machinery for defeating the popular will. At every stage, and under all circumstances, the essence of the struggle is to equalize opportunity, destroy privilege, and give to the life and citizenship of every individual the highest possible value both to himself and to the commonwealth. That is nothing new. All I ask in civil life is what you fought for in the Civil War. I ask that civil life be carried on according to the spirit in which the army was carried on. You never get perfect justice, but the effort in handling the army was to bring to the front the men who could do the job. Nobody grudged promotion to Grant, or Sherman, or Thomas, or Sheridan, because they earned it. The only complaint was when a man got promotion which he did not earn.

Practical equality of opportunity for all citizens, when we achieve it, will have two great results. First, every man will have a fair chance to make of himself all that in him lies; to reach the highest point to which his capacities, unassisted by special privilege of his own and unhampered by the special privilege of others, can carry him, and to get for himself and his family substantially what he has earned. Second, equality of opportunity means that the commonwealth will get from every citizen the highest service of which he is capable. No man who carries the burden of the special privileges of another can give to the commonwealth that service to which it is fairly entitled.

I stand for the square deal. But when I say that I am for the square deal, I mean not merely that I stand for fair play under the present rules of the game, but that I stand for having those rules changed so as to work for a more substantial equality of opportunity and of reward for equally good service. One word of warning, which, I think, is hardly necessary in Kansas. When I say I want a square deal for the poor man, I do not mean that I want a square deal for the man who remains poor because he has not got the energy to work for himself. If a man who has had a chance will not make good, then he has got to quit. And you men of the Grand Army, you want justice for the brave man who fought, and punishment for the coward who shirked his work. Is not that so?

Now, this means that our government, National and State, must be freed from the sinister influence or control of special interests. Exactly as the special interests of cotton and slavery threatened our political integrity before the Civil War, so now the great special business interests too often control and corrupt the men and methods of government for their own profit. We must drive the special interests out of politics. That is one of our tasks to-day. Every special interest is entitled to justice—full, fair, and complete—and, now, mind you, if there were any attempt by mob-violence to plunder and work harm to the special interest, whatever it may be, that I most dislike, and the wealthy man, whomsoever he may be, for whom I have the greatest contempt, I would fight for him, and you would if you were worth your salt. He should have justice. For every special interest is entitled to justice, but not one is entitled to a vote in Congress, to a voice on the bench, or to representation in any public office. The Constitution guarantees protection to property, and we must make that promise good. But it does not give the right of suffrage to any corporation.

The true friend of property, the true conservative, is he who insists that property shall be the servant and not the master of the commonwealth; who insists that the creature of man's making shall be the servant and not the master of the man who made it. The citizens of the United States must effectively control the mighty commercial forces which they have themselves called into being.

There can be no effective control of corporations while their political activity remains. To put an end to it will be neither a short nor an easy task, but it can be done.

We must have complete and effective publicity of corporate affairs, so that the people may know beyond peradventure whether the corporations obey the law and whether their management entitles them to the confidence of the public. It is necessary that laws should be passed to prohibit the use of corporate funds directly or indirectly for political purposes; it is still more necessary that such laws should be thoroughly enforced. Corporate expenditures for political purposes, and especially such expenditures by public-service corporations, have supplied one of the principal sources of corruption in our political affairs.

It has become entirely clear that we must have government supervision of the capitalization, not only of public-service corporations, including, particularly, railways, but of all corporations doing an interstate business. I do not wish to see the nation forced into the ownership of the railways if it can possibly be avoided, and the only alternative is thoroughgoing and effective regulation, which shall be based on a full knowledge of all the facts, including a physical valuation of property. This physical valuation is not needed, or, at least, is very rarely needed, for fixing rates; but it is needed as the basis of honest capitalization.

We have come to recognize that franchises should never be granted except for a limited time, and never without proper provision for compensation to the public. It is my personal belief that the same kind and degree of control and supervision which should be exercised over public-service corporations should be extended also to combinations which control necessaries of life, such as meat, oil, and coal, or which deal in them on an important scale. I have no doubt that the ordinary man who has control of them is much like ourselves. I have no doubt he would like to do well, but I want to have enough supervision to help him realize that desire to do well.

I believe that the officers, and, especially, the directors, of corporations should be held personally responsible when any corporation breaks the law.

Combinations in industry are the result of an imperative economic law which cannot be repealed by political legislation. The effort at prohibiting all combination has substantially failed. The way out lies, not in attempting to prevent such combinations, but in completely controlling them in the interest of the public welfare. For that purpose the Federal Bureau of Corporations is an agency of first importance. Its powers, and, therefore, its efficiency, as well as that of the Interstate Commerce Commission, should be largely increased. We have a right to expect from the Bureau of Corporations and from the Interstate Commerce Commission a very high grade of public service. We should be as sure of the proper conduct of the interstate railways and the proper management of interstate business as we are now sure of the conduct and management of the national banks, and we should have as effective supervision in one case as in the other. The Hepburn Act, and the amendment to the act in the shape in which it finally passed Congress at the last session, represent a long step in advance, and we must go yet further.

There is a wide-spread belief among our people that, under the methods of making tariffs which have hitherto obtained, the special interests are too influential. Probably this is true of both the big special interests and the little special interests. These methods have put a premium on selfishness, and, naturally, the selfish big interests have gotten more than their smaller, though equally selfish, brothers. The duty of Congress is to provide a method by which the interest of the whole people shall be all that receives consideration. To this end there must be an expert tariff commission, wholly removed from the possibility of political pressure or of improper business influence. Such a commission can find the real difference between cost of production, which is mainly the difference of labor cost here and abroad. As fast as its recommendations are made, I believe in revising one schedule at a time. A general revision of the tariff almost inevitably leads to log-rolling and the subordination of the general public interest to local and special interests.

The absence of effective State, and, especially, national, restraint upon unfair money-getting has tended to create a small class of enormously wealthy and economically powerful men, whose chief object is to hold and increase their power. The prime need is to change the conditions which enable these men to accumulate power which it is not for the general welfare that they should hold or exercise. We grudge no man a fortune which represents his own power and sagacity, when exercised with entire regard to the welfare of his fellows. Again, comrades over there, take the lesson from your own experience. Not only did you not grudge, but you gloried in the promotion of the great generals who gained their promotion by leading the army to victory. So it is with us. We grudge no man a fortune in civil life if it is honorably obtained and well used. It is not even enough that it should have been gained without doing damage to the community. We should permit it to be gained only so long as the gaining represents benefit to the community. This, I know, implies a policy of a far more active governmental interference with social and economic conditions in this country than we have yet had, but I think we have got to face the fact that such an increase in governmental control is now necessary.

No man should receive a dollar unless that dollar has been fairly earned. Every dollar received should represent a dollar's worth of service rendered—not gambling in stocks, but service rendered. The really big fortune, the swollen fortune, by the mere fact of its size acquires qualities which differentiate it in kind as well as in degree from what is possessed by men of relatively small means. Therefore, I believe in a graduated income tax on big fortunes, and in another tax which is far more easily collected and far more effective—a graduated inheritance tax on big fortunes, properly safeguarded against evasion and increasing rapidly in amount with the size of the estate.

The people of the United States suffer from periodical financial panics to a degree substantially unknown among the other nations which approach us in financial strength. There is no reason why we should suffer what they escape. It is of profound importance that our financial system should be promptly investigated, and so thoroughly and effectively revised as to make it certain that hereafter our currency will no longer fail at critical times to meet our needs.

It is hardly necessary for me to repeat that I believe in an efficient army and a navy large enough to secure for us abroad that respect which is the surest guaranty of peace. A word of special warning to my fellow citizens who are as progressive as I hope I am. I want them to keep up their interest in our internal affairs; and I want them also continually to remember Uncle Sam's interests abroad. Justice and fair dealing among nations rest upon principles identical with those which control justice and fair dealing among the individuals of which nations are composed, with the vital exception that each nation must do its own part in international police work. If you get into trouble here, you can call for the police; but if Uncle Sam gets into trouble, he has got to be his own policeman, and I want to see him strong enough to encourage the peaceful aspirations of other peoples in connection with us. I believe in national friendships and heartiest good-will to all nations; but national friendships, like those between men, must be founded on respect as well as on liking, on forbearance as well as upon trust. I should be heartily ashamed of any American who did not try to make the American Government act as justly toward the other nations in international relations as he himself would act toward any individual in private relations. I should be heartily ashamed to see us wrong a weaker power, and I should hang my head forever if we tamely suffered wrong from a stronger power.

Of conservation I shall speak more at length elsewhere. Conservation means development as much as it does protection. I recognize the right and duty of this generation to develop and use the natural resources of our land; but I do not recognize the right to waste them, or to rob, by wasteful use, the generations that come after us. I ask nothing of the nation except that it so behave as each farmer here behaves with reference to his own children. That farmer is a poor creature who skins the land and leaves it worthless to his children. The farmer is a good farmer who, having enabled the land to support himself and to provide for the education of his children, leaves it to them a little better than he found it himself. I believe the same thing of a nation.

Moreover, I believe that the natural resources must be used for the benefit of all our people, and not monopolized for the benefit of the few, and here again is another case in which I am accused of taking a revolutionary attitude. People forget now that one hundred years ago there were public men of good character who advocated the nation selling its public lands in great quantities, so that the nation could get the most money out of it, and giving it to the men who could cultivate it for their own uses. We took the proper democratic ground that the land should be granted in small sections to the men who were actually to till it and live on it. Now, with the waterpower, with the forests, with the mines, we are brought face to face with the fact that there are many people who will go with us in conserving the resources only if they are to be allowed to exploit them for their benefit. That is one of the fundamental reasons why the special interests should be driven out of politics. Of all the questions which can come before this nation, short of the actual preservation of its existence in a great war, there is none which compares in importance with the great central task of leaving this land even a better land for our descendants than it is for us, and training them into a better race to inhabit the land and pass it on. Conservation is a great moral issue, for it involves the patriotic duty of insuring the safety and continuance of the nation. Let me add that the health and vitality of our people are at least as well worth conserving as their forests, waters, lands, and minerals, and in this great work the national government must bear a most important part.

I have spoken elsewhere also of the great task which lies before the farmers of the country to get for themselves and their wives and children not only the benefits of better farming, but also those of better business methods and better conditions of life on the farm. The burden of this great task will fall, as it should, mainly upon the great organizations of the farmers themselves. I am glad it will, for I believe they are all well able to handle it. In particular, there are strong reasons why the Departments of Agriculture of the various States, the United States Department of Agriculture, and the agricultural colleges and experiment stations should extend their work to cover all phases of farm life, instead of limiting themselves, as they have far too often limited themselves in the past, solely to the question of the production of crops. And now a special word to the farmer. I want to see him make the farm as fine a farm as it can be made; and let him remember to see that the improvement goes on indoors as well as out; let him remember that the farmer's wife should have her share of thought and attention just as much as the farmer himself.

Nothing is more true than that excess of every kind is followed by reaction; a fact which should be pondered by reformer and reactionary alike. We are face to face with new conceptions of the relations of property to human welfare, chiefly because certain advocates of the rights of property as against the rights of men have been pushing their claims too far. The man who wrongly holds that every human right is secondary to his profit must now give way to the advocate of human welfare, who rightly maintains that every man holds his property subject to the general right of the community to regulate its use to whatever degree the public welfare may require it.

But I think we may go still further. The right to regulate the use of wealth in the public interest is universally admitted. Let us admit also the right to regulate the terms and conditions of labor, which is the chief element of wealth, directly in the interest of the common good. The fundamental thing to do for every man is to give him a chance to reach a place in which he will make the greatest possible contribution to the public welfare. Understand what I say there. Give him a chance, not push him up if he will not be pushed. Help any man who stumbles; if he lies down, it is a poor job to try to carry him; but if he is a worthy man, try your best to see that he gets a chance to show the worth that is in him. No man can be a good citizen unless he has a wage more than sufficient to cover the bare cost of living, and hours of labor short enough so that after his day's work is done he will have time and energy to bear his share in the management of the community, to help in carrying the general load. We keep countless men from being good citizens by the conditions of life with which we surround them. We need comprehensive workmen's compensation acts, both State and national laws to regulate child labor and work for women, and, especially, we need in our common schools not merely education in book-learning, but also practical training for daily life and work. We need to enforce better sanitary conditions for our workers and to extend the use of safety appliances for our workers in industry and commerce, both within and between the States. Also, friends, in the interest of the working man himself we need to set our faces like flint against mob-violence just as against corporate greed; against violence and injustice and lawlessness by wage-workers just as much as against lawless cunning and greed and selfish arrogance of employers. If I could ask but one thing of my fellow countrymen, my request would be that, whenever they go in for reform, they remember the two sides, and that they always exact justice from one side as much as from the other. I have small use for the public servant who can always see and denounce the corruption of the capitalist, but who cannot persuade himself, especially before election, to say a word about lawless mob-violence. And I have equally small use for the man, be he a judge on the bench, or editor of a great paper, or wealthy and influential private citizen, who can see clearly enough and denounce the lawlessness of mob-violence, but whose eyes are closed so that he is blind when the question is one of corruption in business on a gigantic scale. Also remember what I said about excess in reformer and reactionary alike. If the reactionary man, who thinks of nothing but the rights of property, could have his way, he would bring about a revolution; and one of my chief fears in connection with progress comes because I do not want to see our people, for lack of proper leadership, compelled to follow men whose intentions are excellent, but whose eyes are a little too wild to make it really safe to trust them. Here in Kansas there is one paper which habitually denounces me as the tool of Wall Street, and at the same time frantically repudiates the statement that I am a Socialist on the ground that that is an unwarranted slander of the Socialists.

National efficiency has many factors. It is a necessary result of the principle of conservation widely applied. In the end it will determine our failure or success as a nation. National efficiency has to do, not only with natural resources and with men, but it is equally concerned with institutions. The State must be made efficient for the work which concerns only the people of the State; and the nation for that which concerns all the people. There must remain no neutral ground to serve as a refuge for lawbreakers, and especially for lawbreakers of great wealth, who can hire the vulpine legal cunning which will teach them how to avoid both jurisdictions. It is a misfortune when the national legislature fails to do its duty in providing a national remedy, so that the only national activity is the purely negative activity of the judiciary in forbidding the State to exercise power in the premises.

I do not ask for overcentralization; but I do ask that we work in a spirit of broad and far-reaching nationalism when we work for what concerns our people as a whole. We are all Americans. Our common interests are as broad as the continent. I speak to you here in Kansas exactly as I would speak in New York or Georgia, for the most vital problems are those which affect us all alike. The National Government belongs to the whole American people, and where the whole American people are interested, that interest can be guarded effectively only by the National Government. The betterment which we seek must be accomplished, I believe, mainly through the National Government.

The American people are right in demanding that New Nationalism, without which we cannot hope to deal with new problems. The New Nationalism puts the national need before sectional or personal advantage. It is impatient of the utter confusion that results from local legislatures attempting to treat national issues as local issues. It is still more impatient of the impotence which springs from overdivision of governmental powers, the impotence which makes it possible for local selfishness or for legal cunning, hired by wealthy special interests, to bring national activities to a deadlock. This New Nationalism regards the executive power as the steward of the public welfare. It demands of the judiciary that it shall be interested primarily in human welfare rather than in property, just as it demands that the representative body shall represent all the people rather than any one class or section of the people.

I believe in shaping the ends of government to protect property as well as human welfare. Normally, and in the long run, the ends are the same; but whenever the alternative must be faced, I am for men and not for property, as you were in the Civil War. I am far from underestimating the importance of dividends; but I rank dividends below human character. Again, I do not have any sympathy with the reformer who says he does not care for dividends. Of course, economic welfare is necessary, for a man must pull his own weight and be able to support his family. I know well that the reformers must not bring upon the people economic ruin, or the reforms themselves will go down in the ruin. But we must be ready to face temporary disaster, whether or not brought on by those who will war against us to the knife. Those who oppose all reform will do well to remember that ruin in its worst form is inevitable if our national life brings us nothing better than swollen fortunes for the few and the triumph in both politics and business of a sordid and selfish materialism.

If our political institutions were perfect, they would absolutely prevent the political domination of money in any part of our affairs. We need to make our political representatives more quickly and sensitively responsive to the people whose servants they are. More direct action by the people in their own affairs under proper safeguards is vitally necessary. The direct primary is a step in this direction, if it is associated with a corrupt-practices act effective to prevent the advantage of the man willing recklessly and unscrupulously to spend money over his more honest competitor. It is particularly important that all moneys received or expended for campaign purposes should be publicly accounted for, not only after election, but before election as well. Political action must be made simpler, easier, and freer from confusion for every citizen. I believe that the prompt removal of unfaithful or incompetent public servants should be made easy and sure in whatever way experience shall show to be most expedient in any given class of cases.

One of the fundamental necessities in a representative government such as ours is to make certain that the men to whom the people delegate their power shall serve the people by whom they are elected, and not the special interests. I believe that every national officer, elected or appointed, should be forbidden to perform any service or receive any compensation, directly or indirectly, from interstate corporations; and a similar provision could not fail to be useful within the States.

The object of government is the welfare of the people. The material progress and prosperity of a nation are desirable chiefly so far as they lead to the moral and material welfare of all good citizens. Just in proportion as the average man and woman are honest, capable of sound judgment and high ideals, active in public affairs—but, first of all, sound in their home life, and the father and mother of healthy children whom they bring up well—just so far, and no farther, we may count our civilization a success. We must have—I believe we have already—a genuine and permanent moral awakening, without which no wisdom of legislation or administration really means anything; and, on the other hand, we must try to secure the social and economic legislation without which any improvement due to purely moral agitation is necessarily evanescent. Let me again illustrate by a reference to the Grand Army. You could not have won simply as a disorderly and disorganized mob. You needed generals; you needed careful administration of the most advanced type; and a good commissary—the cracker line. You well remember that success was necessary in many different lines in order to bring about general success. You had to have the administration at Washington good, just as you had to have the administration in the field; and you had to have the work of the generals good. You could not have triumphed without that administration and leadership; but it would all have been worthless if the average soldier had not had the right stuff in him. He had to have the right stuff in him, or you could not get it out of him. In the last analysis, therefore, vitally necessary though it was to have the right kind of organization and the right kind of generalship, it was even more vitally necessary that the average soldier should have the fighting edge, the right character. So it is in our civil life. No matter how honest and decent we are in our private lives, if we do not have the right kind of law and the right kind of administration of the law, we cannot go forward as a nation. That is imperative; but it must be an addition to, and not a substitution for, the qualities that make us good citizens. In the last analysis, the most important elements in any man's career must be the sum of those qualities which, in the aggregate, we speak of as character. If he has not got it, then no law that the wit of man can devise, no administration of the law by the boldest and strongest executive, will avail to help him. We must have the right kind of character—character that makes a man, first of all, a good man in the home, a good father, a good husband—that makes a man a good neighbor. You must have that, and, then, in addition, you must have the kind of law and the kind of administration of the law which will give to those qualities in the private citizen the best possible chance for development. The prime problem of our nation is to get the right type of good citizenship, and, to get it, we must have progress, and our public men must be genuinely progressive.

August 31, 1910

★ ★ ★

John Paul Stevens: from Dissent in *Citizens United v. Federal Election Commission*

I. *Antidistortion*

The fact that corporations are different from human beings might seem to need no elaboration, except that the majority opinion almost completely elides it. *Austin* set forth some of the basic differences. Unlike natural persons, corporations have "limited liability" for their owners and managers, "perpetual life," separation of ownership and control, "and favorable treatment of the accumulation and distribution of assets . . . that enhance their ability to attract capital and to deploy their resources in ways that maximize the return on their shareholders' investments." 494 U. S., at 658–659. Unlike voters in U. S. elections, corporations may be foreign controlled.[1] Unlike other interest groups, business corporations have been "effectively delegated responsibility for ensuring society's economic welfare";[2] they inescapably structure the life of every citizen. "'[T]he resources in the treasury of a business corporation,'" furthermore, "'are not an indication of popular support for the corporation's political ideas.'" *Id.*, at 659 (quoting *MCFL*, 479 U. S., at 258). "'They reflect instead the economically motivated decisions of investors and customers. The availability of these resources may make a corporation a formidable political presence, even though the power of the corporation may be no

---

[1] In state elections, even domestic corporations may be "foreign"-controlled in the sense that they are incorporated in another jurisdiction and primarily owned and operated by out-of-state residents.

[2] Regan, Corporate Speech and Civic Virtue, in Debating Democracy's Discontent 289, 302 (A. Allen & M. Regan eds. 1998) (hereinafter Regan).

reflection of the power of its ideas.'" 494 U. S., at 659 (quoting *MCFL*, 479 U. S., at 258).[3]

It might also be added that corporations have no consciences, no beliefs, no feelings, no thoughts, no desires. Corporations help structure and facilitate the activities of human beings, to be sure, and their "personhood" often serves as a useful legal fiction. But they are not themselves members of "We the People" by whom and for whom our Constitution was established.

These basic points help explain why corporate electioneering is not only more likely to impair compelling governmental interests, but also why restrictions on that electioneering are less likely to encroach upon First Amendment freedoms. One fundamental concern of the First Amendment is to "protec[t] the individual's interest in self-expression." *Consolidated Edison Co. of N. Y. v. Public Serv. Comm'n of N. Y.*, 447 U. S. 530, 534, n. 2 (1980); see also *Bellotti*, 435 U. S., at 777, n. 12. Freedom of speech helps "make men free to develop their faculties," *Whitney v. California*, 274 U. S. 357, 375 (1927) (Brandeis, J., concurring), it respects their "dignity and choice," *Cohen v. California*, 403 U. S. 15, 24 (1971), and it facilitates the value of "individual self-realization," Redish, The Value of Free Speech, 130 U. Pa. L. Rev. 591, 594 (1982). Corporate speech, however, is derivative speech, speech by proxy. A regulation

---

[3] Nothing in this analysis turns on whether the corporation is conceptualized as a grantee of a state concession, see, *e.g.*, *Trustees of Dartmouth College v. Woodward*, 4 Wheat. 518, 636 (1819) (Marshall, C. J.), a nexus of explicit and implicit contracts, see, *e.g.*, F. Easterbrook & D. Fischel, The Economic Structure of Corporate Law 12 (1991), a mediated hierarchy of stakeholders, see, *e.g.*, Blair & Stout, A Team Production Theory of Corporate Law, 85 Va. L. Rev. 247 (1999) (hereinafter Blair & Stout), or any other recognized model. *Austin* referred to the structure and the advantages of corporations as "state-conferred" in several places, 494 U. S., at 660, 665, 667, but its antidistortion argument relied only on the basic descriptive features of corporations, as sketched above. It is not necessary to agree on a precise theory of the corporation to agree that corporations differ from natural persons in fundamental ways, and that a legislature might therefore need to regulate them differently if it is human welfare that is the object of its concern. Cf. Hansmann & Kraakman 441, n. 5.

such as BCRA §203 may affect the way in which individuals disseminate certain messages through the corporate form, but it does not prevent anyone from speaking in his or her own voice. "Within the realm of [campaign spending] generally," corporate spending is "furthest from the core of political expression." *Beaumont*, 539 U. S., at 161, n. 8.

It is an interesting question "who" is even speaking when a business corporation places an advertisement that endorses or attacks a particular candidate. Presumably it is not the customers or employees, who typically have no say in such matters. It cannot realistically be said to be the shareholders, who tend to be far removed from the day-to-day decisions of the firm and whose political preferences may be opaque to management. Perhaps the officers or directors of the corporation have the best claim to be the ones speaking, except their fiduciary duties generally prohibit them from using corporate funds for personal ends. Some individuals associated with the corporation must make the decision to place the ad, but the idea that these individuals are thereby fostering their self-expression or cultivating their critical faculties is fanciful. It is entirely possible that the corporation's electoral message will *conflict* with their personal convictions. Take away the ability to use general treasury funds for some of those ads, and no one's autonomy, dignity, or political equality has been impinged upon in the least.

Corporate expenditures are distinguishable from individual expenditures in this respect. I have taken the view that a legislature may place reasonable restrictions on individuals' electioneering expenditures in the service of the governmental interests explained above, and in recognition of the fact that such restrictions are not direct restraints on speech but rather on its financing. See, *e.g.*, *Randall*, 548 U. S., at 273 (dissenting opinion). But those restrictions concededly present a tougher case, because the primary conduct of actual, flesh-and-blood persons is involved. Some of those individuals might feel that they need to spend large sums of money on behalf of a particular candidate to vindicate the intensity of their electoral preferences. This is obviously not the situation with business corporations, as their routine practice of giving "substantial sums to *both* major national parties" makes pellucidly clear. *McConnell*, 540 U. S., at 148. "[C]orporate participation" in elections, any business executive will tell you, "is more transactional than ideological." Supp. Brief for Committee for Economic Development as *Amicus Curiae* 10.

In this transactional spirit, some corporations have affirmatively urged Congress to place limits on their electioneering communications. These corporations fear that officeholders will shake them down for supportive ads, that they will have to spend increasing sums on elections in an ever-escalating arms race with their competitors, and that public trust in business will be eroded. See *id.*, at 10–19. A system that effectively forces corporations to use their shareholders' money both to maintain access to, and to avoid retribution from, elected officials may ultimately prove more harmful than beneficial to many corporations. It can impose a kind of implicit tax.[4]

In short, regulations such as §203 and the statute upheld in *Austin* impose only a limited burden on First Amendment freedoms not only because they target a narrow subset of expenditures and leave untouched the broader "public dialogue," *ante*, at 25, but also because they leave untouched the speech of natural persons. Recognizing the weakness of a speaker-based

---

[4] Not all corporations support BCRA §203, of course, and not all corporations are large business entities or their tax-exempt adjuncts. Some nonprofit corporations are created for an ideological purpose. Some closely held corporations are strongly identified with a particular owner or founder. The fact that §203, like the statute at issue in *Austin*, regulates some of these corporations' expenditures does not disturb the analysis above. See 494 U. S., at 661–665. Small-business owners may speak in their own names, rather than the business', if they wish to evade §203 altogether. Nonprofit corporations that want to make unrestricted electioneering expenditures may do so if they refuse donations from businesses and unions and permit members to disassociate without economic penalty. See *MCFL*, 479 U. S. 238, 264 (1986). Making it plain that their decision is not motivated by a concern about BCRA's coverage of nonprofits that have ideological missions but lack *MCFL* status, our colleagues refuse to apply the Snowe-Jeffords Amendment or the lower courts' *de minimis* exception to *MCFL*. See *ante*, at 10–12.

critique of *Austin*, the Court places primary emphasis not on the corporation's right to electioneer, but rather on the listener's interest in hearing what every possible speaker may have to say. The Court's central argument is that laws such as §203 have "'deprived [the electorate] of information, knowledge and opinion vital to its function,'" *ante*, at 38 (quoting *CIO*, 335 U. S., at 144 (Rutledge, J., concurring in judgment)), and this, in turn, "interferes with the 'open marketplace' of ideas protected by the First Amendment," *ante*, at 38 (quoting *New York State Bd. of Elections* v. *Lopez Torres*, 552 U. S. 196, 208 (2008)).

There are many flaws in this argument. If the overriding concern depends on the interests of the audience, surely the public's perception of the value of corporate speech should be given important weight. That perception today is the same as it was a century ago when Theodore Roosevelt delivered the speeches to Congress that, in time, led to the limited prohibition on corporate campaign expenditures that is overruled today. See *WRTL*, 551 U. S., at 509–510 (Souter, J., dissenting) (summarizing President Roosevelt's remarks). The distinctive threat to democratic integrity posed by corporate domination of politics was recognized at "the inception of the republic" and "has been a persistent theme in American political life" ever since. Regan 302. It is only certain Members of this Court, not the listeners themselves, who have agitated for more corporate electioneering.

Austin recognized that there are substantial reasons why a legislature might conclude that unregulated general treasury expenditures will give corporations "unfai[r] influence" in the electoral process, 494 U. S., at 660, and distort public debate in ways that undermine rather than advance the interests of listeners. The legal structure of corporations allows them to amass and deploy financial resources on a scale few natural persons can match. The structure of a business corporation, furthermore, draws a line between the corporation's economic interests and the political preferences of the individuals associated with the corporation; the corporation must engage the electoral process with the aim "to enhance the profitability of the company, no matter how persuasive the arguments for a broader or conflicting set of priorities," Brief for American Independent Business Alliance as *Amicus Curiae* 11; see also ALI, Principles of Corporate Governance: Analysis and Recommendations §2.01(a), p. 55 (1992) ("[A] corporation . . . should have as its objective the conduct of business activities with a view to enhancing corporate profit and shareholder gain"). In a state election such as the one at issue in *Austin*, the interests of nonresident corporations may be fundamentally adverse to the interests of local voters. Consequently, when corporations grab up the prime broadcasting slots on the eve of an election, they can flood the market with advocacy that bears "little or no correlation" to the ideas of natural persons or to any broader notion of the public good, 494 U. S., at 660. The opinions of real people may be marginalized. "The expenditure restrictions of [2 U. S. C.] §441b are thus meant to ensure that competition among actors in the political arena is truly competition among ideas." *MCFL*, 479 U. S., at 259.

In addition to this immediate drowning out of noncorporate voices, there may be deleterious effects that follow soon thereafter. Corporate "domination" of electioneering, *Austin*, 494 U. S., at 659, can generate the impression that corporations dominate our democracy. When citizens turn on their televisions and radios before an election and hear only corporate electioneering, they may lose faith in their capacity, as citizens, to influence public policy. A Government captured by corporate interests, they may come to believe, will be neither responsive to their needs nor willing to give their views a fair hearing. The predictable result is cynicism and disenchantment: an increased perception that large spenders "'call the tune'" and a reduced "'willingness of voters to take part in democratic governance.'" *McConnell*, 540 U. S., at 144 (quoting *Shrink Missouri*, 528 U. S., at 390). To the extent that corporations are allowed to exert undue influence in electoral races, the speech of the eventual winners of those races may also be chilled. Politicians who fear that a certain corporation can make or break their reelection chances may be cowed into silence about that corporation. On a variety of levels, unregulated corporate electioneering might diminish the ability of citizens to "hold officials accountable to the people," *ante*, at 23, and disserve the goal of a public debate that is "uninhibited, robust, and wide-open," *New York Times Co. v. Sullivan*, 376 U. S. 254, 270 (1964). At the least, I stress again, a legislature is entitled to credit these concerns and to take tailored measures in response.

The majority's unwillingness to distinguish between corporations and humans similarly blinds it to the possibility that corporations' "war chests" and their special "advantages" in the legal realm, *Austin*, 494 U. S., at 659, may translate into special advantages in the market for legislation. When large numbers of citizens have a common stake in a measure that is under consideration, it may be very difficult for them to coordinate resources on behalf of their position. The corporate form, by contrast, "provides a simple way to channel rents to only those who have paid their dues, as it were. If you do not own stock, you do not benefit from the larger dividends or appreciation in the stock price caused by the passage of private interest legislation." Sitkoff, Corporate Political Speech, Political Extortion, and the Competition for Corporate Charters, 69 U. Chi. L. Rev. 1103, 1113 (2002). Corporations, that is, are uniquely equipped to seek laws that favor their owners, not simply because they have a lot of money but because of their legal and organizational structure. Remove all restrictions on their electioneering, and the door may be opened to a type of rent seeking that is "far more destructive" than what noncorporations are capable of. *Ibid.* It is for reasons such as these that our campaign finance jurisprudence has long appreciated that "the 'differing structures and purposes' of different entities 'may require different forms of regulation in order to protect the integrity of the electoral process.'" *NRWC*, 459 U. S., at 210 (quoting *California Medical Assn.*, 453 U. S., at 201).

The Court's facile depiction of corporate electioneering assumes away all of these complexities. Our colleagues ridicule the idea of regulating expenditures based on "nothing more" than a fear that corporations have a special "ability to persuade," *ante*, at 11 (opinion of ROBERTS, C. J.), as if corporations were our society's ablest debaters and viewpoint-neutral laws such as §203 were created to suppress their best arguments. In their haste to knock down yet another straw man, our colleagues simply ignore the fundamental concerns of the *Austin* Court and the legislatures that have passed laws like §203: to safeguard the integrity, competitiveness, and democratic responsiveness of the electoral process. All of the majority's theoretical arguments turn on a proposition with undeniable surface appeal but little grounding in evidence or experience, "that there is no such thing as too much speech," *Austin*, 494 U. S., at 695 (SCALIA, J., dissenting).[5] If individuals in our society had infinite free time to listen to and contemplate every last bit of speech uttered by anyone, anywhere; and if broadcast advertisements had no special ability to influence elections apart from the merits of their arguments (to the extent they make any); and if legislators always operated with nothing less than perfect virtue; then I suppose the majority's premise would be sound. In the real world, we have seen, corporate domination of the airwaves prior to an election may decrease the average listener's exposure to relevant viewpoints, and it may diminish citizens' willingness and capacity to participate in the democratic process.

None of this is to suggest that corporations can or should be denied an opportunity to participate in election campaigns or in any other public forum (much less that a work of art such as *Mr. Smith Goes to Washington* may be banned), or to deny that some corporate speech may contribute significantly to public

---

[5] Of course, no presiding person in a courtroom, legislature, classroom, polling place, or family dinner would take this hyperbole literally.

debate. What it shows, however, is that *Austin's* "concern about corporate domination of the political process," 494 U. S., at 659, reflects more than a concern to protect governmental interests outside of the First Amendment. It also reflects a concern to *facilitate* First Amendment values by preserving some breathing room around the electoral "marketplace" of ideas, *ante*, at 19, 34, 38, 52, 54, the marketplace in which the actual people of this Nation determine how they will govern themselves. The majority seems oblivious to the simple truth that laws such as §203 do not merely pit the anticorruption interest against the First Amendment, but also pit competing First Amendment values against each other. There are, to be sure, serious concerns with any effort to balance the First Amendment rights of speakers against the First Amendment rights of listeners. But when the speakers in question are not real people and when the appeal to "First Amendment principles" depends almost entirely on the listeners' perspective, *ante*, at 1, 48, it becomes necessary to consider how listeners will actually be affected.

In critiquing *Austin's* antidistortion rationale and campaign finance regulation more generally, our colleagues place tremendous weight on the example of media corporations. See *ante*, at 35–38, 46; *ante*, at 1, 11 (opinion of ROBERTS, C. J.); *ante*, at 6 (opinion of SCALIA, J.). Yet it is not at all clear that *Austin* would permit §203 to be applied to them. The press plays a unique role not only in the text, history, and structure of the First Amendment but also in facilitating public discourse; as the *Austin* Court explained, "media corporations differ significantly from other corporations in that their resources are devoted to the collection of information and its dissemination to the public," 494 U. S., at 667. Our colleagues have raised some interesting and difficult questions about Congress' authority to regulate electioneering by the press, and about how to define what constitutes the press. *But that is not the case before us.* Section 203 does not apply to media corporations, and even if it did, Citizens United is not a media corporation. There would be absolutely no reason to consider the issue of media corporations if the majority did not, first, transform Citizens United's as-applied challenge into a facial challenge and, second, invent the theory that legislatures must eschew all "identity"-based distinctions and treat a local nonprofit news outlet exactly the same as General Motors.[6] This calls to mind George Berkeley's description of philosophers: "[W]e have first raised a dust and then complain we cannot see." Principles of Human Knowledge/Three Dialogues 38, ¶3 (R. Woolhouse ed. 1988).

It would be perfectly understandable if our colleagues feared that a campaign finance regulation such as §203 may be counterproductive or self-interested, and therefore attended carefully to the choices the Legislature has made. But the majority does not bother to consider such practical matters, or even to consult a record; it simply stipulates that "enlightened self-government" can arise only in the absence of regulation. *Ante*, at 23. In light of the distinctive features of corporations identified in *Austin*, there is no valid basis for this assumption. The marketplace of ideas is not actually a place where items— or laws—are meant to be bought and sold, and when we move from the realm of economics to the realm of corporate election-eering, there may be no "reason to think the market ordering is intrinsically good at all," Strauss 1386.

The Court's blinkered and aphoristic approach to the First Amendment may well promote corporate power at the cost of the individual and collective self-expression the Amendment was meant to serve. It will undoubtedly cripple the ability of ordinary citizens, Congress, and the States to adopt even lim-ited measures to protect against corporate domination of the electoral process. Americans may be forgiven if they do not feel the Court has advanced the cause of self-government today.

---

[6] Under the majority's view, the legislature is thus damned if it does and damned if it doesn't. If the legislature gives media corporations an exemption from electioneer-ing regulations that apply to other corporations, it violates the newly minted First Amendment rule against identity-based distinctions. If the legislature does not give media corporations an exemption, it violates the First Amendment rights of the press. The only way out of this invented bind: no regulations whatsoever.

_____

V

Today's decision is backwards in many senses. It elevates the majority's agenda over the litigants' submissions, facial attacks over as-applied claims, broad constitutional theories over narrow statutory grounds, individual dissenting opinions over precedential holdings, assertion over tradition, absolutism over empiricism, rhetoric over reality. Our colleagues have arrived at the conclusion that *Austin* must be overruled and that §203 is facially unconstitutional only after mischaracterizing both the reach and rationale of those authorities, and after bypassing or ignoring rules of judicial restraint used to cabin the Court's lawmaking power. Their conclusion that the societal interest in avoiding corruption and the appearance of corruption does not provide an adequate justification for regulating corporate expenditures on candidate elections relies on an incorrect description of that interest, along with a failure to acknowledge the relevance of established facts and the considered judgments of state and federal legislatures over many decades.

In a democratic society, the longstanding consensus on the need to limit corporate campaign spending should outweigh the wooden application of judge-made rules. The majority's rejection of this principle "elevate[s] corporations to a level of deference which has not been seen at least since the days when substantive due process was regularly used to invalidate regulatory legislation thought to unfairly impinge upon established economic interests." *Bellotti*, 435 U. S., at 817, n. 13 (White, J., dissenting). At bottom, the Court's opinion is thus a rejection of the common sense of the American people, who have recognized a need to prevent corporations from undermining self-government since the founding, and who have fought against the distinctive corrupting potential of corporate electioneering since the days of Theodore Roosevelt. It is a strange time to repudiate that common sense. While American democracy is imperfect, few outside the majority of this Court would have thought its flaws included a dearth of corporate money in politics.

I would affirm the judgment of the District Court.

January 21, 2010

QUESTION 5

Protest: Can We Disobey the Law?

★ ★ ★

The largest protest demonstrations in American history have taken place during Donald Trump's term as President. The Women's March, with more than three million participants nationwide, on January 21, 2017, the day after Trump's inauguration, set a new record. The Women's March the following year was in second place. The massive nationwide protests against police violence and racism in the late spring of 2020 are on a similar scale. Ours seems likely to be remembered as an era of protest, in the United States and around the world. There are mass marches to object to government policies and to promote causes, not just anti-racism but also environmentalism, gay rights, and many more. There are actions by groups that take over a public space for an extended period, as Occupy Wall Street did in lower Manhattan for two months in 2011. There are solo activists like the national security leakers Chelsea Manning and Edward Snowden, who, empowered by digital networks, can make vastly significant protests substantially on their own. There are nationwide grassroots groups, like the right-wing Tea Party organizations that appeared in the months after Barack Obama took office as President.

Protest movements were present at the creation of the United States. The Tea Party groups chose their name to associate themselves with the anti-tax, pre-Revolutionary Boston Tea Party, in 1773. Before the Constitution was framed, Shays' Rebellion, another anti-tax protest, by armed bands of

Revolutionary War veterans in western Massachusetts, was test-
ing the authority of the new state's government. Still, if we are
now in a period of especially vigorous and copious protest, it's
worth asking why that is.

Some of it may be the enabling effects of new technologies,
which, when left unimpeded, give voice to any ordinary citizen
and also offer the opportunity to organize very large numbers of
people around a cause rapidly. Also, America's peculiarly durable two-party system forces the everyday politics of a very large
and varied country into Republican and Democratic categories
that necessarily exclude a great many specific and passionately
held concerns; protest provides another avenue. The country
is becoming steadily more politically polarized, and that would
be a sign that an ever larger cohort of Americans is profoundly
dissatisfied with things as they are. Unhappiness with a policy
is a precondition for protest, but so, increasingly, is unhappiness with the entire system. Whatever the reason, if protest is
flowering, then it's worth examining it closely. What is it? Does
it make a difference whether it takes place within the confines
of the law or outside of them? What types of protest produce
lasting effects, and what types are gestures?

Henry David Thoreau's 1849 essay "Civil Disobedience"
has stood for many years as a fundamental manifesto of American protest. Angry about the annexation of Texas, the Mexi-
can-American War, and the complicity of the non-slaveholding
state of Massachusetts in laws prohibiting the harboring of fugitive slaves, Thoreau refused to pay his local poll tax. He spent
a night in jail. The next day, someone paid his tax for him and
he was released. His essay, excerpted here, was inspired by this
experience but doesn't discuss it in any detail; instead, it is a
brief for the general principle that an individual has an obligation to disobey laws that do not comport with his conscience.
The staying power of "Civil Disobedience" is testament to its
eloquence, to the durability of Thoreau's chosen causes of peace
and racial justice, and to the elegant simplicity of his definition
of protest.

"Civil Disobedience" predates the period when American liberalism was as strongly identified as it is now with a large, active government, at least domestically, on behalf of ordinary people's welfare. It reads today as essentially anarchist rather than liberal. Its opposition to specific government actions is rooted in a broader opposition to just about any government action. It presents majority rule as something to fear, not something to strive for. Thoreau's version of protest is based on political objection, but it takes a determinedly nonpolitical form. He does not dream of using protest to try to build a better world. "I came into this world, not chiefly to make this a good place to live in, but to live in it, be it good or bad," he declares. "It is not my business to be petitioning the Governor or the Legislature." Protest to Thoreau is individual, a demonstration of rejection of the idea of membership in a larger society and a duty to try to change those of its rules that one finds abhorrent. As he puts it, "The only obligation which I have a right to assume, is to do at any time what I think right."

Martin Luther King, Jr., said that he was inspired by reading "Civil Disobedience" as a student, but "Letter from Birmingham Jail," his own enduring protest manifesto, written after he had been arrested and incarcerated for violating a judicial order forbidding his organization to stage a public demonstration, could hardly be more different in its tone or its aims. Its stated purpose is to rebut a statement by a group of white Alabama clergymen objecting to the direct-action tactics the civil rights movement was using to fight racial injustice. King surely knew that he was unlikely to change his opponents' minds, but the framing device naturally pushes his tone in the direction of persuasion rather than pure denunciation. He observes that his movement represents a more moderate alternative to other voices in black America. While eloquently conjuring up the daily suffering and humiliation that black people in the South have to endure, he takes pains to ground his argument within the larger traditions of Christianity and of American history. He quotes Christ and Martin Luther, Jefferson and Lincoln.

He makes it clear that he is not operating as an individual but as part of, almost a servant of, a movement. It's impossible to imagine Thoreau declaring, as King does, "I am here because I have organizational ties here."

King represented disenfranchised people, at a moment in American history when, outside the South, the concept of popular sovereignty for African Americans as well as whites was well and widely established. He could argue that his movement's rather minor violations of the law were techniques it had been forced into, because the conventional methods of political participation, organizing, voting, and lobbying, were closed off by the Jim Crow system. His aim was political reform: legislation that would give black people in the South the full citizenship rights they had only briefly during Reconstruction, nearly a century earlier.

"Letter from Birmingham Jail," and even more so the "I Have a Dream" speech he delivered a few months later during a massive protest march in Washington, show King most closely aligned with at least the twenty-first-century version of mainstream opinion. Within a few years, he was advocating for causes that are still controversial, like eliminating "the giant triplets of racism, extreme materialism, and militarism," and protesting against more elusive targets, like the segregation outside the South that was a pervasive practice but not a legally enshrined code. The protest movements of the period were themselves becoming more vigorous and varied in their targets and techniques. Hannah Arendt's essay on civil disobedience, excerpted here, was written only seven years after King's, but it obviously addresses quite a different moment, when the Vietnam War was the subject of protest by millions of people acting individually and also by millions acting en masse, most peacefully but some violently. It is a product of a moment of peak protest.

Thoreau's essay on civil disobedience clearly struck Arendt, a superbly well-educated political philosopher and a refugee from Nazi Germany, as jejune. Meaningful protest, she argued, could not be merely an expression of individual conscience. It had to be aimed at a target in society, something that ought to be changed. To Arendt, all personal convictions do not deserve to be honored merely because they are sincere. A protestor is a citizen and protest should be grounded in a larger principle. Protestors like King, or the opponents of the Vietnam War, occupy a higher plane than Thoreau because they have chosen to organize themselves in the hope of achieving a civic goal that was inaccessible through conventional politics. Arendt was writing during a time of systemic failure of political institutions. In looking for an intellectual guiding spirit for the protests of the late 1960s, she preferred, counterintuitively, Alexis de Tocqueville to Thoreau, and she chose to see antiwar protests as an example of the American tendency to form associations that had made such a strong impression on Tocqueville. Arendt argued that "civil disobedients are nothing but the latest form of voluntary association," and that the breakdown of established institutions had "changed voluntary association into civil dis-obedience and transformed dissent into resistance."

One could argue that Arendt, though she understood protest as being more political than Thoreau did, still under-estimated its political nature. The Tocquevillean voluntary associations that form the core of the American protest tradi-tion, she wrote, "are ad-hoc organizations that pursue short-term goals and disappear when the goal has been reached." Really? Recently a number of scholars, notably the political scientist Theda Skocpol, have argued persuasively that Tocqueville and his latter-day celebrators had it wrong. The voluntary associations of the early republic were not nonpolitical, they were prepolitical. The most effective of them (like the early temperance and sabbatarian societies, or, more recently, the Tea Party groups) organized themselves into national organizations with local and state chapters, achieved their political goals, and remained in business in order to pursue new goals or to protect their gains. And leaders of these associations regularly have gone on to become inside-the-system elected politicians, in the manner of civil rights leaders such as Andrew Young and John

Lewis. Even an evanescent protest movement, like Occupy Wall Street, can help begin a process that leads to politicians being elected to office. Protest can simply raise consciousness, or it can win in the concrete political sense. It can stage itself in flagrant violation of law and politics, or in concert with them. In all instances, though, at its best, it doesn't simply disappear.

Henry David Thoreau: from Civil Disobedience

I heartily accept the motto,—"That government is best which governs least"; and I should like to see it acted up to more rapidly and systematically. Carried out, it finally amounts to this, which also I believe,—"That government is best which governs not at all"; and when men are prepared for it, that will be the kind of government which they will have. Government is at best but an expedient; but most governments are usually, and all governments are sometimes, inexpedient. The objections which have been brought against a standing army, and they are many and weighty, and deserve to prevail, may also at last be brought against a standing government. The standing army is only an arm of the standing government. The government itself, which is only the mode which the people have chosen to execute their will, is equally liable to be abused and perverted before the people can act through it. Witness the present Mexican war, the work of comparatively a few individuals using the standing government as their tool; for, in the outset, the people would not have consented to this measure.

This American government,—what is it but a tradition, though a recent one, endeavoring to transmit itself unimpaired to posterity, but each instant losing some of its integrity? It has not the vitality and force of a single living man; for a single man can bend it to his will. It is a sort of wooden gun to the people themselves. But it is not the less necessary for this; for the people must have some complicated machinery or other, and hear its din, to satisfy that idea of government which they have. Governments show thus how successfully men can be imposed on, even impose on themselves, for their own advantage. It is excellent, we must all allow. Yet this government never of itself furthered any enterprise, but by the alacrity with which it got out of its way. *It* does not keep the country free. *It* does not settle the West. *It* does not educate. The character inherent in the American people has done all that has been accomplished; and it would have done somewhat more, if the government had not sometimes got in its way. For government is an expedient by which men would fain succeed in letting one another alone; and, as has been said, when it is most expedient, the governed are most let alone by it. Trade and commerce, if they were not made of India-rubber, would never manage to bounce over the obstacles which legislators are continually putting in their way; and, if one were to judge these men wholly by the effects of their actions and not partly by their intentions, they would deserve to be classed and punished with those mischievous persons who put obstructions on the railroads.

But, to speak practically and as a citizen, unlike those who call themselves no-government men, I ask for, not at once no government, but *at once* a better government. Let every man make known what kind of government would command his respect, and that will be one step toward obtaining it.

After all, the practical reason why, when the power is once in the hands of the people, a majority are permitted, and for a long period continue, to rule, is not because they are most likely to be in the right, nor because this seems fairest to the minority, but because they are physically the strongest. But a government in which the majority rule in all cases cannot be based on justice, even as far as men understand it. Can there not be a government in which majorities do not virtually decide right and wrong, but conscience?—in which majorities decide only those questions to which the rule of expediency is applicable? Must the citizen ever for a moment, or in the least degree, resign his conscience to the legislator? Why has every man a conscience, then? I think that we should be men first, and subjects afterward. It is not desirable to cultivate a respect for the law, so much as for the right. The only obligation which

I have a right to assume, is to do at any time what I think right. It is truly enough said, that a corporation has no conscience; but a corporation of conscientious men is a corporation *with* a conscience. Law never made men a whit more just; and, by means of their respect for it, even the well-disposed are daily made the agents of injustice. A common and natural result of an undue respect for law is, that you may see a file of soldiers, colonel, captain, corporal, privates, powder-monkeys, and all, marching in admirable order over hill and dale to the wars, against their wills, ay, against their common sense and consciences, which makes it very steep marching indeed, and produces a palpitation of the heart. They have no doubt that it is a damnable business in which they are concerned; they are all peaceably inclined. Now, what are they? Men at all? or small movable forts and magazines, at the service of some unscrupulous man in power? Visit the Navy-Yard, and behold a marine, such a man as an American government can make, or such as it can make a man with its black arts,—a mere shadow and reminiscence of humanity, a man laid out alive and standing, and already, as one may say, buried under arms with funeral accompaniments, though it may be,—

> "Not a drum was heard, not a funeral note,
>   As his corse to the rampart we hurried;
> Not a soldier discharged his farewell shot
>   O'er the grave where our hero we buried."

The mass of men serve the state thus, not as men mainly, but as machines, with their bodies. They are the standing army, and the militia, jailers, constables, posse comitatus, &c. In most cases there is no free exercise whatever of the judgment or of the moral sense; but they put themselves on a level with wood and earth and stones; and wooden men can perhaps be manufactured that will serve the purpose as well. Such command no more respect than men of straw or a lump of dirt. They have the same sort of worth only as horses and dogs. Yet such as these even are commonly esteemed good citizens. Others,—as most legislators, politicians, lawyers, ministers, and office-holders,— serve the state chiefly with their heads; and, as they rarely make any moral distinctions, they are as likely to serve the Devil, without *intending* it, as God. A very few, as heroes, patriots, martyrs, reformers in the great sense, and *men*, serve the state with their consciences also, and so necessarily resist it for the most part; and they are commonly treated as enemies by it. A wise man will only be useful as a man, and will not submit to be "clay," and "stop a hole to keep the wind away," but leave that office to his dust at least:—

> "I am too high-born to be propertied,
> To be a secondary at control,
> Or useful serving-man and instrument
> To any sovereign state throughout the world."

He who gives himself entirely to his fellow-men appears to them useless and selfish; but he who gives himself partially to them is pronounced a benefactor and philanthropist.

How does it become a man to behave toward this American government to-day? I answer, that he cannot without disgrace be associated with it. I cannot for an instant recognize that political organization as *my* government which is the *slave's* government also.

All men recognize the right of revolution; that is, the right to refuse allegiance to, and to resist, the government, when its tyranny or its inefficiency are great and unendurable. But almost all say that such is not the case now. But such was the case, they think, in the Revolution of '75. If one were to tell me that this was a bad government because it taxed certain foreign commodities brought to its ports, it is most probable that I should not make an ado about it, for I can do without them. All machines have their friction; and possibly this does enough good to counterbalance the evil. At any rate, it is a great evil to make a stir about it. But when the friction comes to have its machine, and oppression and robbery are organized, I say, let us not have such a machine any longer. In other words, when a sixth of the population of a nation which has undertaken to be the refuge of liberty are slaves, and a whole country is unjustly overrun and conquered by a foreign army, and subjected to military law, I think that it is not too soon for honest men to rebel and revolutionize. What makes this duty the more urgent is the fact, that the country so overrun is not our own, but ours is the invading army.

Paley, a common authority with many on moral questions, in his chapter on the "Duty of Submission to Civil Government," resolves all civil obligation into expediency; and he proceeds to say, "that so long as the interest of the whole society requires it, that is, so long as the established government cannot be resisted or changed without public inconveniency, it is the will of God that the established government be obeyed, and no longer. . . . This principle being admitted, the justice of every particular case of resistance is reduced to a computation of the quantity of the danger and grievance on the one side, and of the probability and expense of redressing it on the other." Of this, he says, every man shall judge for himself. But Paley appears never to have contemplated those cases to which the rule of expediency does not apply, in which a people, as well as an individual, must do justice, cost what it may. If I have unjustly wrested a plank from a drowning man, I must restore it to him though I drown myself. This, according to Paley, would be inconvenient. But he that would save his life, in such a case, shall lose it. This people must cease to hold slaves, and to make war on Mexico, though it cost them their existence as a people.

In their practice, nations agree with Paley; but does any one think that Massachusetts does exactly what is right at the present crisis?

"A drab of state, a cloth-o'-silver slut,
To have her train borne up, and her soul trail in the dirt."

Practically speaking, the opponents to a reform in Massachusetts are not a hundred thousand politicians at the South, but
a hundred thousand merchants and farmers here, who are
more interested in commerce and agriculture than they are in
humanity, and are not prepared to do justice to the slave and
to Mexico, *cost what it may*. I quarrel not with far-off foes, but
with those who, near at home, co-operate with, and do the
bidding of, those far away, and without whom the latter would
be harmless. We are accustomed to say, that the mass of men are
unprepared; but improvement is slow, because the few are not
materially wiser or better than the many. It is not so important
that many should be as good as you, as that there be some absolute goodness somewhere; for that will leaven the whole lump.
There are thousands who are *in opinion* opposed to slavery and
to the war, who yet in effect do nothing to put an end to them;
who, esteeming themselves children of Washington and Franklin, sit down with their hands in their pockets, and say that
they know not what to do, and do nothing; who even postpone
the question of freedom to the question of free-trade, and quietly read the prices-current along with the latest advices from
Mexico, after dinner, and, it may be, fall asleep over them both.
What is the price-current of an honest man and patriot to-day?
They hesitate, and they regret, and sometimes they petition;
but they do nothing in earnest and with effect. They will wait,
well disposed, for others to remedy the evil, that they may no
longer have it to regret. At most, they give only a cheap vote,
and a feeble countenance and God-speed, to the right, as it
goes by them. There are nine hundred and ninety-nine patrons
of virtue to one virtuous man. But it is easier to deal with the
real possessor of a thing than with the temporary guardian of it.

All voting is a sort of gaming, like checkers or backgam-
mon, with a slight moral tinge to it, a playing with right and
wrong, with moral questions; and betting naturally accompa-
nies it. The character of the voters is not staked. I cast my vote,
perchance, as I think right; but I am not vitally concerned that
that right should prevail. I am willing to leave it to the majority.

Its obligation, therefore, never exceeds that of expediency. Even voting *for the right* is *doing* nothing for it. It is only expressing to men feebly your desire that it should prevail. A wise man will not leave the right to the mercy of chance, nor wish it to prevail through the power of the majority. There is but little virtue in the action of masses of men. When the majority shall at length vote for the abolition of slavery, it will be because they are indifferent to slavery, or because there is but little slavery left to be abolished by their vote. *They* will then be the only slaves. Only *his* vote can hasten the abolition of slavery who asserts his own freedom by his vote.

I hear of a convention to be held at Baltimore, or elsewhere, for the selection of a candidate for the Presidency, made up chiefly of editors, and men who are politicians by profession; but I think, what is it to any independent, intelligent, and respectable man what decision they may come to? Shall we not have the advantage of his wisdom and honesty, nevertheless? Can we not count upon some independent votes? Are there not many individuals in the country who do not attend conventions? But no: I find that the respectable man, so called, has immediately drifted from his position, and despairs of his country, when his country has more reason to despair of him. He forthwith adopts one of the candidates thus selected as the only *available* one, thus proving that he is himself *available* for any purposes of the demagogue. His vote is of no more worth than that of any unprincipled foreigner or hireling native, who may have been bought. O for a man who is a *man*, and, as my neighbor says, has a bone in his back which you cannot pass your hand through! Our statistics are at fault: the population has been returned too large. How many *men* are there to a square thousand miles in this country? Hardly one. Does not America offer any inducement for men to settle here? The American has dwindled into an Odd Fellow,—one who may be known by the development of his organ of gregariousness, and a manifest lack of intellect and cheerful self-reliance; whose first and chief concern, on coming into the world, is to see that the

Almshouses are in good repair; and, before yet he has lawfully donned the virile garb, to collect a fund for the support of the widows and orphans that may be; who, in short, ventures to live only by the aid of the Mutual Insurance company, which has promised to bury him decently.

It is not a man's duty, as a matter of course, to devote himself to the eradication of any, even the most enormous wrong; he may still properly have other concerns to engage him; but it is his duty, at least, to wash his hands of it, and, if he gives it no thought longer, not to give it practically his support. If I devote myself to other pursuits and contemplations, I must first see, at least, that I do not pursue them sitting upon another man's shoulders. I must get off him first, that he may pursue his contemplations too. See what gross inconsistency is tolerated. I have heard some of my townsmen say, "I should like to have them order me out to help put down an insurrection of the slaves, or to march to Mexico;—see if I would go"; and yet these very men have each, directly by their allegiance, and so indirectly, at least, by their money, furnished a substitute. The soldier is applauded who refuses to serve in an unjust war by those who do not refuse to sustain the unjust government which makes the war; is applauded by those whose own act and authority he disregards and sets at naught; as if the State were penitent to that degree that it hired one to scourge it while it sinned, but not to that degree that it left off sinning for a moment. Thus, under the name of Order and Civil Government, we are all made at last to pay homage to and support our own meanness. After the first blush of sin comes its indifference; and from immoral it becomes, as it were, *un*moral, and not quite unnecessary to that life which we have made.

The broadest and most prevalent error requires the most disinterested virtue to sustain it. The slight reproach to which the virtue of patriotism is commonly liable, the noble are most likely to incur. Those who, while they disapprove of the character and measures of a government, yield to it their allegiance and support, are undoubtedly its most conscientious supporters, and so frequently the most serious obstacles to reform. Some are petitioning the State to dissolve the Union, to disregard the requisitions of the President. Why do they not dissolve it themselves,—the union between themselves and the State,—and refuse to pay their quota into its treasury? Do not they stand in the same relation to the State, that the State does to the Union? And have not the same reasons prevented the State from resisting the Union, which have prevented them from resisting the State?

How can a man be satisfied to entertain an opinion merely, and enjoy *it*? Is there any enjoyment in it, if his opinion is that he is aggrieved? If you are cheated out of a single dollar by your neighbor, you do not rest satisfied with knowing that you are cheated, or with saying that you are cheated, or even with petitioning him to pay you your due; but you take effectual steps at once to obtain the full amount, and see that you are never cheated again. Action from principle, the perception and the performance of right, changes things and relations; it is essentially revolutionary, and does not consist wholly with anything which was. It not only divides states and churches, it divides families; ay, it divides the *individual*, separating the diabolical in him from the divine.

Unjust laws exist: shall we be content to obey them, or shall we endeavor to amend them, and obey them until we have succeeded, or shall we transgress them at once? Men generally, under such a government as this, think that they ought to wait until they have persuaded the majority to alter them. They think that, if they should resist, the remedy would be worse than the evil. But it is the fault of the government itself that the remedy *is* worse than the evil. *It* makes it worse. Why is it not more apt to anticipate and provide for reform? Why does it not cherish its wise minority? Why does it cry and resist before it is hurt? Why does it not encourage its citizens to be on the alert to point out its faults, and *do* better than it would have them? Why does it always crucify Christ, and excommunicate Copernicus and Luther, and pronounce Washington and Franklin rebels?

One would think, that a deliberate and practical denial of its authority was the only offence never contemplated by government; else, why has it not assigned its definite, its suitable and proportionate penalty? If a man who has no property refuses but once to earn nine shillings for the State, he is put in prison for a period unlimited by any law that I know, and determined only by the discretion of those who placed him there; but if he should steal ninety times nine shillings from the State, he is soon permitted to go at large again.

If the injustice is part of the necessary friction of the machine of government, let it go, let it go: perchance it will wear smooth,—certainly the machine will wear out. If the injustice has a spring, or a pulley, or a rope, or a crank, exclusively for itself, then perhaps you may consider whether the remedy will not be worse than the evil; but if it is of such a nature that it requires you to be the agent of injustice to another, then, I say, break the law. Let your life be a counter friction to stop the machine. What I have to do is to see, at any rate, that I do not lend myself to the wrong which I condemn.

As for adopting the ways which the State has provided for remedying the evil, I know not of such ways. They take too much time, and a man's life will be gone. I have other affairs to attend to. I came into this world, not chiefly to make this a good place to live in, but to live in it, be it good or bad. A man has not everything to do, but something; and because he cannot do *everything*, it is not necessary that he should do *something* wrong. It is not my business to be petitioning the Governor or the Legislature any more than it is theirs to petition me; and, if they should not hear my petition, what should I do then? But in this case the State has provided no way: its very Constitution is the evil. This may seem to be harsh and stubborn and unconciliatory; but it is to treat with the utmost kindness and consideration the only spirit that can appreciate or deserves it. So is all change for the better, like birth and death, which convulse the body.

I do not hesitate to say, that those who call themselves Abolitionists should at once effectually withdraw their support, both in person and property, from the government of Massachusetts, and not wait till they constitute a majority of one, before they suffer the right to prevail through them. I think that it is enough if they have God on their side, without waiting for that other one. Moreover, any man more right than his neighbors constitutes a majority of one already.

I meet this American government, or its representative, the State government, directly, and face to face, once a year—no more—in the person of its tax-gatherer; this is the only mode in which a man situated as I am necessarily meets it; and it then says distinctly, Recognize me; and the simplest, the most effectual, and, in the present posture of affairs, the indispensablest mode of treating with it on this head, of expressing your little satisfaction with and love for it, is to deny it then. My civil neighbor, the tax-gatherer, is the very man I have to deal with,—for it is, after all, with men and not with parchment that I quarrel,—and he has voluntarily chosen to be an agent of the government. How shall he ever know well what he is and does as an officer of the government, or as a man, until he is obliged to consider whether he shall treat me, his neighbor, for whom he has respect, as a neighbor and well-disposed man, or as a maniac and disturber of the peace, and see if he can get over this obstruction to his neighborliness without a ruder and more impetuous thought or speech corresponding with his action. I know this well, that if one thousand, if one hundred, if ten men whom I could name,—if ten *honest* men only,—ay, if *one* HONEST man, in this State of Massachusetts, *ceasing to hold slaves*, were actually to withdraw from this copartnership, and be locked up in the county jail therefor, it would be the abolition of slavery in America. For it matters not how small the beginning may seem to be: what is once well done is done forever. But we love better to talk about it: that we say is our mission. Reform keeps many scores of newspapers in its service, but not one man. If my esteemed neighbor, the State's ambassador, who will devote his days to the settlement of the question of human rights in the Council Chamber, instead of being threatened with the prisons of Carolina, were to sit down the prisoner of Massachusetts, that State which is so anxious to foist the sin of slavery upon her sister,—though at present she can discover only an act of inhospitality to be the ground of a quarrel with her,—the Legislature would not wholly waive the subject the following winter.

Under a government which imprisons any unjustly, the true place for a just man is also a prison. The proper place to-day, the only place which Massachusetts has provided for her freer and less desponding spirits, is in her prisons, to be put out and locked out of the State by her own act, as they have already put themselves out by their principles. It is there that the fugitive slave, and the Mexican prisoner on parole, and the Indian come to plead the wrongs of his race, should find them; on that separate, but more free and honorable ground, where the State places those who are not *with* her, but *against* her,—the only house in a slave State in which a free man can abide with honor. If any think that their influence would be lost there, and their voices no longer afflict the ear of the State, that they would not be as an enemy within its walls, they do not know by how much truth is stronger than error, nor how much more eloquently and effectively he can combat injustice who has experienced a little in his own person. Cast your whole vote, not a strip of paper merely, but your whole influence. A minority is powerless while it conforms to the majority; it is not even a minority then; but it is irresistible when it clogs by its whole weight. If the alternative is to keep all just men in prison, or give up war and slavery, the State will not hesitate which to choose. If a thousand men were not to pay their tax-bills this year, that would not be a violent and bloody measure, as it would be to pay them, and enable the State to commit violence and shed innocent blood. This is, in fact, the definition of a peaceable revolution, if any such is possible. If the tax-gatherer, or any other public officer, asks me, as one has done, "But what shall I do?" my answer is, "If you really wish to do anything, resign your office." When the subject has refused allegiance, and the officer has resigned his office, then the revolution is accomplished. But even suppose blood should flow. Is there not a sort of blood shed when the conscience is wounded? Through this wound a man's real manhood and immortality flow out, and he bleeds to an everlasting death. I see this blood flowing now.

I have contemplated the imprisonment of the offender, rather than the seizure of his goods,—though both will serve the same purpose,—because they who assert the purest right, and consequently are most dangerous to a corrupt State, commonly have not spent much time in accumulating property. To such the State renders comparatively small service, and a slight tax is wont to appear exorbitant, particularly if they are obliged to earn it by special labor with their hands. If there were one who lived wholly without the use of money, the State itself would hesitate to demand it of him. But the rich man,—not to make any invidious comparison,—is always sold to the institution which makes him rich. Absolutely speaking, the more money, the less virtue; for money comes between a man and his objects, and obtains them for him; and it was certainly no great virtue to obtain it. It puts to rest many questions which he would otherwise be taxed to answer; while the only new question which it puts is the hard but superfluous one, how to spend it. Thus his moral ground is taken from under his feet. The opportunities of living are diminished in proportion as what are called the "means" are increased. The best thing a man can do for his culture when he is rich is to endeavor to carry out those schemes which he entertained when he was poor. Christ answered the Herodians according to their condition. "Show me the tribute-money," said he;—and one took a penny out of his pocket;—if you use money which has the image of Cæsar on it, and which he has made current and valuable, that is, *if you are men of the State*, and gladly enjoy the advantages of Cæsar's government, then pay him back some of his own when he demands it; "Render therefore to Cæsar that which is Cæsar's, and to God those things which are God's,"—leaving them no wiser than before as to which was which; for they did not wish to know.

When I converse with the freest of my neighbors, I perceive that, whatever they may say about the magnitude and seriousness of the question, and their regard for the public tranquillity, the long and the short of the matter is, that they cannot spare the protection of the existing government, and they dread the consequences to their property and families of disobedience to it. For my own part, I should not like to think that I ever rely on the protection of the State. But, if I deny the authority of the State when it presents its tax-bill, it will soon take and waste all my property, and so harass me and my children without end. This is hard. This makes it impossible for a man to live honestly, and at the same time comfortably, in outward respects. It will not be worth the while to accumulate property; that would be sure to go again. You must hire or squat somewhere, and raise but a small crop, and eat that soon. You must live within yourself, and depend upon yourself always tucked up and ready for a start, and not have many affairs. A man may grow rich in Turkey even, if he will be in all respects a good subject of the Turkish government. Confucius said: "If a state is governed by the principles of reason, poverty and misery are subjects of shame; if a state is not governed by the principles of reason, riches and honors are the subjects of shame." No: until I want the protection of Massachusetts to be extended to me in some distant Southern port, where my liberty is endangered, or until I am bent solely on building up an estate at home by peaceful enterprise, I can afford to refuse allegiance to Massachusetts, and her right to my property and life. It costs me less in every sense to incur the penalty of disobedience to the State, than it would to obey. I should feel as if I were worth less in that case.

Some years ago, the State met me in behalf of the Church, and commanded me to pay a certain sum toward the support of a clergyman whose preaching my father attended, but never I myself. "Pay," it said, "or be locked up in the jail." I declined to pay. But, unfortunately, another man saw fit to pay it. I did not see why the schoolmaster should be taxed to support the priest, and not the priest the schoolmaster; for I was not the State's schoolmaster, but I supported myself by voluntary subscription. I did not see why the lyceum should not present its tax-bill, and have the State to back its demand, as well as the Church. However, at the request of the selectmen, I condescended to make some such statement as this in writing:—"Know all men by these presents, that I, Henry Thoreau, do not wish to be regarded as a member of any incorporated society which I have not joined." This I gave to the town clerk; and he has it. The State, having thus learned that I did not wish to be regarded as a member of that church, has never made a like demand on me since; though it said that it must adhere to its original presumption that time. If I had known how to name them, I should then have signed off in detail from all the societies which I never signed on to; but I did not know where to find a complete list.

I have paid no poll-tax for six years. I was put into a jail once on this account, for one night; and, as I stood considering the walls of solid stone, two or three feet thick, the door of wood and iron, a foot thick, and the iron grating which strained the light, I could not help being struck with the foolishness of that institution which treated me as if I were mere flesh and blood and bones, to be locked up. I wondered that it should have concluded at length that this was the best use it could put me to, and had never thought to avail itself of my services in some way. I saw that, if there was a wall of stone between me and my townsmen, there was a still more difficult one to climb or break through, before they could get to be as free as I was. I did not for a moment feel confined, and the walls seemed a great waste of stone and mortar. I felt as if I alone of all my townsmen had paid my tax. They plainly did not know how to treat me, but behaved like persons who are underbred. In every threat and in every compliment there was a blunder; for they thought that my chief desire was to stand the other side of that stone wall.

I could not but smile to see how industriously they locked the door on my meditations, which followed them out again without let or hindrance, and *they* were really all that was dangerous. As they could not reach me, they had resolved to punish my body; just as boys, if they cannot come at some person against whom they have a spite, will abuse his dog. I saw that the State was half-witted, that it was timid as a lone woman with her silver spoons, and that it did not know its friends from its foes, and I lost all my remaining respect for it, and pitied it.

Thus the State never intentionally confronts a man's sense, intellectual or moral, but only his body, his senses. It is not armed with superior wit or honesty, but with superior physical strength. I was not born to be forced. I will breathe after my own fashion. Let us see who is the strongest. What force has a multitude? They only can force me who obey a higher law than I. They force me to become like themselves. I do not hear of *men* being *forced* to live this way or that by masses of men. What sort of life were that to live? When I meet a government which says to me, "Your money or your life," why should I be in haste to give it my money? It may be in a great strait, and not know what to do: I cannot help that. It must help itself; do as I do. It is not worth the while to snivel about it. I am not responsible for the successful working of the machinery of society. I am not the son of the engineer. I perceive that, when an acorn and a chestnut fall side by side, the one does not remain inert to make way for the other, but both obey their own laws, and spring and grow and flourish as best they can, till one, perchance, overshadows and destroys the other. If a plant cannot live according to its nature, it dies; and so a man.

A Yankee in Canada, with Anti-Slavery and Reform Papers (1866)

★ ★ ★

Martin Luther King, Jr.: Letter from Birmingham Jail

April 16, 1963

MY DEAR FELLOW CLERGYMEN:

While confined here in the Birmingham city jail, I came across your recent statement calling my present activities "unwise and untimely." Seldom do I pause to answer criticism of my work and ideas. If I sought to answer all the criticisms that cross my desk, my secretaries would have little time for anything other than such correspondence in the course of the day, and I would have no time for constructive work. But since I feel that you are men of genuine good will and that your criticisms are sincerely set forth, I want to try to answer your statement in what I hope will be patient and reasonable terms.

I think I should indicate why I am here in Birmingham, since you have been influenced by the view which argues against "outsiders coming in." I have the honor of serving as president of the Southern Christian Leadership Conference, an organization operating in every southern state, with headquarters in Atlanta, Georgia. We have some eighty-five affiliated

AUTHOR'S NOTE: This response to a published statement by eight fellow clergymen from Alabama (Bishop C. C. J. Carpenter, Bishop Joseph A. Durick, Rabbi Hilton L. Grafman, Bishop Paul Hardin, Bishop Holan B. Harmon, the Reverend George M. Murray, the Reverend Edward V. Ramage and the Reverend Earl Stallings) was composed under somewhat constricting circumstances. Begun on the margins of the newspaper in which the statement appeared while I was in jail, the letter was continued on scraps of writing paper supplied by a friendly Negro trusty, and concluded on a pad my attorneys were eventually permitted to leave me. Although the text remains in substance unaltered, I have indulged in the author's prerogative of polishing it for publication.

organizations across the South, and one of them is the Alabama Christian Movement for Human Rights. Frequently we share staff, educational and financial resources with our affiliates. Several months ago the affiliate here in Birmingham asked us to be on call to engage in a nonviolent direct-action program if such were deemed necessary. We readily consented, and when the hour came we lived up to our promise. So I, along with several members of my staff, am here because I was invited here. I am here because I have organizational ties here.

But more basically, I am in Birmingham because injustice is here. Just as the prophets of the eighth century B.C. left their villages and carried their "thus saith the Lord" far beyond the boundaries of their home towns, and just as the Apostle Paul left his village of Tarsus and carried the gospel of Jesus Christ to the far corners of the Greco-Roman world, so am I compelled to carry the gospel of freedom beyond my own home town. Like Paul, I must constantly respond to the Macedonian call for aid.

Moreover, I am cognizant of the interrelatedness of all communities and states. I cannot sit idly by in Atlanta and not be concerned about what happens in Birmingham. Injustice anywhere is a threat to justice everywhere. We are caught in an inescapable network of mutuality, tied in a single garment of destiny. Whatever affects one directly, affects all indirectly. Never again can we afford to live with the narrow, provincial "outside agitator" idea. Anyone who lives inside the United States can never be considered an outsider anywhere within its bounds.

You deplore the demonstrations taking place in Birmingham. But your statement, I am sorry to say, fails to express a similar concern for the conditions that brought about the demonstrations. I am sure that none of you would want to rest content with the superficial kind of social analysis that deals merely with effects and does not grapple with underlying causes. It is unfortunate that demonstrations are taking place in Birmingham, but it is even more unfortunate that the city's white power structure left the Negro community with no alternative.

In any nonviolent campaign there are four basic steps: collection of the facts to determine whether injustices exist; negotiation; self-purification; and direct action. We have gone through all these steps in Birmingham. There can be no gainsaying the fact that racial injustice engulfs this community. Birmingham is probably the most thoroughly segregated city in the United States. Its ugly record of brutality is widely known. Negroes have experienced grossly unjust treatment in the courts. There have been more unsolved bombings of Negro homes and churches in Birmingham than in any other city in the nation. These are the hard, brutal facts of the case. On the basis of these conditions, Negro leaders sought to negotiate with the city fathers. But the latter consistently refused to engage in good-faith negotiation.

Then, last September, came the opportunity to talk with leaders of Birmingham's economic community. In the course of the negotiations, certain promises were made by the merchants—for example, to remove the stores' humiliating racial signs. On the basis of these promises, the Reverend Fred Shuttlesworth and the leaders of the Alabama Christian Movement for Human Rights agreed to a moratorium on all demonstrations. As the weeks and months went by, we realized that we were the victims of a broken promise. A few signs, briefly removed, returned; the others remained.

As in so many past experiences, our hopes had been blasted, and the shadow of deep disappointment settled upon us. We had no alternative except to prepare for direct action, whereby we would present our very bodies as a means of laying our case before the conscience of the local and the national community. Mindful of the difficulties involved, we decided to undertake a process of self-purification. We began a series of workshops on nonviolence, and we repeatedly asked ourselves: "Are you able to accept blows without retaliating?" "Are you able to endure the ordeal of jail?" We decided to schedule our direct-action program for the Easter season, realizing that except for Christmas, this is the main shopping period of the year. Knowing that a strong economic-withdrawal program would be the by-product of direct action, we felt that this would be the best time to bring pressure to bear on the merchants for the needed change.

Then it occurred to us that Birmingham's mayoral election was coming up in March, and we speedily decided to postpone action until after election day. When we discovered that the Commissioner of Public Safety, Eugene "Bull" Connor, had piled up enough votes to be in the run-off, we decided again to postpone action until the day after the run-off so that the demonstrations could not be used to cloud the issues. Like many others, we waited to see Mr. Connor defeated, and to this end we endured postponement after postponement. Having aided in this community need, we felt that our direct-action program could be delayed no longer.

You may well ask: "Why direct action? Why sit-ins, marches and so forth? Isn't negotiation a better path?" You are quite right in calling for negotiation. Indeed, this is the very purpose of direct action. Nonviolent direct action seeks to create such a crisis and foster such a tension that a community which has constantly refused to negotiate is forced to confront the issue. It seeks so to dramatize the issue that it can no longer be ignored. My citing the creation of tension as part of the work of the nonviolent-resister may sound rather shocking. But I must confess that I am not afraid of the word "tension." I have earnestly opposed violent tension, but there is a type of constructive, nonviolent tension which is necessary for growth. Just as Socrates felt that it was necessary to create a tension in the mind so that individuals could rise from the bondage of myths and half-truths to the unfettered realm of creative analysis and objective appraisal, so must we see the need for nonviolent gadflies to create the kind of tension in society that will help men rise from the dark depths of prejudice and racism to the majestic heights of understanding and brotherhood.

The purpose of our direct-action program is to create a situation so crisis-packed that it will inevitably open the door to negotiation. I therefore concur with you in your call for negotiation. Too long has our beloved Southland been bogged down in a tragic effort to live in monologue rather than dialogue.

One of the basic points in your statement is that the action that I and my associates have taken in Birmingham is untimely. Some have asked: "Why didn't you give the new city administration time to act?" The only answer that I can give to this query is that the new Birmingham administration must be prodded about as much as the outgoing one, before it will act. We are sadly mistaken if we feel that the election of Albert Boutwell as mayor will bring the millennium to Birmingham. While Mr. Boutwell is a much more gentle person than Mr. Connor, they are both segregationists, dedicated to maintenance of the status quo. I have hope that Mr. Boutwell will be reasonable enough to see the futility of massive resistance to desegregation. But he will not see this without pressure from devotees of civil rights. My friends, I must say to you that we have not made a single gain in civil rights without determined legal and nonviolent pressure. Lamentably, it is an historical fact that privileged groups seldom give up their privileges voluntarily. Individuals may see the moral light and voluntarily give up their unjust posture; but, as Reinhold Niebuhr has reminded us, groups tend to be more immoral than individuals.

We know through painful experience that freedom is never voluntarily given by the oppressor; it must be demanded by the oppressed. Frankly, I have yet to engage in a direct-action campaign that was "well timed" in the view of those who have not suffered unduly from the disease of segregation. For years now I have heard the word "Wait!" It rings in the ear of every Negro with piercing familiarity. This "Wait" has almost always meant "Never." We must come to see, with one of our distinguished jurists, that "justice too long delayed is justice denied."

We have waited for more than 340 years for our constitutional and God-given rights. The nations of Asia and Africa are moving with jetlike speed toward gaining political independence, but we still creep at horse-and-buggy pace toward gaining a cup of coffee at a lunch counter. Perhaps it is easy for those who have never felt the stinging darts of segregation to say, "Wait." But when you have seen vicious mobs lynch your mothers and fathers at will and drown your sisters and brothers at whim; when you have seen hate-filled policemen curse, kick and even kill your black brothers and sisters; when you see the vast majority of your twenty million Negro brothers smothering in an airtight cage of poverty in the midst of an affluent society; when you suddenly find your tongue twisted and your speech stammering as you seek to explain to your six-year-old daughter why she can't go to the public amusement park that has just been advertised on television, and see tears welling up in her eyes when she is told that Funtown is closed to colored children, and see ominous clouds of inferiority beginning to form in her little mental sky, and see her beginning to distort her personality by developing an unconscious bitterness toward white people; when you have to concoct an answer for a five-year-old son who is asking: "Daddy, why do white people treat colored people so mean?"; when you take a cross-country drive and find it necessary to sleep night after night in the uncomfortable corners of your automobile because no motel will accept you; when you are humiliated day in and day out by nagging signs reading "white" and "colored"; when your first name becomes "nigger," your middle name becomes "boy" (however old you are) and your last name becomes "John," and your wife and mother are never given the respected title "Mrs."; when you are harried by day and haunted by night by the fact that you are a Negro, living constantly at tiptoe stance, never quite knowing what to expect next, and are plagued with inner fears and outer resentments; when you are forever fighting a degenerating sense of "nobodiness"—then you will understand why we find it difficult to wait. There comes a time when the cup of endurance runs over, and men are no longer willing to be plunged into the abyss of despair. I hope, sirs, you can understand our legitimate and unavoidable impatience.

You express a great deal of anxiety over our willingness to break laws. This is certainly a legitimate concern. Since we so diligently urge people to obey the Supreme Court's decision of 1954 outlawing segregation in the public schools, at first glance it may seem rather paradoxical for us consciously to break laws. One may well ask: "How can you advocate breaking some laws and obeying others?" The answer lies in the fact that there are two types of laws: just and unjust. I would be the first to advocate obeying just laws. One has not only a legal but a moral responsibility to obey just laws. Conversely, one has a moral responsibility to disobey unjust laws. I would agree with St. Augustine that "an unjust law is no law at all."

Now, what is the difference between the two? How does one determine whether a law is just or unjust? A just law is a man-made code that squares with the moral law or the law of God. An unjust law is a code that is out of harmony with the moral law. To put it in the terms of St. Thomas Aquinas: An unjust law is a human law that is not rooted in eternal law and natural law. Any law that uplifts human personality is just. Any law that degrades human personality is unjust. All segregation statutes are unjust because segregation distorts the soul and damages the personality. It gives the segregator a false sense of superiority and the segregated a false sense of inferiority. Segregation, to use the terminology of the Jewish philosopher Martin Buber, substitutes an "I–it" relationship for an "I–thou" relationship and ends up relegating persons to the status of things. Hence segregation is not only politically, economically and sociologically unsound, it is morally wrong and sinful. Paul Tillich has said that sin is separation. Is not segregation an existential expression of man's tragic separation, his awful estrangement, his terrible sinfulness? Thus it is that I can urge men to obey the 1954 decision of the Supreme Court, for it is morally right; and I can urge them to disobey segregation ordinances, for they are morally wrong.

Let us consider a more concrete example of just and unjust laws. An unjust law is a code that a numerical or power majority group compels a minority group to obey but does not make binding on itself. This is *difference* made legal. By the same token, a just law is a code that a majority compels a minority to follow and that it is willing to follow itself. This is *sameness* made legal.

Let me give another explanation. A law is unjust if it is inflicted on a minority that, as a result of being denied the right to vote, had no part in enacting or devising the law. Who can say that the legislature of Alabama which set up that state's segregation laws was democratically elected? Throughout Alabama all sorts of devious methods are used to prevent Negroes from becoming registered voters, and there are some counties in which, even though Negroes constitute a majority of the population, not a single Negro is registered. Can any law enacted under such circumstances be considered democratically structured?

Sometimes a law is just on its face and unjust in its application. For instance, I have been arrested on a charge of parading without a permit. Now, there is nothing wrong in having an ordinance which requires a permit for a parade. But such an ordinance becomes unjust when it is used to maintain segregation and to deny citizens the First-Amendment privilege of peaceful assembly and protest.

I hope you are able to see the distinction I am trying to point out. In no sense do I advocate evading or defying the law, as would the rabid segregationist. That would lead to anarchy. One who breaks an unjust law must do so openly, lovingly, and with a willingness to accept the penalty. I submit that an individual who breaks a law that conscience tells him is unjust, and who willingly accepts the penalty of imprisonment in order to arouse the conscience of the community over its injustice, is in reality expressing the highest respect for law.

Of course, there is nothing new about this kind of civil disobedience. It was evidenced sublimely in the refusal of Shadrach, Meshach and Abednego to obey the laws of Nebuchadnezzar, on the ground that a higher moral law was at stake. It was practiced superbly by the early Christians, who were willing to face hungry lions and the excruciating pain of chopping blocks rather than submit to certain unjust laws of the Roman Empire. To a degree, academic freedom is a reality today because Socrates practiced civil disobedience. In our own nation, the Boston Tea Party represented a massive act of civil disobedience.

We should never forget that everything Adolf Hitler did in Germany was "legal" and everything the Hungarian freedom fighters did in Hungary was "illegal." It was "illegal" to aid and comfort a Jew in Hitler's Germany. Even so, I am sure that, had I lived in Germany at the time, I would have aided and comforted my Jewish brothers. If today I lived in a Communist country where certain principles dear to the Christian faith are suppressed, I would openly advocate disobeying that country's antireligious laws.

I must make two honest confessions to you, my Christian and Jewish brothers. First, I must confess that over the past few years I have been gravely disappointed with the white moderate. I have almost reached the regrettable conclusion that the Negro's great stumbling block in his stride toward freedom is not the White Citizen's Counciler or the Ku Klux Klanner, but the white moderate, who is more devoted to "order" than to justice; who prefers a negative peace which is the absence of tension to a positive peace which is the presence of justice; who constantly says: "I agree with you in the goal you seek, but I cannot agree with your methods of direct action"; who paternalistically believes he can set the timetable for another man's freedom; who lives by a mythical concept of time and who constantly advises the Negro to wait for a "more convenient season." Shallow understanding from people of good will is more frustrating than absolute misunderstanding from people of ill will. Lukewarm acceptance is much more bewildering than outright rejection.

I had hoped that the white moderate would understand that law and order exist for the purpose of establishing justice

and that when they fail in this purpose they become the danger-
ously structured dams that block the flow of social progress. I
had hoped that the white moderate would understand that the
present tension in the South is a necessary phase of the transi-
tion from an obnoxious negative peace, in which the Negro
passively accepted his unjust plight, to a substantive and positive peace, in which all men will respect the dignity and worth
of human personality. Actually, we who engage in nonviolent
direct action are not the creators of tension. We merely bring
to the surface the hidden tension that is already alive. We bring
it out in the open, where it can be seen and dealt with. Like
a boil that can never be cured so long as it is covered up but
must be opened with all its ugliness to the natural medicines of
air and light, injustice must be exposed, with all the tension its
exposure creates, to the light of human conscience and the air
of national opinion before it can be cured.

In your statement you assert that our actions, even though
peaceful, must be condemned because they precipitate violence. But is this a logical assertion? Isn't this like condemning
a robbed man because his possession of money precipitated
the evil act of robbery? Isn't this like condemning Socrates
because his unswerving commitment to truth and his philo-
sophical inquiries precipitated the act by the misguided popu-
lace in which they made him drink hemlock? Isn't this like
condemning Jesus because his unique God-consciousness and
never-ceasing devotion to God's will precipitated the evil act
of crucifixion? We must come to see that, as the federal courts
have consistently affirmed, it is wrong to urge an individual to
cease his efforts to gain his basic constitutional rights because
the quest may precipitate violence. Society must protect the
robbed and punish the robber.

I had also hoped that the white moderate would reject the
myth concerning time in relation to the struggle for freedom.
I have just received a letter from a white brother in Texas.
He writes: "All Christians know that the colored people will
receive equal rights eventually, but it is possible that you are

in too great a religious hurry. It has taken Christianity almost two thousand years to accomplish what it has. The teachings of Christ take time to come to earth." Such an attitude stems from a tragic misconception of time, from the strangely irrational notion that there is something in the very flow of time that will inevitably cure all ills. Actually, time itself is neutral; it can be used either destructively or constructively. More and more I feel that the people of ill will have used time much more effectively than have the people of good will. We will have to repent in this generation not merely for the hateful words and actions of the bad people but for the appalling silence of the good people. Human progress never rolls in on wheels of inevitability; it comes through the tireless efforts of men willing to be co-workers with God, and without this hard work, time itself becomes an ally of the forces of social stagnation. We must use time creatively, in the knowledge that the time is always ripe to do right. Now is the time to make real the promise of democracy and transform our pending national elegy into a creative psalm of brotherhood. Now is the time to lift our national policy from the quicksand of racial injustice to the solid rock of human dignity.

You speak of our activity in Birmingham as extreme. At first I was rather disappointed that fellow clergymen would see my nonviolent efforts as those of an extremist. I began thinking about the fact that I stand in the middle of two opposing forces in the Negro community. One is a force of complacency, made up in part of Negroes who, as a result of long years of oppression, are so drained of self-respect and a sense of "somebodiness" that they have adjusted to segregation; and in part of a few middle-class Negroes who, because of a degree of academic and economic security and because in some ways they profit by segregation, have become insensitive to the problems of the masses. The other force is one of bitterness and hatred, and it comes perilously close to advocating violence. It is expressed in the various black nationalist groups that are springing up across the nation, the largest and best-known being Elijah

Muhammad's Muslim movement. Nourished by the Negro's frustration over the continued existence of racial discrimination, this movement is made up of people who have lost faith in America, who have absolutely repudiated Christianity, and who have concluded that the white man is an incorrigible "devil."

I have tried to stand between these two forces, saying that we need emulate neither the "do-nothingism" of the complacent nor the hatred and despair of the black nationalist. For there is the more excellent way of love and nonviolent protest. I am grateful to God that, through the influence of the Negro church, the way of nonviolence became an integral part of our struggle.

If this philosophy had not emerged, by now many streets of the South would, I am convinced, be flowing with blood. And I am further convinced that if our white brothers dismiss as "rabble-rousers" and "outside agitators" those of us who employ nonviolent direct action, and if they refuse to support our nonviolent efforts, millions of Negroes will, out of frustration and despair, seek solace and security in black-nationalist ideologies—a development that would inevitably lead to a frightening racial nightmare.

Oppressed people cannot remain oppressed forever. The yearning for freedom eventually manifests itself, and that is what has happened to the American Negro. Something within has reminded him of his birthright of freedom, and something without has reminded him that it can be gained. Consciously or unconsciously, he has been caught up by the *Zeitgeist*, and with his black brothers of Africa and his brown and yellow brothers of Asia, South America and the Caribbean, the United States Negro is moving with a sense of great urgency toward the promised land of racial justice. If one recognizes this vital urge that has engulfed the Negro community, one should readily understand why public demonstrations are taking place. The Negro has many pent-up resentments and latent frustrations, and he must release them. So let him march; let him make prayer pilgrimages to the city hall; let him go on freedom rides—and try to understand why he must do so. If his repressed emotions are not released in nonviolent ways, they will seek expression through violence; this is not a threat but a fact of history. So I have not said to my people: "Get rid of your discontent." Rather, I have tried to say that this normal and healthy discontent can be channeled into the creative outlet of nonviolent direct action. And now this approach is being termed extremist.

But though I was initially disappointed at being categorized as an extremist, as I continued to think about the matter I gradually gained a measure of satisfaction from the label. Was not Jesus an extremist for love: "Love your enemies, bless them that curse you, do good to them that hate you, and pray for them which despitefully use you, and persecute you." Was not Amos an extremist for justice: "Let justice roll down like waters and righteousness like an ever-flowing stream." Was not Paul an extremist for the Christian gospel: "I bear in my body the marks of the Lord Jesus." Was not Martin Luther an extremist: "Here I stand; I cannot do otherwise, so help me God." And John Bunyan: "I will stay in jail to the end of my days before I make a butchery of my conscience." And Abraham Lincoln: "This nation cannot survive half slave and half free." And Thomas Jefferson: "We hold these truths to be self-evident, that all men are created equal . . ." So the question is not whether we will be extremists, but what kind of extremists we will be. Will we be extremists for hate or for love? Will we be extremists for the preservation of injustice or for the extension of justice? In that dramatic scene on Calvary's hill three men were crucified. We must never forget that all three were crucified for the same crime—the crime of extremism. Two were extremists for immorality, and thus fell below their environment. The other, Jesus Christ, was an extremist for love, truth and goodness, and thereby rose above his environment. Perhaps the South, the nation and the world are in dire need of creative extremists.

I had hoped that the white moderate would see this need. Perhaps I was too optimistic; perhaps I expected too much. I suppose I should have realized that few members of the oppressor race can understand the deep groans and passionate yearnings of the oppressed race, and still fewer have the vision to see that injustice must be rooted out by strong, persistent and determined action. I am thankful, however, that some of our white brothers in the South have grasped the meaning of this social revolution and committed themselves to it. They are still all too few in quantity, but they are big in quality. Some—such as Ralph McGill, Lillian Smith, Harry Golden, James McBride Dabbs, Ann Braden and Sarah Patton Boyle—have written about our struggle in eloquent and prophetic terms. Others have marched with us down nameless streets of the South. They have languished in filthy, roach-infested jails, suffering the abuse and brutality of policemen who view them as "dirty nigger-lovers." Unlike so many of their moderate brothers and sisters, they have recognized the urgency of the moment and sensed the need for powerful "action" antidotes to combat the disease of segregation.

Let me take note of my other major disappointment. I have been so greatly disappointed with the white church and its leadership. Of course, there are some notable exceptions. I am not unmindful of the fact that each of you has taken some significant stands on this issue. I commend you, Reverend Stallings, for your Christian stand on this past Sunday, in welcoming Negroes to your worship service on a nonsegregated basis. I commend the Catholic leaders of this state for integrating Spring Hill College several years ago.

But despite these notable exceptions, I must honestly reiterate that I have been disappointed with the church. I do not say this as one of those negative critics who can always find something wrong with the church. I say this as a minister of the gospel, who loves the church; who was nurtured in its bosom; who has been sustained by its spiritual blessings and who will remain true to it as long as the cord of life shall lengthen.

When I was suddenly catapulted into the leadership of the bus protest in Montgomery, Alabama, a few years ago, I felt we would be supported by the white church. I felt that the white ministers, priests and rabbis of the South would be among our strongest allies. Instead, some have been outright opponents, refusing to understand the freedom movement and misrepresenting its leaders; all too many others have been more cautious than courageous and have remained silent behind the anesthetizing security of stained-glass windows.

In spite of my shattered dreams, I came to Birmingham with the hope that the white religious leadership of this community would see the justice of our cause and, with deep moral concern, would serve as the channel through which our just grievances could reach the power structure. I had hoped that each of you would understand. But again I have been disappointed.

I have heard numerous southern religious leaders admonish their worshipers to comply with a desegregation decision because it is the law, but I have longed to hear white ministers declare: "Follow this decree because integration is morally right and because the Negro is your brother." In the midst of blatant injustices inflicted upon the Negro, I have watched white churchmen stand on the sideline and mouth pious irrelevancies and sanctimonious trivialities. In the midst of a mighty struggle to rid our nation of racial and economic injustice, I have heard many ministers say: "Those are social issues, with which the gospel has no real concern." And I have watched many churches commit themselves to a completely otherworldly religion which makes a strange, un-Biblical distinction between body and soul, between the sacred and the secular.

I have traveled the length and breadth of Alabama, Mississippi and all the other southern states. On sweltering summer days and crisp autumn mornings I have looked at the South's beautiful churches with their lofty spires pointing heavenward. I have beheld the impressive outlines of her massive religious-education buildings. Over and over I have found myself asking: "What kind of people worship here? Who is their God? Where were their voices when the lips of Governor Barnett dripped with words of interposition and nullification? Where were they when Governor Wallace gave a clarion call for defiance and hatred? Where were their voices of support when bruised and weary Negro men and women decided to rise from the dark dungeons of complacency to the bright hills of creative protest?"

Yes, these questions are still in my mind. In deep disappointment I have wept over the laxity of the church. But be assured that my tears have been tears of love. There can be no deep disappointment where there is not deep love. Yes, I love the church. How could I do otherwise? I am in the rather unique position of being the son, the grandson and the great-grandson of preachers. Yes, I see the church as the body of Christ. But, oh! How we have blemished and scarred that body through social neglect and through fear of being nonconformists.

There was a time when the church was very powerful—in the time when the early Christians rejoiced at being deemed worthy to suffer for what they believed. In those days the church was not merely a thermometer that recorded the ideas and principles of popular opinion; it was a thermostat that transformed the mores of society. Whenever the early Christians entered a town, the people in power became disturbed and immediately sought to convict the Christians for being "disturbers of the peace" and "outside agitators." But the Christians pressed on, in the conviction that they were "a colony of heaven," called to obey God rather than man. Small in number, they were big in commitment. They were too God-intoxicated to be "astronomically intimidated." By their effort and example they brought an end to such ancient evils as infanticide and gladiatorial contests.

Things are different now. So often the contemporary church is a weak, ineffectual voice with an uncertain sound. So often it is an archdefender of the status quo. Far from being disturbed by the presence of the church, the power structure of the average community is consoled by the church's silent—and often even vocal—sanction of things as they are.

But the judgment of God is upon the church as never before. If today's church does not recapture the sacrificial spirit of the early church, it will lose its authenticity, forfeit the loyalty of millions, and be dismissed as an irrelevant social club with no meaning for the twentieth century. Every day I meet young people whose disappointment with the church has turned into outright disgust.

Perhaps I have once again been too optimistic. Is organized religion too inextricably bound to the status quo to save our nation and the world? Perhaps I must turn my faith to the inner spiritual church, the church within the church, as the true *ekklesia* and the hope of the world. But again I am thankful to God that some noble souls from the ranks of organized religion have broken loose from the paralyzing chains of conformity and joined us as active partners in the struggle for freedom. They have left their secure congregations and walked the streets of Albany, Georgia, with us. They have gone down the highways of the South on tortuous rides for freedom. Yes, they have gone to jail with us. Some have been dismissed from their churches, have lost the support of their bishops and fellow ministers. But they have acted in the faith that right defeated is stronger than evil triumphant. Their witness has been the spiritual salt that has preserved the true meaning of the gospel in these troubled times. They have carved a tunnel of hope through the dark mountain of disappointment.

I hope the church as a whole will meet the challenge of this decisive hour. But even if the church does not come to the aid of justice, I have no despair about the future. I have no fear about the outcome of our struggle in Birmingham, even if our motives are at present misunderstood. We will reach the goal of freedom in Birmingham and all over the nation, because the goal of America is freedom. Abused and scorned though we may be, our destiny is tied up with America's destiny. Before the pilgrims landed at Plymouth, we were here. Before the pen of Jefferson etched the majestic words of the Declaration of Independence across the pages of history, we were here. For more than two centuries our forebears labored in this country without wages; they made cotton king; they built the homes of their masters while suffering gross injustice and shameful humiliation—and yet out of a bottomless vitality they continued to thrive and develop. If the inexpressible cruelties of slavery could not stop us, the opposition we now face will surely fail. We will win our freedom because the sacred heritage of our nation and the eternal will of God are embodied in our echoing demands.

Before closing I feel impelled to mention one other point in your statement that has troubled me profoundly. You warmly commended the Birmingham police force for keeping "order" and "preventing violence." I doubt that you would have so warmly commended the police force if you had seen its dogs sinking their teeth into unarmed, nonviolent Negroes. I doubt that you would so quickly commend the policemen if you were to observe their ugly and inhumane treatment of Negroes here in the city jail; if you were to watch them push and curse old Negro women and young Negro girls; if you were to see them slap and kick old Negro men and young boys; if you were to observe them, as they did on two occasions, refuse to give us food because we wanted to sing our grace together. I cannot join you in your praise of the Birmingham police department.

It is true that the police have exercised a degree of discipline in handling the demonstrators. In this sense they have conducted themselves rather "nonviolently" in public. But for what purpose? To preserve the evil system of segregation. Over the past few years I have consistently preached that nonviolence demands that the means we use must be as pure as the ends we seek. I have tried to make clear that it is wrong to use immoral means to attain moral ends. But now I must affirm that it is just as wrong, or perhaps even more so, to use moral means to preserve immoral ends. Perhaps Mr. Connor and his policemen have been rather nonviolent in public, as was Chief Pritchett in Albany, Georgia, but they have used the moral means of nonviolence to maintain the immoral end of racial injustice. As T. S. Eliot has said: "The last temptation is the greatest treason: To do the right deed for the wrong reason."

I wish you had commended the Negro sit-inners and demonstrators of Birmingham for their sublime courage, their willingness to suffer and their amazing discipline in the midst of great provocation. One day the South will recognize its real heroes. They will be the James Merediths, with the noble sense of purpose that enables them to face jeering and hostile mobs, and with the agonizing loneliness that characterizes the life of the pioneer. They will be old, oppressed, battered Negro women, symbolized in a seventy-two-year-old woman in Montgomery, Alabama, who rose up with a sense of dignity and with her people decided not to ride segregated buses, and who responded with ungrammatical profundity to one who inquired about her weariness: "My feets is tired, but my soul is at rest." They will be the young high school and college students, the young ministers of the gospel and a host of their elders, coura-geously and nonviolently sitting in at lunch counters and will-ingly going to jail for conscience' sake. One day the South will know that when these disinherited children of God sat down at lunch counters, they were in reality standing up for what is best in the American dream and for the most sacred values in our Judaeo-Christian heritage, thereby bringing our nation back to those great wells of democracy which were dug deep by the founding fathers in their formulation of the Constitution and the Declaration of Independence.

Never before have I written so long a letter. I'm afraid it is much too long to take your precious time. I can assure you that it would have been much shorter if I had been writing from a comfortable desk, but what else can one do when he is alone in a narrow jail cell, other than write long letters, think long thoughts and pray long prayers?

If I have said anything in this letter that overstates the truth and indicates an unreasonable impatience, I beg you to forgive me. If I have said anything that understates the truth and indicates my having a patience that allows me to settle for anything less than brotherhood, I beg God to forgive me.

I hope this letter finds you strong in the faith. I also hope that circumstances will soon make it possible for me to meet each of you, not as an integrationist or a civil-rights leader but as a fellow clergyman and a Christian brother. Let us all hope that the dark clouds of racial prejudice will soon pass away and the deep fog of misunderstanding will be lifted from our fear-drenched communities, and in some not too distant tomorrow the radiant stars of love and brotherhood will shine over our great nation with all their scintillating beauty.

Yours for the cause of Peace and Brotherhood,
MARTIN LUTHER KING, JR.

Why We Can't Wait (1964)

★ ★ ★

Hannah Arendt: from Civil Disobedience

The Bar Association of the City of New York celebrated its centennial this year with a symposium on the rather dismal question "Is the law dead?" The participants, divided into two panels, were asked by Eugene V. Rostow to prepare papers on "the citizen's moral relation to the law in a society of consent" and on "the capacity of American society to meet changing demands for social justice in peace, and through the processes of law and of democratic policymaking"—two topics that seemed to encourage a somewhat brighter outlook. The following remarks are in answer to the first question.

Asked to consider the citizen's *moral* relation to the law, one is inclined to think first of two men in prison—Socrates, in Athens, and Thoreau, in Concord, both of whom appear regularly in the literature on the subject. Many, indeed, share Senator Philip A. Hart's position: "Any tolerance that I might feel toward the disobeyer is dependent on his willingness to accept whatever punishment the law might impose"—an argument whose plausibility gains in strength in a country where, as Edward H. Levi has pointed out, "an individual, through one of the most serious oddities of our law, is encouraged or in some sense compelled to establish a significant legal right through a personal act of civil disobedience." Yet all these models of civil disobedience may be seriously misleading when we try to come to terms with our present predicament, and not only because "the distinction between such acts"—in which an individual breaks the law in order to test its Constitutionality or legitimacy—"and ordinary violations becomes much more fragile in a period of turmoil."

As for Socrates, the argument in the "Crito" is less unequiv-
ocal than it is usually accepted as being. Socrates had never
challenged the laws themselves—only this particular miscar-
riage of justice, which he spoke of as the "accident" ($τύχη$)
that had befallen him. His personal misfortune did not entitle
him to "break his contracts and agreements" with the laws; his
quarrel was not with the laws but with the judges. Moreover,
as Socrates pointed out to Crito (who tried to persuade him
to escape and go into exile) at the time of the trial, the laws
themselves had offered him this choice: "At that time you
could have done with the state's consent what you are trying
now to do without it. But then you gloried in being willing
to die. You said that you preferred death to exile." We also
know, from the "Apology," that he had the option of desisting
from his public examination of things, which doubtless spread
uncertainty about established customs and beliefs, and that
again he had preferred death, because "an unexamined life is
not worth living." That is, Socrates would not have honored
his own words if he had tried to escape; he would have undone
all he had done during his trial—would have "confirmed the
judges in their opinion, and made it seem that their verdict was
a just one." He owed it *to himself* as well as to the citizens he
had addressed to stay and die. "We have tried to explain why
Socrates chooses death in the 'Crito,'" N. A. Greenberg has
written in an excellent analysis. "To say that it is because he
despises death has seemed to us inhuman. . . . It is the payment
of a debt of honor, the payment of a gentleman who has lost
a wager and who pays because he cannot otherwise live with
himself. There has indeed been a contract, and the notion of
a contract pervades the latter half of the 'Crito,' but . . . the
contract which is binding is . . . *the commitment involved in the
trial.*" (My italics.)

Thoreau's case, though much less dramatic (he spent one
night in jail for refusing to pay his poll tax to a government that
permitted slavery, but he let his aunt pay it for him the next
morning), seems at first glance more pertinent to our current

debates, for, in contradistinction to Socrates, he protested against the injustice of the laws themselves. The trouble with this example is that in "On the Duty of Civil Disobedience," the famous essay that grew out of the incident and made the term "civil disobedience" part of our political vocabulary, he argued his case not on the ground of a *citizen's* moral relation to the law but on the ground of individual conscience and conscience's moral obligation: "It is not a man's duty, as a matter of course, to devote himself to the eradication of any, even the most enormous, wrong; he may still properly have other concerns to engage him; but it is his duty, at least, to wash his hands of it, and, if he gives it no thought longer, not to give it practically his support." Thoreau did not pretend that a man's washing his hands of it would make the world better or that a man had any obligation to do so. He "came into this world, not chiefly to make this a good place to live in, but to live in it, be it good or bad." Indeed, this is how we all come into the world—lucky if the world and the part of it we arrive in is a good place to live in at the time of our arrival, or at least a place where the wrongs committed are not "of such a nature that it requires you to be the agent of injustice to another." For only if this is the case, "then, I say, break the law." And Thoreau was right: individual conscience requires nothing more.

Here, as elsewhere, conscience is unpolitical. It is not primarily interested in the world where the wrong is committed or in the consequences that the wrong will have for the future course of the world. It does not say, with Jefferson, "I tremble *for my country* when I reflect that God is just; that His justice cannot sleep forever," because it trembles for the individual self and its integrity. It can therefore be much more radical and say, with Thoreau, "This people must cease to hold slaves, and to make war on Mexico, *though it cost them their existence as a people* [my italics]," whereas for Lincoln "the paramount object," even in the struggle for the emancipation of the slaves, remained, as he wrote in 1862, "to save the Union, and . . . not either to save or to destroy slavery." This does not mean that Lincoln was unaware of "the monstrous injustice of slavery itself," as he had called it eight years earlier; it means that he was also aware of the distinction between his "official duty" and his "personal wish that all men every where could be free." And this distinction, if one strips it of the very complex and equivocal historical circumstances, is ultimately the same as Machiavelli's when he said, "I love my native city more than my own soul." The discrepancy between "official duty" and "personal wish" in Lincoln's case no more indicates a lack of moral commitment than the discrepancy between city and soul indicates that Machiavelli was an atheist and did not believe in eternal salvation and damnation.

This possible conflict between "the good man" and "the good citizen" (according to Aristotle, the good man could be a good citizen only in a good state), between the individual self, with or without belief in an afterlife, and the member of the community, or, as we would say today, between morality and politics, is very old—older, even, than the word "conscience," which in its present connotation is of relatively recent origin. And almost equally old are the justifications for the position of either. Thoreau was consistent enough to recognize and admit that he was open to the charge of irresponsibility, the oldest charge against "the good man." He said explicitly that he was "not responsible for the successful working of the machinery of society," was "not the son of the engineer." The adage "*Fiat justitia et pereat mundus*"—"Let justice be done even if the world perishes"—which is usually invoked rhetorically against the defenders of absolute justice, often for the purpose of excusing wrongs and crimes, neatly expresses the gist of the dilemma.

———

Consent—meaning that voluntary membership must be assumed for every citizen in the community—is obviously (except in the case of naturalization) at least as open to the reproach of being a fiction as the aboriginal contract. The argument is correct legally and theoretically but not existentially. Every man is born a member of a particular community and can survive only if he is welcomed and made at home within it. A kind of consent is implied in every newborn's factual situation; namely, a kind of conformity to the rules under which the great game of the world is played in the particular group to which he belongs by birth. We all live and survive by a kind of tacit consent, which, however, it would be difficult to call voluntary. How can we will what is there anyhow? We might call it voluntary, though, when the child happens to be born into a community in which dissent is also a legal and de-facto possibility once he has grown into a man. Dissent implies consent, and is the hallmark of free government; one who knows that he may dissent knows also that he somehow consents when he does not dissent.

Consent as it is implied in the right to dissent—the spirit of American law and the quintessence of American government—spells out and articulates the tacit consent given in exchange for the community's tacit welcome of new arrivals, of the inner immigration through which it constantly renews itself. Seen in this perspective, tacit consent is not a fiction; it is inherent in the human condition. This *consensus universalis* (as Tocqueville called it) does not, however, cover consent to specific laws or specific policies, even if they are the result of majority decisions. It is often argued that the consent to the Constitution, the *consensus universalis*, implies consent to statutory laws as well, because in representative government the people have helped to make them. This consent, I think, is indeed entirely fictitious; under the present circumstances, at any rate, it has lost all plausibility. Representative government itself is in a crisis today, partly because it has lost, in the course of time, all institutions that permitted the citizens' actual participation, and partly because it is now gravely affected by the disease from which the party system suffers: bureaucratization and the two parties' tendency to represent nobody except the party machines.

At any rate, the current danger of rebellion in the United States arises not from dissent and resistance to particular laws, and not even from denunciation of the "system" or the "establishment," but from the challenge to the Constitution (partly from the side of the Administration) and the unwillingness of certain sections of the population to recognize the *consensus universalis*. Tocqueville predicted almost a hundred and fifty years ago that "the most formidable of all the ills that threaten the future of the Union arises" not from slavery, whose abolition he foresaw, but "from the presence of a black population upon its territory." And the reason he could predict the future of Negroes and Indians for more than a century lies in the simple and frightening fact that these people had never been included in the original *consensus universalis* of the American republic. (It was the tragedy of the abolitionist movement that it could appeal only to conscience, and not to the law of the land. There was nothing in the Constitution or in the intent of the framers that could be so construed as to include the slave people in the original compact. And the strong anti-institutional bias of the anti-slavery movement—its abstract morality, which condemned all institutions as evil because they tolerated the evil of slavery—certainly did not help in promoting those elementary measures of humane reform by which in all other countries the slaves were gradually emancipated into the free society.) We know that this original crime could not be remedied by the Fourteenth and Fifteenth Amendments; on the contrary, the tacit exclusion from the tacit consensus was made more conspicuous by the inability or unwillingness of the federal government to enforce its own laws, and as time went by and wave after wave of immigrants came to the country, it grew more poignant that blacks, now free, and born and bred in the country, were the only ones for whom it was not true that, in Bancroft's words, "the welcome of the Commonwealth was as wide as sorrow." We know the result, and we need not be surprised that the present belated attempts to welcome the black population explicitly into the otherwise tacit *consensus universalis* of the nation are not trusted. (An explicit Constitutional amendment, addressed specifically to the black people of America, might have underlined the great change more dramatically for these people who had never been welcome, assuring them of its finality. Supreme Court decisions are Constitutional interpretations, of which the Dred Scott decision is one. The failure of Congress to propose such an amendment is striking in the light of the overwhelming vote for a Constitutional amendment to cure the infinitely milder discriminatory practices against women.) At any rate, such attempts are met by rebuffs from black organizations, which care little about the rules of non-violence for civil disobedience and, often, just as little about the issues at stake—the Vietnam war, specific defects in our institutions—because they are in open rebellion against all of them. And although they have been able to attract to their cause the extreme fringe of radical disobedience, which without them would probably have withered away long ago, their instinct tells them to disengage themselves even from these supporters, who, their rebellious spirit notwithstanding, were included in the original contract out of which rose the tacit *consensus universalis*.

Consent, in the American understanding of the term, relies on the horizontal version of the social contract, and not on majority decisions. (On the contrary, much of the thinking of the framers of the Constitution concerned safeguards for dissenting minorities.) The moral content of this consent is like the moral content of all agreements and contracts; namely, the obligation to keep them. This obligation is inherent in all promises. Thoreau's often quoted statement "The only obligation which I have a right to assume is to do at any time what I think right" might well be varied to: The only obligation which I as a citizen have a right to assume is to make and to keep promises. Promises are the uniquely human way of ordering the future, making it predictable and reliable to the extent that this is humanly possible. And since the predictability of the future can never be absolute, promises are qualified by two tacit limitations. We are bound to keep our promises provided that no unexpected circumstances arise, and provided that the mutuality inherent in all promises is not broken. There exist a great number of circumstances that may cause a promise to be broken, the most important one in our context being the general circumstance of change. And violation of the inherent mutuality of promises can also be caused by many factors, the only relevant one in our context being the failure of the established authorities to keep to the original conditions. Examples of such failures have become only too numerous; there is the case of an "illegal and immoral war," the case of an increasingly impatient claim to power by the executive branch of government, and the case of violations (in the form of war-oriented or other government-directed research) of the specific trust of the universities which gave them protection against political interference and social pressure. As to the debates about the last, those who attack these misuses and those who defend them unfortunately incline to agree on the basically wrong premise that the universities are mere "mirrors for the larger society," an argument best answered by Edward H. Levi, the president of the University of Chicago: "It is sometimes said that society will achieve the kind of education it deserves. Heaven help us if this is so."

"The spirit of the laws," as Montesquieu understood it, is the principle by which people living under a particular legal system act and are inspired to act. Consent, the spirit of American laws, is based on the notion of a mutually binding contract, which established first the individual colonies and then the Union. A contract presupposes a plurality of at least two, and every association established and acting according to the principle of consent, based on mutual promise, presupposes a plurality that does not dissolve but is shaped into the form of a union—*e pluribus unum*. If the individual members of the community thus formed should choose not to retain a restricted autonomy, if they should choose to disappear into complete unity, such as the *unité sacrée* of the French nation, all talk about the citizen's *moral* relation to the law would be mere rhetoric.

Consent and the right to dissent became the inspiring and organizing principles of action that taught the inhabitants of this continent the "art of associating together," from which sprang those voluntary associations whose role Tocqueville was the first to notice, with amazement, admiration, and some misgiving; he thought it the peculiar strength of the American political system. The few chapters he devoted to them are still by far the best in the not very large literature on the subject. The words with which he introduced it—"In no country in the world has the principle of association been more successfully used or applied to a greater multitude of objects than in America"—are no less true today than they were nearly a hundred and fifty years ago; and neither is the conclusion that "nothing . . . is more deserving of our attention than the moral and intellectual associations of America." Voluntary associations are not parties; they are ad-hoc organizations that pursue short-term goals and disappear when the goal has been reached. Only in the case of their prolonged failure and of an aim of great importance may they "constitute, as it were, a separate nation in the midst of the nation, a government within the government." (This happened in 1861, about thirty years after Tocqueville wrote these words, and it could happen again; the challenge of the Massachusetts Legislature to the foreign policy of the Administration is a clear warning.) Alas, it is no longer true that their spirit "pervades every act of social life," and while this may have resulted in a certain decline in the huge number of joiners in the population—of Babbitts, who are the specifically American version of Philistines—the refusal to form associations "for the smallest undertakings" is paid for by an evident decline in the appetite for action. For Americans still regard association as "the only means they have for acting," and rightly so. In short, "as soon as several of the inhabitants of the United States have taken up an opinion or a feeling which they wish to promote in the world," or have found some fault they wish to correct, "they look out for mutual assistance, and as soon as they have found one another out, they combine. *From that moment, they are no longer isolated men but a power seen from afar* [my italics], whose actions serve for an example and whose language is listened to."

It is my contention that civil disobedients are nothing but the latest form of voluntary association, and that they are thus quite in tune with the oldest traditions of the country. What could better describe them than Tocqueville's words "The citizens who form the minority associate in order, first, to show their numerical strength and so to diminish the moral power of the majority"? To be sure, it has been a long time since "moral and intellectual associations" could be found among voluntary associations—which, on the contrary, seem to have been formed only for the protection of special interests, of pressure groups and the lobbyists who represented them in Washington. I do not doubt that the dubious reputation of the lobbyists is deserved, just as the dubious reputation of the politician in this country has frequently been amply deserved. However, the fact is that the pressure groups are also voluntary associations, and that they are recognized in Washington, where their influence is sufficiently great to be called an "assistant government;" indeed, the number of registered lobbyists exceeds by far the number of congressmen. (This public recognition is no small matter, for, surprisingly, such "assistance," like the freedom of association in general, was in no way foreseen in the Constitution and its First Amendment, which protects no more than a kind of negative right—"peaceably to assemble and to petition the Government for a redress of grievances.")

The dangers inherent in civil disobedience are no greater than the dangers inherent in the right to free association, and of these Tocqueville, his admiration notwithstanding, was not unaware. (John Stuart Mill, in his review of the first volume of "Democracy in America," interpreted them: "The capacity of coöperation for a common purpose, heretofore a monopolized instrument of power in the hands of the higher classes, is now a most formidable one in those of the lowest.") Tocqueville knew that "the tyrannical control that these societies exercise is often far more insupportable than the authority possessed over society by the government which they attack." But he knew also that "the liberty of association has become a necessary guarantee against the tyranny of the majority," that "a dangerous expedient is used to obviate a still more formidable danger," and, finally, that "it is by the enjoyment of dangerous freedom that the Americans learn the art of rendering the dangers of freedom less formidable." In any event, "if men are to remain civilized or to become so, the art of associating together must grow and improve *in the same ratio in which the equality of conditions is increased.*" (My italics.)

We need not go into the old debates about the glories and the dangers of equality, the good and the evil of democracy, to understand that all evil demons could be let loose if the original contractual model of the associations—mutual promises with the moral imperative *pacta sunt servanda*—should be lost. Under today's circumstances, this could happen if these groups, like their counterparts in other countries, were to substitute ideological commitments, political or other, for actual goals. When an association is no longer capable or willing to unite "into one channel the efforts of *divergent* minds" (as Tocqueville wrote), it has lost its gift for action. What threatens the student movement, the chief civil-disobedience group of the moment, is not just vandalism, violence, bad temper, and worse manners but the growing infection of the movement with ideologies (Maoism, Castroism, Stalinism, Marxism-Leninism, and the like), which in fact split and dissolve the association.

Civil disobedience and voluntary association are phenomena practically unknown anywhere else. (The political terminology that surrounds them yields only with great difficulty to translation.) It has often been said that the genius of the English people is to muddle through and that the genius of the American people is to disregard theoretical considerations in favor of pragmatic experience and practical action. However that may be, the fact is that the phenomenon of voluntary association has been neglected and that the notion of civil disobedience has only recently received the attention it deserves. In contrast to the conscientious objector, the civil disobedient is a member of a group, and this group, whether we like it or not, is formed in accordance with the same spirit that has informed voluntary associations. The greatest fallacy in the present debate seems to me the assumption that we are dealing with individuals, who pit themselves subjectively and conscientiously against the laws and customs of the community—an assumption that is shared by the defenders and the detractors of civil disobedience. The fact is that we are dealing with organized minorities, who stand against assumed and non-vocal, though hardly "silent," majorities, and I think it is undeniable that these majorities have changed in mood and opinion to an astounding degree under the pressure of the minorities. It has been the misfortune of recent debates that they have been dominated largely by jurists—lawyers, judges, and other men of law—for they must find it difficult to recognize the civil disobedient as a member of a group rather than to see him as an individual lawbreaker, and hence a potential defendant in court. It is, indeed, the grandeur of court procedure that it is concerned with meting out justice to an individual, and remains unconcerned with everything else—with the *Zeitgeist* or with opinions that the defendant may share with others and try to present in court. The only non-criminal lawbreaker the court recognizes is the conscientious objector, and the only group adherence it is aware of is called conspiracy—an utterly misleading charge in such cases, since conspiracy requires not only "breathing together" but secrecy, and civil disobedience occurs in public.

As I noted earlier, civil disobedience, though it is compatible with the spirit of American laws, has not yet found a niche in the American legal system. The first step would be to obtain the same recognition for the civil-disobedient minorities that is accorded the numerous special interests (minority interests, by definition) in the country, and to deal with civil-disobedient groups in the same way as with pressure groups, which, through their representatives—that is, registered lobbyists—are permitted to influence and "assist" Congress by means of persuasion, qualified opinion, and the numbers of their constituents. These minorities of opinion would thus be able to establish themselves as a power that not only is "seen from afar" during demonstrations and other dramatizations of their viewpoint but is always present and to be reckoned with. The next step would be to admit publicly that the First Amendment covers neither in language nor in spirit the right of association as it is actually practiced in this country—this precious privilege whose exercise has in fact been (as Tocqueville noted) "incorporated with the manners and customs of the people" for centuries. If there is anything that urgently requires a new Constitutional amendment and is worth all the trouble that goes with it, it is certainly this.

Perhaps an emergency was needed before we could find a home for civil disobedience not only in our political language but in our legal system as well. An emergency is certainly at hand when the established institutions of a country fail to function properly and its authority loses its power, and it is such an emergency in the United States today that has changed voluntary association into civil disobedience and transformed dissent into resistance. It is common knowledge that this condition prevails at present—and, indeed, has prevailed for some time—in large parts of the world; what is new is that this country is no longer an exception. Whether our form of government will survive this century is uncertain, but it is also uncertain that it will not. Wilson Carey McWilliams has wisely said, "When institutions fail, political society depends on men, and men are feeble reeds, prone to acquiesce in—if not to commit—iniquity." Ever since the Mayflower Compact was drafted and signed under a different kind of emergency, voluntary associations have been the specifically American remedy for the failure of institutions, the unreliability of men, and the uncertain nature of the future. As

distinguished from other countries, this republic, despite the
great turmoil of change and of failure through which it is going
at present, may still be in possession of its traditional instru-
ments for facing the future with some measure of confidence.

The New Yorker, September 12, 1970

Sources and Acknowledgments

George Washington to the Hebrew Congregation of Newport, Rhode Island. The George Washington Papers at Founders Online (https://founders.archives.gov/content/volumes#Washington, accessed April 6, 2020).

Frederick Douglass: *from* What to the Slave is the 4th of July? *Oration, Delivered in Corinthian Hall, Rochester, by Frederick Douglass, July 5th, 1852* (Rochester, NY: Lee, Mann & Co., 1852), 13–21.

Elizabeth Cady Stanton: Solitude of Self. *Hearing of the Woman Suffrage Association before the Committee on the Judiciary, Monday, January 18, 1892* (Washington, DC: Government Printing Office, 1892), 1–5.

Henry Cabot Lodge: Speech in the Senate on Immigration. Henry Cabot Lodge, *Speeches and Addresses, 1884–1909* (Boston: Houghton Mifflin Company, 1909), 243–66.

Randolph S. Bourne: Trans-National America. *The Atlantic Monthly*, July 1916.

Horace Mann: *from* Twelfth Annual Report to the Massachusetts Board of Education. *Twelfth Annual Report of the Board of Education, together with the Twelfth Annual Report of the Secretary of the Board* (Boston: Dutton & Wentworth, 1849), 53–60.

Abraham Lincoln: Speech to the 166th Ohio Regiment. *New York Herald*, August 23, 1864.

Jane Addams, *from* The Subtle Problems of Charity. *The Atlantic Monthly*, July 1916, 163–69.

W.E.B. Du Bois, from *Black Reconstruction*. W. E. Burghardt Du Bois, *Black Reconstruction: An Essay Toward a History of the Part Which Black Folk Played in the Attempt to Reconstruct Democracy in America, 1860–1880* (New York: Harcourt, Brace and Company, 1935), 700–708. Copyright © 1935, 1962, W. E. Burghardt Du Bois. Reprinted with the permission of Scribner, a division of Simon & Schuster, Inc. All rights reserved.

James Madison: The Federalist No. 51. The Papers of James Madison at Founders Online (https://founders.archives.gov/about/Madison, accessed April 24, 2020).

John Marshall: *from* Opinion for the Court in *McCulloch v. Maryland*. Henry Wheaton, *Reports of Cases Argued and Adjudged in the Supreme Court of the United States*, vol. IV (New York: R. Donaldson, 1819), 405–7, 413–21.

Alexis de Tocqueville: from *Democracy in America*. *Alexis de Tocqueville: Democracy in America*, trans. Arthur Goldhammer, ed. Olivier Zunz (New York: Library of America, 2004), 816–21. Translation copyright © 2004 by Literary Classics of the United States, Inc.

Franklin D. Roosevelt: Address to the Commonwealth Club of California. *The Public Papers and Addresses of Franklin D. Roosevelt*, ed. Samuel I. Rosenman, vol. I (New York: Random House, 1938), 742–56. Copyright © 1938 by Franklin Delano Roosevelt.

Paul Nitze et al.: *from* NSC-68: United States Objectives and Programs for National Security. U.S. Department of State, *Foreign Relations of the United States, 1950, Vol. I: National Security Affairs, Foreign Economic Policy* (Washington, DC: Government Printing Office, 1977), 237–44.

Andrew Jackson: *from* Veto of the Bank Charter. *A Compilation of the Messages and Papers of the Presidents, 1789–1897*, vol. II, ed. James D. Richardson (Washington, DC: Government Printing Office, 1896), 576–78, 590–91.

Carl Schurz: *from* Address on Civil Service Reform. *The Necessity and Progress of Civil Service Reform. An address delivered at the annual meeting of the National Civil-Service Reform League, December 12, 1894, by the president Hon. Carl Schurz* (Washington, DC: National Civil-Service Reform League, 1894), 3–5, 6–8, 17–20.

Theodore Roosevelt: The New Nationalism. *The Works of Theodore Roosevelt: National Edition*, vol. XVII, ed. Hermann Hagedorn (New York: Charles Scribner's Sons, 1926), 5–22. Copyright © 1925 by Charles Scribner's Sons.

John Paul Stevens: *from* Dissent in *Citizens United v. Federal Election Commission*. *Citizens United v. Federal Election Commission*, 558 U.S. 310 (2010), 465–75, 478–79.

Henry David Thoreau: *from* Civil Disobedience. Henry D. Thoreau, *A Yankee in Canada, with Anti-Slavery and Reform Papers* (Boston: Ticknor and Fields, 1866), 123–42.

Martin Luther King, Jr.: Letter from Birmingham Jail. Martin Luther King, Jr., *Why We Can't Wait* (New York: Harper & Row, 1964),

The text in this book is set in 10½ point Goudy Old Style. In 1915, after designing two dozen typefaces, Illinois native Frederic W. Goudy (1865–1947) released his eponymous font as his first project for American Type Founders. It became not only the best known of the ninety fonts he issued during his storied career but also one of the most popular fonts ever created. When it appeared, one type archivist proclaimed that art directors can "now cease to worry about the impending doom of the typefounding industry in America." A perennial choice of designers and typophiles, the font has been widely featured in advertising and will be especially familiar to readers of *Harper's Magazine*. Fifteen years after the appearance of his Old Style, Goudy designed the display type Goudy Sans, used in this volume for chapter openings, drop caps, and running heads.

The paper is an acid-free Forest Stewardship Council–certified stock that exceeds the requirements for permanence of the American National Standards Institute. The binding material is Arrestox, a cotton-based cloth with an aqueous acrylic coating manufactured by Holliston, Church Hill, Tennessee. Text design and composition by Publishers' Design and Production Services, Inc., Sagamore Beach, Massachusetts. Printing by McNaughton & Gunn, Saline, Michigan, with cloth binding by Dekker Bookbinding, Wyoming, Michigan.